SCHOOLING COMPREHENSIVE KIDS

For my mother who never lost her faith in me
and my father who did not live to see
this work completed.

Schooling Comprehensive Kids

Pupil responses to education

AMANDA PALMER

LONDON AND NEW YORK

First published 1998 by Ashgate Publishing

Reissued 2018 by Routledge
2 Park Square, Milton Park, Abingdon, Oxon, OX14 4RN
711 Third Avenue, New York, NY 10017, USA

Routledge is an imprint of the Taylor & Francis Group, an informa business

Copyright © A.M. Palmer 1998

All rights reserved. No part of this book may be reprinted or reproduced or utilised in any form or by any electronic, mechanical, or other means, now known or hereafter invented, including photocopying and recording, or in any information storage or retrieval system, without permission in writing from the publishers.

Notice:
Product or corporate names may be trademarks or registered trademarks, and are used only for identification and explanation without intent to infringe.

Publisher's Note
The publisher has gone to great lengths to ensure the quality of this reprint but points out that some imperfections in the original copies may be apparent.

Disclaimer
The publisher has made every effort to trace copyright holders and welcomes correspondence from those they have been unable to contact.

A Library of Congress record exists under LC control number: 97077643

ISBN 13: 978-1-138-34803-5 (hbk)
ISBN 13: 978-1-138-34805-9 (pbk)
ISBN 13: 978-0-429-43679-6 (ebk)

Contents

Figures and tables vi
Preface viii
Acknowledgements x
Abbreviations and terminology xi

1 Introduction 1
2 Introduction to Bridgehurst and Leafield comprehensive 17
3 Boys and girls - different but equal? 53
4 Black and white - unite or fight? 82
5 Classes within classes 103
6 Choosing for the future 137
7 Expectations and destinations 169
8 Summary and conclusion 199

Appendices

1 Leafield 5th form pro-forma questionnaire 215
2 Names and groupings of the twenty in-depth informants 217

Bibliography 219

Figures and tables

Table 3.1	Catering subjects, examination entries by gender, summer 1985	57
Table 3.2	Science subjects, O-level entries by gender, summer 1985	58
Table 5.1	Fathers' and mothers' occupations for in-depth informants	107
Table 5.2	Parental occupations and career aspirations of Leafield 5th form working class achievers	132
Table 6.1	Exam group informants by ethnicity, to show parental occupations and career aspirations	139
Table 6.2	Parental occupations and job aspirations of less-achieving working class informants, by ethnicity	147
Table 6.3	First and second choice occupations of 5th formers, by gender, as cited on 5th form questionnaire	150
Figure 6.4	Titles of career talks at Leafield school, autumn term, 1984	158
Table 6.5	First and second choice occupations of Leafield non-white 5th formers, by gender, as cited on 5th form questionnaire	160
Table 6.6	Pupils' suggestions for improving careers provision in school, by gender, as cited on 5th form questionnaire	163

Table 7.1	Destinations of Leafield 5th formers (as at 31st October 1985) compared with pupils originally aspiring to those destinations from earlier questionnaire		170
Table 7.2	Destinations of 5th formers who entered YTS one year after commencing training (as at 31st October 1986)		171
Table 7.3	Less-achievers: first destinations of informants upon leaving 5th form, by gender and ethnic origin		173
Table 7.4	Achievers: first destinations of informants upon leaving 5th form, by gender and ethnic origin		174
Figure 7.5	Diagram to show hierachy of success in job attainment for Leafield informants according to gender, race and class factors		197

Preface

This book is based upon an ethnographic study of white and black pupils in a mixed comprehensive school conducted during the 1980s. The research was designed to identify what pupils really thought about school, what they wanted from it and what they hoped for in their adult, working lives. In the process, gender, race and class factors were considered for their impact upon pupils' attitudes, academic achievement and early post-school destinations.

The findings are discussed in the light of the strong debate within the sociology of education that took place during the 1970s and 1980s concerning academic achievement and underachievement. The research is documented here as a contibution to that debate.

Since the research was completed, there have been major changes in education including the introduction of a new National Curriculum and the replacement of the Certificate of School Education (CSE) and O-levels with the General Certificate of School Education (GCSE). However, despite these changes, the findings in this study still have resonance in explaining why pupils do or do not thrive in the school environment of the 1990s. The grading system within GCSEs, the higher or lower levels at which subjects can be studied and the continuation of both mixed ability and ability-led classes, between them serve to create scenarios for pupils in the 1990s not dissimilar to those for the pupils in this study. It is, therefore, in the spirit of learning from what pupils can tell us that this work is published.

Ethnographic data comprise both classroom observations and discussions with 20 informants. These are supplemented by questionnaire data from the entire 5th form year.

Chapter 1 outlines the nature of existing research in this field and argues for the need to look at gender, race and class simultaneously to understand the impact of such factors on the lives of pupils. It also addresses methodological considerations and the problem of gaining access. Chapter 2 describes the school, its local context and its internal organisation. It also provides an introduction to the 5th year and their teachers drawing largely on classroom observations.

Gender, race and class receive individual attention in Chapters 3, 4 and 5 respectively. Chapter 3 indicates that gender was a powerful discriminator in classroom and breaktime interactions whilst Chapter 4 shows that racist humour and beliefs were a regular feature of school life despite a lack of racial discord at the school. Chapter 5 demonstrates that class consciousness existed amongst pupils and informed their attitudes towards school and work.

Chapter 6 concentrates on career choices and the quality of careers advice concluding that career choices were highly realistic in the main and that they were both gender and class-specific. Chapter 7 focuses on pupils' early destinations after the 5th form finding that girls were more likely than boys to utilise 6th form to gain entry into middle-class occupations. For those seeking employment, personal contacts were a great advantage. Black, job-seeking girls fared least well being more reliant on YTS and suffering greater unemployment whilst job-seeking boys were more likely to experience many jobs in quick succession. Only half of pupils overall achieved the destinations they had intended.

The conclusion reached in Chapter 8 is that gender and class had greatest impact on school experiences and career choices whilst race in conjunction with gender, affected actual destinations.

Acknowledgements

My thanks go, posthumously, to Barry Troyna who supported me as my supervisor in the early stages of this research and to Professor Robert Burgess whose encouragement and commitment to ethnographic research in schools led to the completion of this project. Thanks also go to the many pupils who shared their world with me so eagerly and without whom I would have had nothing to say. They also go to the teaching staff who stood back so that this research could take place. Thanks also to Caroline Henson for her pains-taking word processing and to Ali Black for her careful proof-reading.

Abbreviations and terminology

Abbreviations

A-level	-	Advanced level GCE (see below)
B.Tec	-	Business and Technical Education Council
CSE	-	Certificate of School Education
DES	-	Department of Education and Science
F.E.	-	Further Education
GCE	-	General Certificate of Education
HND	-	Higher National Diploma
LEA	-	Local Education Authority
O-level	-	Ordinary level GCE (see above)
RSA	-	Royal Society of Arts
OND	-	Ordinary National Diploma
RSA	-	Royal Society of Arts
TVEI	-	Training & Vocational Education Initiative
YOP	-	Youth Opportunities Programme
YTS	-	Youth Training Scheme
W.I.	-	West Indian origin (see below)

Terminology

Asian	=	Individuals of Asian origin irrespective of actual country of birth
West Indian	=	Individuals of West Indian origin irrespective of actual country of birth
Black	=	Pupils of West Indian origin only, unless otherwise stated
Achievers	=	Pupils sitting predominantly O-levels, with or without CSEs
Less-achievers	=	Pupils sitting predominantly CSEs, with or without the occasional O-level

1 Introduction

Ethnography has only become an important feature of research in the sociology of education since the 1960s. Studies by Hargreaves (1967) and Lacey (1970) are among the earliest examples of participant observation inside school walls and within the 'closed' confines of the classroom. This is perhaps surprising, considering the enormous importance of ethnographic participant observation studies some decades before in the pioneering anthropological accounts of Malinowski (1922) and Evans-Pritchard (1940) and in view of the in-depth insights gained by early sociologists such as Whyte (1955) and Becker (1963) in their respective studies of people on the margins of society.

During the 1970s, however, there was a growing incidence of ethnographic research in the classroom, aimed at understanding the processes and interactions taking place. The earliest school ethnographies focussed not only on boys but also on 'problem' boys. The early work of Hargreaves (1967) concentrated on the school experiences of secondary modern boys and described an emerging anti-school culture among the boys in the lowest streams. Similarly, Lacey (1970) observed the 'differentiation and polarisation' between top and bottom streams in a boys' grammar school, identifying similar pro-school and anti-school cultures associated with either academic success or relative failure. The work of Lambart (1976) is one exception to this being research conducted with girls parallel to the studies of Hargreaves and Lacey, but girls' experiences of education did not receive much attention prior to the 1980s. As a result, research on boys was invariably taken to be research on pupils per se. From this we can deduce that girls were seen as being either as no different to boys or as unimportant. Either way, they did not require special attention. That this attitude continued late into the 1970s is confirmed by Griffin (1987) who, speaking about her research with schoolgirls conducted in 1979, says:

> Exclusively male studies pass without comment, accepted as perfectly normal, whereas my work was seen as unusual from the start (Griffin, 1987, p. 219).

Invisible girls

That this is true for a number of ethnographic researches in schools during the 1970s can be illustrated by the quiet invisibility of girls in the work of Ball (1981). His Beachside Comprehensive was heralded as an important insight into the effects of banding in one of the new comprehensives, and therefore as an important sequel to Hargreaves (1967) and Lacey (1970). It passed virtually unnoticed in the book that the school under scrutiny was a mixed comprehensive and no attempt was made to separate out the different experiences and reactions of girls.

Many other examples exist to demonstrate the preponderance of boys' studies (e.g. Willis 1977, Corrigan 1979) and these have served to highlight a predominantly male, working-class culture and perspective in the literature. Whilst there may well be sound methodological reasons why male researchers should concentrate on male respondents (e.g. for reasons of easier access and better rapport with members of the same sex), it has to be recognised that the earlier work conducted with boys provided formative frameworks for analysis that were taken to be common truths for the subsequent analysis of pupils from different groups. Thus, later studies on girls laboured under the preconceptions and precedents set by earlier work conducted solely with boys. The problems encountered by Griffin (1987) serve to clarify this point and de-mystify the importance of the pioneering studies:

> I also felt the pressure to fit young women's experiences into the dominant cultural paradigm, ... At first I too searched for female equivalents to Willis' 'lads' and 'earoles', striving to identify female pro- and anti-school cultures .... I tried in vain to fit the young women's experiences into this 'gang of lads' format, but their lives were far too complex (Griffin, 1987, p. 218).

Fortunately, Griffin has not been alone in trying to redress the balance by bringing girls' experience of school onto the sociologists' agenda. Many researchers (e.g. Burgess 1986, Purvis 1984, Delamont 1980) have highlighted the need for research with girls and some (e.g. Sharpe 1976, Delamont 1980 and Stanley 1986) have begun the systematic observation of young women at school and in the transition to work, training, domesticity or unemployment in order to understand their world.

Black and white

Just as gender in general, and girls in particular, have until recently been ignored in ethnographic studies, so has race received scant attention. The work of Hargreaves, Lacey, Ball, Willis and many others concerned not just boys but indigenous white boys. Riley (1985a) remarks on this in her study of black South London schoolgirls. She writes:

> Girls at school are assumed either to be non-existent or just pale reflections of the male pupils. Black girls are doubly invisible (Riley, 1985a, p. 63).

Even where researchers have incorporated the male/female dimension in their work they have more often than not looked only at white pupils or left ethnicity unspecified (e.g. Stanworth 1981, Measor 1984 and Davies 1979).

Yet as Wright (1985) states:

> Studies on gender and classroom interaction which have failed to give some consideration to the participants' race (or ethnicity) as an important variable run the risk of either projecting too simplistic or distorted a picture of classroom dynamics (Wright, 1985, p. 184).

Exceptions to this include Griffin (1985) and Furlong (1984) who conducted interviews and conversations with both white and non-white pupils in order to understand the factors important in shaping their school lives. With Griffin's work, however, there is the fact that black, white and Asian girls were researched without any comparison with boys. With Furlong, there is the same lack of comparison but from the opposite perspective, for in his study white and black boys received attention without reference to the experiences of girls attending the same school. A similar, but more restrictive problem arises in studies that confine themselves to an analysis of black pupils' experiences alone as in the article by Fuller (1980). Though much rich data can be obtained in studies that concentrate on one particular ethnic group, there is always the danger that what is discovered is then attributed to that group and that group alone, when comparative research might have indicated that some of the findings were in fact common to other groups of pupils, and not due solely to racial or ethnic factors.

Wright's (1986) ethnographic study sought to offer a comprehensive account of black and Asian pupils' experiences in comparison with those of their white peers. Male and female, Asian, black and white pupils in two Midlands comprehensives were thoroughly researched through eighteen hundred hours of classroom observation, formal and informal interviews and school records. This, it could be argued, is a thorough ethnography which compares and contrasts the experiences of British school pupils according to their race (ethnicity) and gender. Yet here once more there is a deficit inasmuch as class receives scant attention. Indeed, Wright (1986), in describing her two schools where research was conducted merely states:

> Schools A and B are mixed comprehensives, approximately three miles apart. The ethnic compositions of the two schools vary considerably .... Despite the variation in the percentage of ethnic minority groups in the two schools, the school experiences of the Afro-Caribbean pupils in both schools appears [sic] not dissimilar (Wright, 1986, p. 218).

A three-mile distance in a British city can spell an enormous difference in catchment area and, in consequence, in the class origins of pupils.

The class dimension

What is required here is the additional analysis of the social class (or class consciousness/aspirations) of the pupils concerned for as Troyna (1984) says with regards to studies of West Indian underachievement:

> Social class is clearly a critical factor yet rarely have the data been standardised to take this into account (Troyna, 1984, p. 162).

Paradoxically, it was the earlier studies of such researchers as Hargreaves (1967), Willis (1977) and Corrigan (1979) which acknowledged the role played by working class values and culture as mediated through parents, family life and peer group influences. Thus, it would appear that as subsequent researchers elaborated on the gender and race dimensions of life in school they allowed the significance of class to recede. King (1987) notes the importance of this oversight as follows:

> Generalisations about men and women, or boys and girls, including their education, without reference to social class, are as limited as those about the social classes without reference to sex (King, 1987, p. 298).

This oversight is particularly important in the area of race and education where much research (e.g. Swann 1985, Eggleston et al. 1986) has demonstrated West Indian children to be underachieving vis-á-vis their white peers. Here, it is argued by such authors as Troyna (1984) and Reeves and Chevannes (1981), that it is crucial to understand the working class position of most West Indian families in Britain and to view the achievements of pupils from such families against a matched sample of working class whites. Reeves and Chevannes (1981) specifically make this point in their critique of the Rampton Committee's Interim Report (later Swann Report, 1985). They state:

> .... the figures are unstandardised for such crucial factors as parental social class or educational level.... The only variable mentioned in the case of the Rampton figures is that of racial (geographical?) group, but the significance of this factor can only be demonstrated after other well-established factors affecting educational performance have been allowed for (Reeves and Chevannes, 1981, p. 37).

Since the Swann Report, some researchers (e.g. Brewer and Haslum, 1986, Plewis, 1987) have addressed themselves to the interaction of race and class in affecting pupils' educational performance. Their work has highlighted the importance of home background and social class origins, factors indicated to have some importance in the research of previous authors such as Bagley (1971) and Driver (1980). However, their work has been based on quantitative data (e.g. measurable performance in reading tests and examinations) and not on ethnographic accounts of pupils' lives. Achievement relative to others is therefore established but not explained in terms of how these factors operate to affect life chances. In this respect, both Swann (1985) and Taylor (1981) have indicated the need for detailed research to determine the processes involved, with Taylor advocating studies of:

> the attitudes of pupils to teachers, and their perceptions of home and school differences, especially on the issue of differential expectation and aspiration which has been postulated (Taylor, 1981, p. 241).

An additional point concerning these studies is that again, they only take two of the three key variables of gender, race and class into account; in these cases just race and class are assessed without reference to gender.

Burgess (1986) has noted this deficit in the literature in relation to gender, race and class stating:

> ... the evidence has been reviewed separately yet in reality individuals experience the interaction of class, gender and race as the product of their membership of different social groups (Burgess, 1986, p. 126).

Towards integration

It is mindful of this deficit that this study attempts to deal simultaneously with the three variables of gender, race and class as they affected the lives of very 'ordinary' British-born white and black pupils during their final year of compulsory education (and beyond) at a mixed comprehensive in the south of England.

By 'ordinary' is meant those pupils who do not have privileged backgrounds or very high academic ability. The term is used in a similar way to Brown (1987) and his findings are compared with this study in relation to pupils' attitudes to school and their career or job choices. These ordinary pupils are further divided, in this study, into 'achievers' and 'less-achievers'. The former refers to pupils primarily taking 0-levels and the latter to pupils taking primarily CSEs or no examinations at all.

The term 'black' refers only to pupils of West Indian/Afro-Caribbean origin unless otherwise stated in the text. Where the term 'West Indian' appears this also signifies West Indian origin irrespective of place of birth. Where Asian pupils are involved they are referred to specifically as 'Asian' and not incorporated within the usage of the term 'black'. As Modood (1988) states, this falls in line with the actual practice of many researchers who use the term black solely to refer to people of West Indian origin. It also takes into account the fact that many Asian pupils do not see themselves as black but instead define themselves in terms of an Asian ethnicity and identity (Hanson, 1987). See Appendix 3 for a full list of terminology used.

This study examines race, class and gender issues both individually and in combination with each other, and uses an ethnographic and predominantly participant observation approach in order to understand what actually 'happened' in the daily lives of informants, both in and out of lessons.

Insufficient attention has been paid to the 'consumers' of education, yet it is crucial to listen to their voices in order to understand the pupils' world, hopes and ambitions and how school either serves or fails them. As Stebbins et al. (1987) state on the ritual of school:

> It is rare for a social scientist to enter and observe the world of the student as this world unfolds both inside and outside the classroom (Stebbins et al., 1987, p. 86).

Who, where and how?

By wishing to focus on attitudes to school, choices regarding staying on and career choices, 5th formers became the target group for study. A small group of 20 pupils were tracked both in their final year of compulsory schooling and beyond. This enabled the study of their reactions to school, their levels of achievement and their career choices, their exam results (if any), decisions regarding any further schooling or other education, and, finally, the search for work.

The school was selected to provide the highest proportions of black pupils in the area whilst simultaneously yielding a group of white and black informants who shared similar surroundings, housing and economic constraints. It was considered important that all pupils participating as in-depth informants in the research should come from one school and have received all their secondary education at that establishment.

The research which emanates from such a study can be said to be idiosyncratic with dubious representativeness of pupils 'in general'. It then follows that if the researcher has any aspirations for the findings to be utilised in changing policy or practice within the education system, those hopes are likely to be dashed. But in-depth work of this kind is constructive on two accounts. Firstly, as Wolcott (1975) indicates, ethnography can be used as an individual building block in the whole process of documenting and theorising education. Secondly, as Woods (1979) states, it is possible to achieve:

> Both rich and sensitive description and generalisability. The more 'representative' the school, the greater the chances of the external validity of the results (Woods, 1979, p. 268).

In this respect the school selected was an 'ordinary' southern English comprehensive, and the pupils selected as informants were a representative cross section of their year. The school was neither very old nor brand new, it had a mixture of 'progressive' and 'conservative' teachers, interested and disinterested pupils. It was not in an economically 'run-down' area with attendant unemployment problems, nor was it in a thriving middle-class suburb. It did not have large proportions of ethnic minority pupils such that its ethnic mix could be said to be higher than the UK average. In addition, out of all the possible pupils who could have become informants, great care was taken to avoid the 'special cases'. For example, the final group of some 20 informants did not include two pupils with special histories of bad attendance linked to (a) a car accident, and (b) poor home circumstances even though teachers had suggested they were 'interesting'. Similarly, a disproportionate number of high-flyers was avoided, despite teachers being keen that they should be included. In short, a basically commonsense approach was adopted in developing a good rapport with a representative group of pupils, some bright, others not, some keen, others disinterested in school work. The number of informants was restricted according to what was manageable in the time available, and in order to achieve a balance between the sexes and between white and black pupils. Finally, a group of 10 white and 10 West Indian origin pupils was selected.

So that the main in-depth work with informants could be properly set in context and analysed it was necessary to supplement the ethnographic and participant-observer approach using other research methods. This mostly occurred in the area of careers information, job placements and 'proving' academic achievement. Firstly, in order to gain a fuller understanding of the careers advice offered at the school it was necessary to 'interview' careers staff based on questions which arose out of observation. Secondly, hard statistical data was required as a backdrop to the individual experiences of informants. As a result, the research project also involved seeking out and analysing statistical information on exam results for the entire 5th form year.

The 5th form questionnaire

A questionnaire was also administered to the entire 5th form concerning their opinions on school and future employment issues. (See Appendix 1). This represented a more formal and quantifiable part of the research which involved the administering of a questionnaire to all 5th year pupils. It was given or sent to all registered 5th formers whether attending school or not.

The questionnaire was administered in March 1985, before the Easter vacation when some pupils would be officially leaving school. It was at this time of year, that the Head had a brief interview with every pupil about their future plans. The interviews were, indeed, very brief, approximately three minutes each. However, in this time the Head would establish whether each pupil was fixed up with a job or YTS, had taken advantage of the various careers services available both in school and at the local Careers Office, or intended to continue with education in the 6th form or College of Further Education. It was whilst waiting for this interview that all pupils were asked to complete a questionnaire. Of the 251 pupils in the 5th form 155 were present for the Head's interview and of these, 152 completed the form. Of the remaining 96 pupils, some 41 were known to be absent for long term reasons as follows:

- 13 poor attenders
- 10 school refusers
- 2 suspended
- 2 pregnant
- 3 in Special Needs education outside normal classes
- 11 on long term work experience

Postal questionnaires were sent out in May 1985 to these 96 pupils and after a second reminder 41 postal replies to the questionnaire were received. Thus in total 193 replies were received representing 77 per cent of the entire 5th form year.

The purpose of the questionnaire was to establish pupils' likes and dislikes about school and their opinions of the careers advice available to them. It was also aimed at obtaining data on their work experience (if any), job choices and work aspirations upon leaving school. A sample of the questionnaire appears as Appendix I. The questionnaire data proved most useful in identifying trends in pupils' opinions and job choices that could then be illustrated and explained by more descriptive data gained from in-depth informants.

Thus, although the primary objective was to identify the in-depth perspectives of informants, the data gleaned could also be viewed against the whole of which they were part. This, it was hoped, would add to the 'generalisability' and practical utility of the study. In addition, in seeking to examine the 'reality' for informants from different angles (as well as employing varying methods to get at their own perceived reality), it can be argued that there was an attempt at triangulation which should serve to further validate the research findings.

Overall then, the research consisted of casual observation, discussions, structured and unstructured interviews, participant observation, collection and analysis of statistical data and compilation, administration and analysis of a questionnaire. The intention throughout was to make proper sense of the world of these comprehensive school pupils, relating it primarily in their own words but using gender, race and class paradigms.

Gaining access

Gaining access to the school did not prove difficult. An initial enquiry followed up by a letter and subsequent meeting with the Head was sufficient to convince him that the study was worthwhile. The research idea was then put to staff at a school meeting and they voted to permit the researcher open access. Making personal contacts within the school proved far less problematic than had been anticipated. Certainly some teachers and pupils were more forthcoming than others but there was never any danger of the research project grinding to a halt due to limited or faltering access.

Teachers were, in the main, genuinely keen to co-operate. Sometimes they were too keen, desiring access to the data being collected which they could not have in order to protect the anonymity of informants.

Pupils rarely have the opportunity to express their views and the fact that someone actually cared about their point of view and had time to listen to them made for open and easy rapport with both black and white boys and girls. This can perhaps be attributed to the sincere interest the researcher had in them as people and in what they thought and felt. This was something that came across and as a result they were more than willing to discuss their ideas and hopes and grievances.

Initial access

Upon entering the school, it was made clear by the Head, that the researcher was 'on her own', therefore links had to be forged with individual teachers and pupils negotiating access with them directly as and when required. There were no obstacles placed in the way and the request for access to school records and reports were answered in the affirmative. All office staff were very helpful and in fact, their knowledge was also immense concerning the whereabouts of individuals. Thus, if any difficulty was being experienced in tracing a particular pupil or member of staff, relevant information could usually be gained from the General Office.

After some initial fact-finding at the school, the following research schedule was adopted:-

From half term to Christmas 1984

1 week spent alongside Section 11 teacher
4 weeks following one individual pupil per week
1 week of general observation and teacher contacts

January 1985 to Summer 1985

Informal, in-depth interviews with informants
Administration of questionnaire to 5th form
Recourse to teachers and school records

Autumn 1985 to Christmas 1985

Follow up with school leavers and those who entered 6th form
Analysis of questionnaire data

The researchers role

Being a researcher and not a teacher was a distinct advantage in conducting this research. It is difficult, if not impossible to gain access to the private thoughts and private lives of pupils whilst occupying the role of teacher, especially when pupils' actions and perspectives are considered illegitimate by the school. Corrigan (1979) is right when he states:

> Those readers who are teachers and those who remember their school days will be aware, I hope, of the impossibility of actually gaining accurate information from pupils if you are a teacher. Being labelled as such breaks the possibility of gaining certain sorts of information at all. What happens if a pupil smokes? (Corrigan, 1979, p. 12).

Corrigan's comment here about smoking was borne out exactly in this study because smoking was a big issue for some informants. They wanted the right to smoke at break times, but took every opportunity to have a quick cigarette between lessons anyway. Teachers on the other hand were quite clear on this issue. Smoking was not to be tolerated. As a result break time could evolve into a 'them and us' situation of patrolling teachers and furtive smokers.

Birkstead (1976) has also asserted that teacher status is problematic where pupil accounts are required, and certainly in this study (where pupil perspectives were essential to the research) it would not have been possible to gain the respect and trust of many of the informants if their researcher had not stood with them on the smoking issue. Basically it was necessary to take risks alongside them whilst being neither a true pupil nor a teacher. It was important neither to be an active part of their stand, nor a public supporter of school policy in order to avoid the sanctions of both camps.

Over the first week alone, however, word spread among the pupils that this researcher was 'alright'. Pupils stopped pretending they had something special to do at break time in order to get away for a 'quick fag', but simply said 'We're off to 'X' for a smoke'. Pupils' acceptance of the researcher was confirmed when it became possible to turn the corner of 'X' and not be met with hurried stubbing out activity. Nevertheless pupils did test the researcher's allegiance over the smoking issue by subtly 'dropping her in it' in front of staff, presumably to gauge the reaction.

'Got any fags Miss?' the researcher was asked by one boy during a very quiet part of a Geography lesson, whereupon a number of pairs of eyes were upon her. A silent shaking of the head sufficed for a reply. 'Just thought you might have, that's all.' came the casual reply. The teacher in this lesson could not help overhearing this but very tactfully ignored the episode, mindful of the researcher's ambiguous position.

Being neither pupil nor teacher did pose some problems in maintaining a good working relationship with staff. For example, once a patrolling teacher at break time did interrupt a smoking session among a group of girls whilst they were being shadowed by thr researcher. Fortunately this teacher was sympathetic to the researcher's role and gracefully retreated from the scene. Nevertheless, it was possible to feel very split by such a 'confrontation' of values, and recourse to the Staff Room to 'patch things up' in due course was sometimes called for. The feeling of being a go-between was ever present however, especially as in some instances, pupils wanted to use the research opportunity for representations to be made to staff on their behalf; and teachers (perhaps ingenuously), wanted feedback on pupils' views of their lessons and pupils' comments. It was important to take great care in not giving away information that would negate the absolute anonymity that pupils had been promised. Again, 'a sit-on-the-fence' approach seemed the best. A topic could be discussed in general terms with teachers without reference to specific individuals so as to avoid being seen as obstructive or hostile. It was at this time, however, that it became clear how much teachers valued feedback from pupils, and some articulated how fortunate they thought the researcher was in being able to get 'closer' to the pupils than they could. Some were quite envious of this position.

Viewed from the pupils' angle, the researcher was also seen as fortunate, it was possible to engage in their world but with an 'escape' route to a different life outside of school. Although many trusted the researcher from the outset and were prepared to be outspoken, others 'tested' her, as in Burgess (1984), in subtle ways. Mention has already been made of the pupil who made reference to smoking in class to see what reaction it would gain. Other tests included being invited into the pupils' social circles and life outside school (e.g. invited to go swimming) and being asked questions about personal life to see if reciprocity was in the offing.

The week spent following a female, white CSE-taker was particularly fruitful. This was a girl who had already indicated her willingness to be involved in the study and her eagerness made it important to double check with both her teachers and her friends that her observed behaviour was characteristic and not for the researcher's benefit alone. She was definitely delighted to be shadowed for a week to the point of showing off about it. On one occasion she chose to taunt a group of boys outside the toilets:

> 'My friend Mandy and I are going in 'ere for a chat' (indicating towards the girls' toilet).
>
> 'Go on then, go and have your fucking book written about you then!'

derided one of the boys amid other jeering and whistling.

The introductions that ensued to her friends and to some black boys were invaluable albeit that that it ran the risk of alienating other pupils not in her clique. Woods (1979) sees this as inevitable. In developing contacts with one group, the impressions given to others are unavoidable. This can be reconciled on the basis that ethnographic data had to be rich and truthful, and that excellent rapport with a small cluster of respondents is more fruitful than shallow contact with many.

Original fears of not being able to develop enough contacts among the boys and amongst the black pupils because of being female and white proved quite unfounded. Boys struck up conversations during breaks and the lessons that lent themselves to talking, such as woodwork and metalwork. One boy who was shadowed was a 'problem' to the school, a persistent non-attender. This itself gave other pupils cause to comment, and friendships were struck up out of such initial comments as:

> 'Old Terry's a dosser, what you following him for?'

Contacts among the boys developed well and breaktime conversations with them were more informative and constructive than with the girls. This, however, was due in part to the slant of the research interests (i.e. career and work) and there was a distinct drying up on such matters amongst the girls. This aspect of a gender divide is discussed later in Chapter 3.

The week shadowing a black girl was also formative in creating introductions to a number of her black female friends. All the black pupils knew each other well and they formed a small, though not segregated, clique at breaktimes. Contacts with black boys developed either through white girls or by direct approaches. With the black girls, however, there was something of Burgess's 'snowball effect', whereby one contact led to others within the same set. This raised a concerned about bias in the sample, but later research served to allay those fears because it transpired that whilst this group of girls did socialise together and know each other outside school, they were not necessarily a cohesive unit in terms of friendship groups or ability. Indeed, the black girls spanned the whole range of the academic achievement spectrum and some never saw each other outside school. More importantly, however, the final group of 20 informants include all 10 black pupils in the 5th year. Thus, sampling difficulties were avoided, for the entire cohort of black pupils was included in the study.

Hitting it off in the early stages with a black pupil who was shadowed for a week taught the value, indeed absolute necessity, of giving of oneself in order to develop a good relationship. It was important to share with this girl details of the researcher's private life including views on and activities to combat racism. All of this was appreciated, and it helped her to relax. Only then did her conversations open out and become more honest and did she offer assistance in getting to know the other black girls.

Burgess (1984) argues that to remain totally 'impartial' and not comment or give of oneself is impossible if good relationships are to be maintained. This study bears out that point. A two-way flow has to be perceived by the informant for trust to develop, let alone the desire to participate in discussions. Without such giving of self, discussions become sterile events.

Teachers have already been said to be keen for feedback, but pupils also wanted to discuss with the researcher things that mattered to them. Boys wanted opinions on unemployment and girls wanted more personal information from the researcher. Griffin (1985) had similar experiences in her study of female school leavers, and her sentiments are echoed entirely:

> At school, young women had asked how I had got the research job, and how I felt about leaving school. After leaving school, they tended to ask

more about their ex-school friends, using me as a means of keeping in touch. I never treated these questions as irrelevant or unwanted intrusions ....Young women used me as a source of information, ... as well as 'someone to moan to' when they were depressed (Griffin, 1985, pp. 108-9).

In terms of making good pupil contacts for later in-depth discussions, the most unproductive week was the one spent with a top-achieving female pupil. This girl did not open out and was generally too busy with her academic interests to spend time talking to a researcher. Her lack of enthusiasm to be involved in the study blocked her friends in deciding to volunteer due to her influence among her peers. Timing, however, was of critical importance. For this girl and her main associates, the 5th year was one huge build up to 'O' levels. Primary objectives were getting through the syllabus, completing project work and having enough free periods for revision. Many of her friends voiced their willingness to talk 'after exams' and made it clear that nobody was going to get in their way in the meantime. Although CSE-takers were similarly locked into a syllabus and time schedule, they did not display the same fervour or interest in their exams and were prepared to take time out to talk about themselves. Indeed, many positively preferred taking time out to talk rather than concentrate on lessons. Brown (1987) found a similar ease of access with his 'tidy lads' who did their 'own thing' at school and were always ready for a chat. As a result, CSE-takers and potential Easter-leavers were early targets for the research and arrangements were made to talk at length with a number of top achieving pupils upon their return to the 6th form, after the summer break.

Interactions with staff

Although the views of staff and observations of them were only peripheral to the study, teachers themselves played an important part in access to pupils, records and operational matters and so relationships with them were of vital importance.

The Head

The Head has already been described as a busy person who gave the researcher a free hand within the school. The only negative effect of this was that he was difficult to contact later on in the research process, to authorise letters to parents, when their permission to interview their children was needed. In addition, it took some patience and fortitude to wait until the Head was sufficiently free of work commitments to spare the time for an interview. A spare slot would be weeks, rather than days ahead. However, his tacit support was always present.

The teachers

The general atmosphere among staff was one of being open and able to speak one's mind. It proved possible to circulate among and gain the co-operation of everyone approached. Only two teachers refused permission for the researcher to sit in on their lessons with pupils during the weeks of participant observation. (An advance notice had been pinned up in the staffroom asking for any dissenters to notify the Head of 5th Year immediately). One teacher's reason was that she was having difficulty with the particular pupil being shadowed and felt that the researcher's presence would be detrimental. The other had not read the advance warning notice, and turned the researcher away from his classroom before the lesson began. Afterwards pupils confided that he was a real stickler for discipline and probably did not want his treatment of pupils to be on record. It came as no surprise to pupils that he refused, in fact, it served to confirm their negative opinion of him.

Some staff were positively helpful in not only granting access to their lessons, but also granting valuable lesson time in which the research could be described to pupils and their questions answered. Others offered opinions on how sexism and/or racism was operating in the school, providing useful hints for things to follow up. Then again, simple conversation and eavesdropping in the staffroom was often very informative, especially in gleaning the reputations of individual pupils and the attitudes of various teachers towards them.

Overview

This discussion of the literature available in the 1980s indicates a real need to research the reality of pupils' lives inside school whilst taking account of their gender, race and class origins. The actual research stategy selected for this study has been identified and its effectiveness considered whilst some potentially problematic areas concerning access and methodology have been highlighted and discussed. A fuller introduction to the school selected for study and its pupils is now called for. This is the subject of Chapter 2.

2 Introduction to Bridgehurst and Leafield comprehensive

The city of Bridgehurst

Bridgehurst is a small city of some 100,000 inhabitants in southern England. The city features three industrial estates, central and suburban shopping area, some private colleges and a university. It has a popular football team and offers various cinemas, theatres and leisure centres. Bridgehurst is not noted for high levels of unemployment, nor does it have a run-down inner-city area with high concentrations of ethnic minority families. Data from the 1981 Census (OPCS 1982a, b) reveal that the New Commonwealth and Pakistan-born population is around 3.5 per cent from which an estimate of some 7 per cent can be made to include British-born black and Asian citizens that remain invisible in Census statistics.

Ethnic minorities are not evenly distributed throughout the city and its suburbs. An unpublished Ph.D. Thesis (1975)[1] examining spatial segregation in the city demonstrates that the early post-war Indian immigrants were, by the mid-1970s, settled into a highly fashionable suburb characterised by expensive and spacious Victorian properties. Arriving slightly later, West Indian (black) families had settled initially in inexpensive rented accommodation near the city centre but had, by the 1970s, shifted towards council housing, primarily on Leafield estate on the southern edge of the city. Subsequent immigrants arriving from Pakistan and Bangladesh were clustered in private, rented and private, owner-occupied, run-down Victorian terraced houses close to, but not in, the city centre.

Leafield estate

Leafield estate is a housing estate initiated by the city council in the 1950s as part of their Development Plan subsequent to the Town and Country Planning Act of 1947. Originally the objective was that this estate should provide rented accommodation for the expanding workforce of major industries situated nearby. By the early 1980s some 10,000 people were resident on the estate and some houses had passed into private owner-occupation due to the council's policy of selling to tenants. Nevertheless the vast majority of families remained as tenants of the council.

In a further unpublished Ph.D. Thesis (1967)[2] there were no 'coloured' (sic) children on the school rolls in the older part of the estate in 1967. At that time there was only one 'black' member of the Social Club and two 'West Indian' boys in the Boy Scouts. By 1983, some 10 per cent of pupils at the local middle school were of West Indian origin, there was a thriving West Indian youth club, and varied services offered to the black community including a supplementary Saturday school initiative. Two interesting features of this estate at this time were its youthful age structure and increasing proportion of West Indian-origin families. As the estate developed during the 1960s it was mostly younger couples with small children who were housed there. As a result, in 1983 the retired population was still low, and the estate still comprised mainly middle-aged families plus their now-adult children and their respective very young children. In addition, the number of West Indian-origin families on the estate had risen out of proportion to the figures for the city as a whole. Using the 1981 Census data cited above, the number of Caribbean-born persons in the city as a whole totalled 1.2 per cent of the total population. Yet, taking the estate alone from the OPCS Small Area Statistics, no less than 7 per cent of the estate's population was Caribbean-born. Furthermore, one third of the city's Caribbean-born population was clustered on Leafield estate giving it the highest density of black families of any area in the city. Leafield estate provided half the school intake at Leafield School.

Hillrise

This area is, in effect, two council estates, providing some 20 per cent of the intake at Leafield school. It is comprised of mostly pre-war council housing of concrete unit construction together with other 1930s brick-built council houses. Towards the city-side edge of the estates the houses give way to larger 1930s semi-detached properties in private ownership. Originally the two estates were totally council owned but in accordance with council policy, a small proportion were sold to tenants and eventually entered the house market. As the origins of Hillrise are some twenty or thirty years earlier than Leafield, the area has a higher proportion of elderly residents. In addition, the Caribbean-born population stood at less than 1 per cent of the total population in the 1980s. Situated just a short cycle ride from the industrial area and major factories, this estate also serves as housing for many manual workers.

Rushmead

The once separate village of Rushmead was by 1984, hardly distinguishable from the various suburbs of Bridgehurst. In the 19th century it had comprised both stone and brick-built terraced cottages, a Sanatorium for mentally ill patients, and a cluster of wealthy land-owners, clergy and squires. At that time the Sanatorium provided a good deal of unskilled employment for the local residents and children attended the typically Victorian village school. Leafield School is located on flat meadow land between Rushmead and Leafield Estate and is the 'natural' choice of upper school for both these areas. Rushmead itself has a large council estate of pre-war origins. Houses are mostly constructed of concrete slabs with asbestos-tiled roofing, giving a bleak appearance. These houses abut one side of the school premises.

The population characteristics of Rushmead are similar to those of Hillrise but with a slightly increased elderly population and higher proportion of detached properties where it adjoins open countryside and farm-land. The proportion of West Indian-origin families in the 1980s was under 1 per cent.

Leafield School's catchment area

The major council estates of Leafield, Hillrise and Rushmead, inhabited as they are by predominantly manual and unskilled workers (OPCS, 1982b), provide a mainly working class catchment area for Leafield School. Houses that have been purchased by tenants still remain mainly in the hands of manual workers such that Leafield School's intake throughout the 1980s included a majority of pupils from working class backgrounds. Indeed, a study of the occupation of 5th formers' parents taken from school records revealed something close to 90 per cent of all pupils having an unskilled, manual working father and/or mother. Half of Leafield's intake came from Leafield Estate with a further one-fifth coming from Hillrise. Rushmead accounted for a further one-tenth of the school intake such that these three heavily working class areas provided the home environment for 80 per cent of Leafield pupils.

Leafield School

Leafield School was formed in 1968 when the two co-existing grammar and secondary modern schools, on sites adjacent to each other, were merged to form one, new comprehensive school. Local Government Reorganisation in 1974 created a new County Council responsible for the school and by 1977 a major building programme was completed turning the original grammar and secondary modern blocks into part of an integrated and modern complex of buildings and quadrangles.

By 1984, the school accommodated some 900 pupils with approximately 100 in the two 6th form years combined. There were some 60 teachers and 30 support staff including office, technical, cleaning and kitchen personnel.

To the newcomer, the school appeared to be a strange mixture of 1960s-style 'modern' concrete and glass blocks, two to four storeys high with open plan staircases, in combination with single storey unit-construction or timber-framed buildings reminiscent of army camps and Nissen huts. These buildings contained Maths, Science and Technical Blocks, a library and 6th form Centre, specialist subject suites and leisure/study facilities. Initially the layout seemed sprawling and the architecture incongruous.

Pupils were very aware of their surroundings and the most vociferous comments concerned the upkeep of buildings and condition of the classrooms. For example, one observed lesson was interrupted as follows:

Eileen (out loud): 'This place is a dump, have you seen the state of it?'

Liz (to teacher): 'Look at this disgusting roof', [the teacher agrees].

Indeed, the room being occupied at the time was depressing. Located in a dark-stained, ship-lapped timber, single-storey building in the middle of the school site, it looked, from the outside, like a large Boy Scouts' hut. Field notes at the time say about the classroom:

Rather drab and austere by first and middle school standards I have seen locally. Ceiling construction is soft-board panels and the paint on 50 per cent of these is flaking. There are holes in the ceiling; large, brown water stains and black mould on two of the six panels (roof leaking?) and one such bad patch surrounds a fluorescent light.

The walls and radiators are acid yellow/green and the latter are old-fashioned, 'institutional' radiators. There is a lot of visible, chunky pipe work. Wood block, herring-bone flooring and partition walls complete the room. Tables are wood-grain formica on four metal legs, chairs to match on metal legs, the room seats around 30 people. Desks are slightly damaged at the edges, some edging strips are missing but there is very little graffiti, no cuts or inking on table tops. Windows go the length of one wall making it hot and stuffy today with the radiators on. Windows open in pairs using a winding handle soon creating a cold draught. Two thin blue curtains hang at one set of windows but they are missing from the other.........

The three lockable cupboards housing text books are a mixture. One old, dirty-looking tall pine cupboard; one modern, glass-topped low cupboard and a further white laminated one. The teacher's desk is a light oak table, very plain, standing directly in front of the chalk board.

A connecting door to another classroom (presently unoccupied) blows open because the door jamb is split and the lock cannot connect into its housing. It is wedged shut with a chair. (Field notes, 8 November 1984)

Aims of the school

The aim of the school, as stated in the 1984 handbook to parents, was:

> to provide the best possible secondary education for every one of our pupils (A Guide for Parents, 1984).

Emphasis was placed on giving each pupil a good start in adult life not only in terms of qualifications obtained at school but also in:

> equipping them for continuous education at Further or Higher level, for their work, for their leisure-time, for their relationships with other

individuals and for their community responsibilities (A Guide for Parents, 1984).

The school handbook went further to explain in detail the skills and issues it hoped to promote during each pupil's time at the school. An longer extract reads:

> Listed below are the skills, the concerns and the various kinds of awareness that we wish each student to acquire in the maximum measure that intelligence, temperament, aptitude and supporting background make possible.
>
> Numeracy, literacy and the communication skills associated with them.
>
> Respect for the worth and dignity of all people whatever their race, nationality or creed.
>
> Respect for the truth and the ability to exercise the human capacities for curiosity, criticism, reasoning and sensitivity in establishing it over falsehood and in making judgements about the values of different truths.
>
> A good general knowledge drawn from areas of human learning that are generally accessible and that our society has deemed important. These are likely to embrace the arts, sciences, humanities and the social sciences and to include moral, political and aesthetic learning.
>
> The capacity to develop a concern for what is important and worthwhile and to persevere in the pursuit of such excellence.
>
> The capacity to find enjoyment in all good learning experiences.
>
> Appreciation of the sensitivity and the social skills that are likely to lead to successful relationships with others.
>
> A respect for Beauty and a concern to enjoy it and, if possible, help create it for others in whatever activity the individual may discover talent or ability.
>
> A regard for the natural environment and a determination to preserve it for future generations.

A regard for healthy recreational activities and a willingness to participate in and promote these in the interest of human wellbeing, co-operation and higher endeavour.

An understanding of those communities at home and at work in which our students are likely to find themselves and a readiness to work constructively within those communities (A Guide for Parents, 1984).

From this it is clear that the school was far more than a strictly academically-orientated one. There was a keen desire to broaden the nature of the education the pupils received particularly in the area of awareness of, and sensitivity towards, the needs of others, especially in the community. There was a desire to make the education on offer relevant to the needs and aspirations of the mostly working class pupils who attended the school.

Much of this could be attributed to the appointment of a new Head in 1982. His philosophy was one of removing traditional boundaries between academic disciplines, aiming instead for an integrated syllabus. In addition, he favoured mixed ability teaching and had implemented a common core curriculum in some subjects. Details of this are contained in the next section.

The Head also favoured the idea of the 'community' school, the objective being that Leafield should be open for local residents to use its facilities and that parents should be actively encouraged to have a say in their children's education via the Parents Association. Whilst there was some local uptake of the school's swimming pool, coffee mornings and adult learning centre, there was little parental involvement in school matters save for the conscientious efforts of a committed few. Indeed, such was the low level of parental involvement that teachers often judged a good, supportive home background by whether or not a mother or father bothered to turn up to parents' evenings, there being little or no expectation that any other involvement would be forthcoming:

> Form teacher (said of Sylvia - a white pupil): 'Oh yes. Nice family, plenty of encouragement. Mother always comes to parents' evenings and responds to letters.'

Leafield School then, set out to 'reach' its public and provide useful community services. From observations, however, this meant little to the pupils attending the school.

The curriculum

All pupils joining the school followed courses in the following areas:

English Language and Literature
Expressive Art - (Art, Drama, Music and Dance)
Science and Technology
Modern Languages
Mathematics
Community Studies - (including History, Geography, Religious Education)
Home Studies - (incorporating Needlecraft and Domestic Science)
Games and Physical Education

All the main examination subjects were offered at G.C.E. O-level and/or C.S.E. together with a variety of courses in Russian, Latin, Environment Studies, Economics, Humanities, Sociology, Social Studies, Statistics, Computer Studies, Commerce, Parentcraft, Engineering Drawing, Motor Mechanics, Control Technology, Photography, Movement Studies and Christian Ethics.

Apart from this, the school also offered its own local Certificate of Educational Achievement to all students joining the school after September 1983. This certificate provided an assessment of qualities other than pure academic abilities and ensured that each pupil left school with some measurable assessment of their achievements. The certificate did not, however, relate to the pupils in this study who were the last year to come through under a more traditional system. Apart from the Certificate of Educational Achievement, the new pupils after September 1983 also had greater lateral flexibility in the subjects offered. Either exam or non-exam modules could be followed in a way not possible before. However, as curriculum content was not the focus of this study, and indeed this new initiative did not affect the informants in this research (viz: students finishing compulsory education in 1985), it will not be discussed in any detail. Suffice it to say, that in the Head's opinion, subsequent pupils would have a better deal out of their subjects and more choices open to them. Whether this would, in time, affect levels of satisfaction with schooling is impossible to say, and would need a further study with younger cohorts of pupils finishing their compulsory schooling no earlier than 1988. However, judging by early observation of the 4th year who were following this revised curriculum, they found school equally as boring as their 5th form peers. School was still compulsory, it had set hours and set lessons. Pupils did not appreciate the niceties of curriculum reform and integrated studies, failing to see any relevance in the new-style syllabus and the good intentions of teachers. The new Records of Achievement were a vague irrelevance.

In the 6th form, pupils could follow a fairly standard range of A-level subjects including English, Mathematics, Science subjects, Languages, Art, Music, Religious Education, History, Geography, Woodwork, Economics and General Studies. Special tuition was also available for those sitting Oxford and Cambridge University entrance examinations but no-one aspired to such heights from the 5th form year documented in this study.

Pupils were also very much encouraged to stay on in the 6th form to re-take O-levels if necessary. Business Education Council (BEC) courses, Secretarial (RSA) and City and Guilds courses were also offered. These two factors contributed towards the high uptake of 6th form studies for a school which had very few high-flyers.

Indeed Summer 1985 O-level results revealed only four grade A's out of 280 entrants. Nevertheless the two 6th form years usually totalled some 100-120 pupils, approximately half of the number in the 5th form year. The precise reasons for this high uptake, including whether 6th form was utilised to avoid YTS or unemployment are considered later in Chapter 7.

In addition to the standard curriculum, the school prided itself in a number of special projects and activities. The school had its own residential centre for weekend and holiday ventures, conducted field studies at county-funded outward bound centres as well as engaging in skiing, hill walking and surfing expeditions. Foreign exchange visits were available to language students and school trips abroad were organised for the summer vacations. In 1985 there was a major study trip to a school in East Africa and many school projects were organised around this theme, including major fund-raising events. Beyond this the school presented dramatic and musical productions throughout the year and had an excellent reputation for its sporting achievements.

One particularly interesting feature of the school calendar was an Activities Week. Held every year after the summer examination sittings, all lessons stopped and students could sign up to learn various skills or participate in a multitude of activities offered according to the interests and expertise of members of staff. 1985 Activities Week include cycling trips in the local countryside, mural painting, foreign foods, sailing, fantasy adventure games, pottery, bridge and egg races. (This list is by no means exhaustive.)

Careers advice

Leafield School offered careers advice to its pupils in a number of different ways. The school had a 'Head of Careers and Industrial Liaison', a full-time member of staff with additional responsibility for:

(a) arranging and timetabling visiting speakers with a variety of industrial and commercial employers who recruit new staff in the area,

(b) organising talks in school by the local careers officer,

(c) industrial liaison both to secure work experience placements for most members of the 5th form and, occasionally, to lobby for equipment or finances to assist the school,

(d) individual career interviews with every member of the 5th form to advise on their interests and ambitions.

In recognition of these duties, the teacher concerned received an additional two hours per week on his timetable, but the actual work load involved many more hours than that. Many of his free periods were spent telephoning prospective visiting speakers and setting up work experience opportunities. In addition, his presence was required at career talks held, on average, once per week for the 5th formers during their final, compulsory year at school.

Pupil perspectives on the careers advice and world of work are contained in Chapter 6 together with observational and interview data on the careers service. Discussion of this important area is therefore postponed until then. For the present, suffice it to say that staff appreciated the importance of both work experience and careers advice and operated a system designed to benefit the pupils in this respect. This system was found to be lacking by many informants, a view confirmed by the researcher's observations and responses in questionnaire.

School organisation

The form group system

Each year group, which numbered around 250 pupils, was split into form groups each with its own Form Tutor. The Form Tutors were reponsible for checking the daily registers and for giving out twice-weekly bulletins and messages to their classes before they left each morning to attend various lessons in both mixed-ability and ability groups. Form Tutors had prime responsibility for the pastoral care of pupils in their Tutor Group including giving praise and encouragement, collecting merits awarded by other teachers to members of their form, and effecting any sanctions (see next section). The Form Tutor was also responsible for inviting parents to organised meetings and contacting them personally at other times as deemed necessary. During the course of this study, the 5th form contained 251 pupils and was split into 10 form groups, giving each member of staff responsibility for, on average, 25 pupils.

One level up from the Form Tutors were the Senior Tutors. They had responsibility for supervising the effectiveness of a group of tutors and checking that all agreed procedures were duly carried whilst also operating as a Form Tutor themselves. The Senior Tutors also formed the next stage in the referral system of sanctions discussed in the next section. In general there were two Senior Tutors for each year group.

The final link in the form group system was the Year Tutor. The Year Tutor chaired regular meetings concerned with organisation and administration of the year group and also had responsibility for initiating school report programmes, assessments, and parental contacts. Further responsibilities included bringing issues to the attention of the Head that could not be resolved at Year Group meetings. This person also organised their year group's assemblies and allocated pupils to their form groups.

Overall, the form group system represented a hierarchical system of control through which matters arising at the level of the classroom could be referred upwards for decision making or action where necessary, and through which matters of policy and practice could be filtered downwards from the Head and Deputy Heads to all members of the teaching staff. A series of fortnightly Year Group meetings preceded by Senior Year Staff meetings created a channel for the dissemination of information. Similarly in subject Departments, there were fortnightly Departmental meetings running alternatively with the Year Group meetings at which matters arising at a preceding Head of Departments meeting could be discussed. Throughout the term then, all staff, whatever their status in the Department or Form System, would find themselves scheduled to attend meetings once a week at which they could inform others of events and be informed themselves.

The School Council

The School Council represented the pupil voice in the decision making process at Leafield School. Each form had an elected representative on the council which met four times each term and was chaired by a senior pupil. The staff also had two representatives and the Head and other senior staff were ex-officio members.

On a wide range of matters directly concerned with the interests of the pupils (e.g. school rules, punishment) the School Council's views were fully accepted and it offered its opinions on other matters of wider concern. Its agenda arose from proposals, recommendations and requests for information formulated by Form Groups. Although the Head had a veto, it was rarely, if ever, used.

The Council also had control over the spending of the School Fund (yearly contribution by parents). This normally amounted to about £350 annually.

Each Form Tutor was responsible for ensuring that the election of the form's representative was carried out in a serious manner, and that the representative attended all meetings. The Form Tutor also had to provide opportunities for the group to discuss matters important to them and to encourage them in using the School Council to voice their opinions or grievances. In practice, however, very few pupils had an interest in participating in this 'pupil voice'. Volunteers to be form representative were not always forthcoming and few informants knew or cared who their representative was.

Rules, regulations and rewards

Rules and regulations were kept to a minimum at Leafield, and those that were in force concerning conduct had been agreed between the Head, teaching staff and School Council as being acceptable norms of behaviour both within the classroom and around the school generally. They included rules of courtesy and politeness, attention in lessons and orderly conduct at all times. There was no school uniform although pupils were expected to attend suitably dressed in a neat and tidy condition. Smoking was completely forbidden and being found smoking led automatically to a detention. Other forms of misbehaviour outside lesson time (e.g. fighting) could also lead to a detention. Within the classroom situation, disruptive behaviour was first dealt with by a verbal warning from the teacher. From there, a referral system operated, whereby a further offence led to the pupil being sent out of the classroom to report to the Year Tutor, the Deputy or Head teacher. Cases of persistent underachievement or misbehaviour were reported to the Senior Tutor for investigation and corrective action.

Where necessary, a pupil could be placed 'on report'. This involved the pupil carrying a pro-forma to every lesson over a specified period of time for each teacher to enter comments upon concerning the pupil's behaviour in their class.

Extra work could also be set as a sanction for messing about and low output, but instructions to staff stated that this must be of a 'constructive nature'. The same document also stated:

> The Head insists that there be no corporal punishment in this school (Folder of Supplementary Information for New Staff, 1984).

Instead, pupils who perpetually misbehaved or who were repeatedly in detention were considered for suspension. Such action was, however, seen as drastic and would not occur without much staff and parental consultation. During my time at the school there was just one suspension, of a boy who let off a shot gun near a girl pupil injuring the side of her face. Even then, the Head had been reluctant to suspend the boy but felt he had no option but to impose the ultimate sanction.

The other side of the coin to sanctions and discipline was praise and rewards. Staff were at all times urged to give verbal praise where it was due and to consolidate this by awarding merit points for individual pieces of work:

> deemed to be of very high standard for the pupil concerned (Folder of Supplementary Information for New Staff, 1984)

When five merit points had been achieved the Senior Tutor could endorse them by awarding a commendation. Twelve commendations in one year qualified for a School Prize. In addition, there were several school cups, shields and trophies that could be won for outstanding achievements in sport and other competitions throughout the year. The school always tried to bring good achievements to the attention of both parents and the pupil's peers by announcing such things in bulletins and at meetings. From observations such rewards meant nothing to informants in this study and were not regarded as motivators. The majority of pupil informants stood little chance of receiving twelve commendations in a year and did not actively strive to do so. Far more likely for them, was the chance of being placed in detention for smoking or insolence. Overall though, Leafield presented itself as a school largely unencumbered by petty rules and regulations although its pupils did not have a point of comparison that helped them appreciate this.

School hours

To the utter dismay of many pupils, school started at the early hour of 8.30am each day and the only redeeming feature of this was that it provided a half day on Wednesdays when school finished at 1.00pm. Officially this early finish on Wednesdays gave staff time to plan future lessons on half a day per week, whilst also affording time for pupils' extra-curricular sporting activities. In reality most teachers were exhausted by 1.00pm, having crammed four shortened periods into the morning session, as a result they were soon off the premises. Of course, leaving the school premises did not necessarily mean that teachers were not working and some indicated that they relied on the peace and quiet of their homes for marking and preparation, there being little time set aside in their timetables for such duties. In addition, space was at a premium at the school and only a small room attached to the staffroom was available for paper work. This was totally inadequate to meet the needs of sixty teachers.

Each school day (except Wednesday) consisted of four periods. There were three x 1 hour 10 minute periods in the morning and a longer 1 hour 20 minute period in the afternoon. No bells rang to signal the end of each lesson and in consequence, both teachers and pupils watched watches. The lack of school bells was a feature of Leafield School that developed more by default than design. The Head explained that the sprawling site had never been fully fitted for bells in every area and so, when one of the major bells broke down, staff were already familiar with gauging the time for themselves. During attempts to repair the bells, it became apparent that lesson changes carried on as normal without their clanging and so they fell into disuse.

However, pupils were not slow to exploit the opportunity for 'skiving' that this lack of a school bell afforded them. Pupils arriving late for lessons were able to blame their watches, and during one particularly disruptive afternoon lesson observed, two boys tricked their teacher into an early finish to the day. This they achieved by climbing onto a cupboard and altering the hands of the classroom clock while the teacher was in the corridor sanctioning another boy for rude behaviour. Their sense of amused victory was highly apparent as they sauntered nonchalently off the school premises, ten minutes early, watched through classroom windows by puzzled teachers and pupils still engaged in their lessons.

In general, however, it was with great precision that all pupils would erupt from their classrooms and spill out into the corridors and thoroughfares at exactly the right time, pivoting themselves 'en masse' towards their next port of call.

Noise levels in the corridors along with the general bustle was a striking first image of this scene. The sheer volume of people milling about was quite overpowering to an uninitiated observer. 'Organised or disorganised chaos?' was a comment written in field notes on Day Two of the initial observation period whilst waiting in a corridor with 25 boisterous teenagers for their teacher to arrive.

This movement between lessons did in fact eat into teaching time to a considerable degree in many of the classes observed. To begin with, all classrooms had to be unlocked by the teacher upon occupation and locked again upon vacation, even if the gap between teachers being in attendance was only a matter of minutes. This gave early arrivals the opportunity to lounge around outside the locked doors, leaning against the walls talking and shouting in groups with their bags blocking the corridor. Frequently there would be a hold-up for other pupils and teachers trying to get past 'en route' to other destinations. Pushing and shoving would break out causing a 'domino effect' on those standing in line and general disruption ensued, such that other classes, perhaps already settled, could not concentrate because of the rumpus.

At the start of a lesson it often took five or ten minutes for a new group to settle down before teaching could begin. A typical entrance would be for the boys to crash into the room first, thumping bags down on the tables, scraping chairs across the floor, tussling with each other for the seats they wanted to occupy. This process was timed at the start of one lesson in which the pupils arrived to find the tables rearranged in an unusable configuration. The teacher asked the class to put the tables and chairs back into the normal U-shaped formation, whereupon the noise of the upheaval became quite deafening. It was some twenty minutes into the lesson before all was quiet and the lesson content could be started.

Similarly, at the end of lessons, pupils would start to check their watches regularly within ten minutes of the end of the period. Restlessness set in and some would start to pack away their pens, shuffle their papers and reorganise their bags. All of these ploys were aimed at time-wasting, for pupils knew precisely what the time was and some teachers would make a stand about packing up by insisting all books remained open and all bags on the floor until they gave permission to pack away. However, many either did not, or could not, control this time slippage, and combined with their own need to call in books and lock them away in classroom cupboards before the end of the lesson, the net result was that a seventy-minute period was often reduced to fifty minutes of actual teaching time.

Similarly in transit, pupils knew precisely how much time they could take getting from A to B. A number of pupils intent on 'getting the odd fag in' between lessons would be the first out of the door, speedily behind the sheds for a few drags on a shared cigarette, and back among the final stragglers arriving for the next lesson.

The smoking issue

The main bone of contention between pupils and staff that could be discerned was about smoking. There was a total ban on smoking throughout the school premises with an automatic detention for pupils caught in the act. This rankled and was a hot issue with many 5th formers who were now sixteen (or nearly so) and wished to smoke. A hard-core of smokers existed, both male and female, and these were exclusively lower-achieving CSE and non-exam pupils.

Smoking went on in the toilets, behind the bicycle sheds, behind the Technical Block, at the far end of the playing fields and in other odd corners. Cigarettes were often handed around and here girls would 'cadge a drag' off the boys and vice versa according to who had supplies.

This appropriation of school time and property for personal purposes was to reveal itself in other ways (see p. 41). Furlong (1984) refers to a West Indian male appropriation of school space in this way, which suggests that this was a peculiar feature among West Indian youth. However, observations at Leafield revealed that both male and female, white and West Indian pupils would make space for themselves in this way. The opportunity was taken by many separate groups of friends who could be categorised more by their negative attitude to school and its petty rules than by gender or racial groupings. Thus, black and white pupils hung around together and would be involved in 'passing around'. The pupils that would come together to smoke at any one spot at a given time tended to be a loose group based on who they were teamed up with from the last lesson and where they were heading next. These spots, however, were only frequented by those who wanted a quick smoke and their friends, and not by other 'goody-goodies' as Natalie, one of the informants, put it.

This researcher's acceptance by the pupils was demonstrated by the reception she received the first time she turned the corner behind the Technical Block and was confronted by seven boys having a smoke.

Arriving with Natalie and two of her girlfriends, the boys' immediate reaction was one of being 'found out'. Their faces dropped, one neatly passed the smouldering cigarette to his mate who placed it behind his back whilst turning his head away to exhale the smoke. 'Ah, shit!' exclaimed another, assuming the worst. 'It's OK, Mandy's with us' explained Natalie, 'She won't say nothing'.

This testimonial from another pupil was sufficient for everybody. They immediately relaxed and continued their shared cigarette. Natalie and friends lit up and offered their cigarette to all around, researcher included. Being a non-smoker proved fortunate at this point for it was possible to decline the offer without causing offence whilst also not compromising the delicate position of the researcher betwixt staff and pupils by being caught on a staff check both witnessing and participating in a forbidden activity. The pupils found the reason for refusal acceptable. 'You're lucky then!' was the response, for many of them had been smoking whenever they had enough money to by a packet of cigarettes for two, three or even five years.

It was extremely gratifying to be accepted so readily and trusted by the group on this occasion, nevertheless pupils tested this trust later on in a classroom situation as has been discussed already in Chapter 1.

Another favourite place for smoking was the girls' toilets. Many of these, in different blocks, were supposed to be locked at break or lunch times to avoid vandalism and general mucking about, but smokers were well-informed about which ones tended to be left open by omission or design. The girls would lean on the basins smoking and chatting with one non-smoking girl strategically positioned to see who came in the door. A non-verbal signal of stiffening and trying to look innocent was sufficient to send smokers shooting into cubicles to douse their cigarettes and pretend to be using the toilets. False alarms were always treated with relieved amusement.

One small clique of girls had a good routine sussed out with the school caretaker:

> White female pupil: 'He's OK is Leonard. He gives us 10p to stay in here and make sure no-one bungs toilet rolls down the loo or breaks the seats and then we buy cigarettes with it.'

Leonard was indeed party to letting the girls have untroubled access to a particular set of toilets on the basis that they would 'look after them for him'. However, some of the tricks these girls got up to could easily have led to the accidental damage or vandalism he so wanted to avoid (see p. 41).

It was striking that these persistent smokers were not just working class youngsters, but low-achieving or non-achieving into the bargain. Johnson et al. (1985) found a link between school pupils' smoking and social class with peer group influence also playing an important part in encouraging smoking as part of a desired image of adulthood the pupils wanted to project. At Leafield it would appear that not being an O-level taker was another important variable in combination with coming from a working class background. Thus, being an 'academic failure' gave the pupils more need to 'prove' themselves in other spheres, and displaying adulthood via the right to indulge in a habit forbidden to children was an important part of 'being somebody'. Smoking provided an assumed adult status and also defied the school rules in line with an anti-school culture that most non-achievers and less-achievers ascribed to. It was also a way of rejecting the control of teachers whom they saw as having no right to dictate actions outside the realm of the classroom.

The smoking battle was therefore not simply about the right to enjoy a cigarette, it was about a larger freedom and autonomy and about being accepted as an adult on equal terms with teachers. This theme of freedom and autonomy is now taken up via an exploration of pupil/teacher interactions and the accommodation and resistance employed by pupils in negotiating their way through each school day.

The fifth form and their teachers

For their part, pupils could and did have some choice and flexibility in their daily lives at school. Both legitimate and illegitimate choices were exercised in the classroom and illegitimate choices were made at break times to appropriate school space for their own ends. The remaining sections of this chapter explore some of those choices and pupils' needs before moving on to a discussion of teachers' perspectives and staffroom life.

The 5th form in action

The most noticeable evidence of pupil choice within the classroom was in seating arrangements. Pupils always sat with their friends, although sometimes a teacher would split up a group who were not working. They chose to sit with friends in order to chat or 'have a laugh' as they worked. Naturally enough, teachers' styles and tolerance levels varied between individuals, but there was a large degree of free and easy discussion, even banter, permitted in most lessons. Pupils clearly appreciated this freedom evidenced later by the questionnaire returns from the whole 5th year in which pupils rated friendly and fair teachers quite highly. Woods (1983) emphasises the fact that pupils value teachers according to whether they are fair, can take a joke and teach. Certainly Leafield pupils utilised similar criteria in evaluating their teachers.

Pupils were not in awe of their teachers and felt free to voice their opinions and feelings in the classroom situation. As a result, dissatisfaction was rarely contained, taking instead the overt form of either disruption, open criticism or complaint.

Responses to teachers

One unintended consequence of this open style of teaching was that the pupils who chose to had plenty of scope to muck about. Events observed ranged from throwing bags across the room to uncontrollable laughter at an in-lesson joke, and from doodling and chewing gum to telling the teacher to 'Fuck off!'.

Beynon (1984) cites all of these ploys as pupils' means of 'sussing out' teachers and establishing just how far they can go. Leafield pupils were adept at testing teachers in this way.

Individual teachers coped in different ways and with one particularly authoritarian male teacher there was no overt mucking about, or so the pupils said. (This was the only teacher to refuse the researcher access to 'sit in' on his lessons.) The general conclusions from six weeks of observations in the classroom situation was that female teachers had to fight harder to be taken seriously by pupils and so gain control, and that their reliance on shouting led to greater degrees of 'winding-up' and derision from the class, not greater authority and control. Pupils would indeed, take a teacher's shouting as an indication that they (the pupils) had 'got her to lose her rag' and as a victory for them. Male teachers on the other hand could raise their deeper voices and be authoritative. Whether the latter led to work being achieved was debatable, but classroom order was maintained allowing peace and quiet for those who wished to work.

However, some male and female teachers using a quiet, gentle approach, could obtain the respect and co-operation of their classes. One male science teacher in particular never raised his voice or appeared angry yet he never had problems of control. He would explain, wait quietly, mention that breaktime would be lost if work was not completed, and slowly the lesson would progress satisfactorily. Another female English teacher was able to maintain an orderly class by means of quiet sarcasm. For example, in one lesson a boy was day dreaming and not paying attention to the class reading of the book Animal Farm. The teacher spotted this and asked him a question which he could not answer:

> Teacher: 'That's great isn't it! A few weeks off the exam but you've got time to gaze out of the window and not listen. Brilliant!'

Suitably shamed this boy at least looked at the book for the rest of the lesson.

Teachers who shouted to display authority or gain silence rarely achieved their objective. Indeed, a few minutes of grudging silence could be extracted from pupils by such techniques but the feeling of resentment from them was all too apparent, leading to further disturbances.

'How dare you come into my lesson like this still?' shrieked one female teacher as her class rolled in, talking loudly and making a great deal of noise over the settling in process.

She eventually got silence from rows of dead-pan, resilient faces, had bags placed on the floor and pupils sat 'nicely' waiting to start the lesson but she did not have the respect of the class and her lesson kept erupting in minor incidents to do with pens, rubbers, comments from the class and expressions of boredom.

Pupils, for their part, could really dish out the hard treatment if they chose to. The constant barrage of noise, insolence, mucking about, and general resistance to doing any work reduced some teachers (female) to tears. One such teacher left shortly after observation of her class, deeply disillusioned about teaching teenagers. A whole set of complex antecedents had evolved between this teacher and the pupils such that she was 'written off' by them and stood little chance of gaining their respect.

On another occasion, Julia, a girl designated as 'brain-damaged' and 'difficult' following a head injury, erupted in fury during a lesson on Parentcraft. The female teacher was taking an all-girls class for this subject, the only sex-segregated one in the school apart from P.E. During the teacher's explanation of the various signs of pregnancy, Julia vehemently disagreed with the teacher that menstruation ceased during pregnancy. Her friend sitting next to her raised the query but Julia persisted with it, getting louder and louder:

> Julia: 'You're talking out of your arse! I'm not fucking listening!'

Julia was challenged to behave or be sent to the referral tutor as part of the disciplinary system. She quietened down on the following condition:

Julia: 'Only if you'll stop lying!'

The teacher explained afterwards that she was more lenient with Julia because of her 'problem' and because all staff agreed that her outbursts should be tolerated to enable her to stay in mainstream schooling. She had never behaved this way before her accident so staff could forgive her.

This researcher spent many an interesting break-time talking to Julia and found her intelligent and inquiring. She wanted to know about politics and discuss CND (she sported a CND badge) and bore all the marks of an angry, frustrated teenager wanting to know and do things and not knowing how to go about them. This girl in particular used the researcher as a source of information in the way Griffin (1987) describes. Schooling certainly was not fulfilling her needs, and yet she could be lively-minded, soul-searching and friendly. Three years later she was to be seen in the town centre enthusing to a friend she had met on the street about the date of her forthcoming marriage. She was full of life and exuberance, looked good in some smart but casual clothes and was clearly looking forward to the change of status in her life. No enquiries into the actual medical evidence of Julia's condition were made for the purpose of this research but ignoring the 'brain damaged' label staff gave her at school, there was nothing in her behaviour that suggested anything other than her being a boisterous and over-zealous teenager with a penchant for bad language. Her change of mood could be attributed to the onset of adolescent dissent. Staff, however, felt protected by her label of 'brain damaged' and it assisted them in coping with her otherwise embarrassing and unacceptable behaviour.

Pupils engaged in other forms of disrupting or delaying lessons and in testing the teacher. 'Miss can't teach!' stated an Asian boy from the back of one class in a mischievous tone. This created great amusement and the female teacher, struggling for command of the class, sent him out of the room to stand in the corridor. 'It's Guy Fawkes Day today,' announced one girl out of the blue in a Parentcraft lesson. 'I'm going to the pub tonight to get pissed. Excuse my language, Miss!' 'No, I don't Brenda, so watch it please!' came the teacher's warning shot.

This lesson was punctuated with other tests of endurance aimed at the teacher and it slowly disintegrated. After some ineffective shouting the teacher wrote up a long passage from a text book on the board for copying and obtained some degree of order by initiating this rote task. Comments like 'I'm bored!' or 'I can't bloody see!' came and went for the rest of the lesson with a minimum amount of commitment to learn and effort displayed by most of the 25 girls present.

Pupils would provide supplementary information about classroom incidents such as these, usually with a view to putting their side of a situation forward or putting down the teacher concerned. For example:

> Natalie: 'I bet you think we're all awful after yesterday' (referring to Julia's swearing incident over the pregnancy issue).
> Researcher: 'No, not really. I'm just interested that's all.'
>
> Natalie: 'We just get bored sometimes, but we're interested in what you're doing. Are you going to follow me?'

Yet again, after being turned away from observing a geography lesson:

> Toni: 'Mr Stedman's always like that, strict he is. Not surprised he didn't want you in his class. He didn't want you to see how he treats us.'

Another pupil volunteered the following after a particularly chaotic lesson:

> Anne: 'Miss can't control us really. The men have got better control I think, but some female teachers can do it.'

Teacher control from the pupils' perspective is discussed further in Chapter 3, but for now, the point is that pupils provided the researcher with privileged access to their analyses of situations and to themselves; the self of friend, confidante, humorist, trouble-maker and 'dosser'. It is difficult not to feel beholden to those pupils who provided access to their private circles, and there is a feeling of responsibility towards them regarding usage of the data gathered. All informants were guaranteed anonymity yet graphical accounts of their activities and opinions would lay open areas of operation and points of view that were previously unknown to staff, even though individuals would never be discovered. Pupils were also aware of this but their concern was for their personal protection now, combined with a deep desire that their voices should be heard. For non-achieving pupils this desire to be heard was all the more poignant because they wanted those in control of their education to listen to their grievances and save future generations of pupils from experiencing something as irrelevant and boring. They were more than happy that their views should be documented for all to see.

Coping strategies

Boredom was something frequently alluded to aloud in class and also in later private discussions with the researcher. It cannot be emphasised enough how much meaning and weight pupils could attached in verbalising the word 'boring' by drawing out the sound, droning and sighing:

> 'I'm so bored' sighed one young man rocking back on his chair and gazing at the ceiling.
>
> Researcher: 'Why's that?'
>
> Boy: 'Cos I'm at school of course. That's boring'.

Pupils explained that teachers were boring, lessons were boring and that coming to school altogether was boring. Such statements predominantly came from less-achieving pupils not involved in preparing for O-levels. A full discussion of their boredom appears in Chapter 5, but for the present, suffice it to say that 'turned off' pupils had a whole repertoire of verbal and non-verbal signals ranging from sighs to insults and fiddling to falling asleep over the desk by which they conveyed their lack of interest.

However, some pupils were prepared to challenge the status quo rather than acquiesce or 'cut off' from the proceedings. Such challenges took the form of criticism or complaint and with these the appeal was still very definitely to the teacher with a view to obtaining modifications or assistance to 'improve' the work at hand. Sometimes, the appeal fell on deaf ears and pupils would mutter and curse to themselves and friends, but on other occasions some amendment of the task in hand was achieved. Pupils sought to re-negotiate the task in hand, for example:

> Female pupil: 'Miss, why can't we read something else that's interesting. This is boring' (said in an English lesson),
>
> Female pupil: 'Why can't we have a film?' (said in a Geography lesson)

Frequently the criticism seemed justified and the suggested alternative a viable option, but in observations at Leafield teachers did no more than pay lip service to such appeals. Teachers might nod sympathetically or directly agree with a pupil's comment but took no steps to alter their lesson plan or content. As a result, the less academic pupils, (who will be discussed in

Chapter 5) were the ones who lost interest in their lessons and failed to see their relevance. Such pupils then opted for other diversions including mucking about in class. Eventually they were not entered for exams.

The library represented another way in which pupils could exercise some choice over the day's activities as teachers would sometimes ask for volunteers to work quietly in the library. Invariably most hands in the class shot up at such an offer and difficulty ensued over who should be privileged enough to go to the library and who should remain. The unlucky, unselected ones frequently groused about it. Both boys and girls would elect to work in the library, but the majority chosen tended to be the girls. Teachers were inclined to think that the girls could be trusted to work quietly in the library without supervision. Boys were more likely to turn it into 'a doss', especially collectively, and it was for this reason that the library was out of bounds for 'ad hoc' usage and locked at breaktimes.

The pupils sent off to work in the library were observed on two occasions some fifteen minutes after their departure. They were talking quietly amongst themselves but also working, having already selected relevant books from the shelves:

Researcher: 'Why did you want to come here to work?'

Female Pupil: 'Because of the noise in class, you can't think in that row.'

Researcher: 'Why did you choose to work in the library?'

Another Female Pupil: 'The boys just muck about in class, I can't concentrate and the teacher can't do anything.'

It was clear that most of the pupils valued the opportunity to 'work on their own' out of the classroom environment, and that whilst some just wanted more freedom to chat quietly whilst they worked others deeply wanted a more peaceful, undisturbed working environment and saw the library as a means of achieving this.

From pupils' comments and responses on the questionnaire there was a great deal of concern about the control of noise so as to assist studying, especially from the more able and achieving pupils. This use of the library was one small way in which pupils could take control of noise for themselves and so 'manage' their own interests.

Other things pupils found important included greater freedom of subject choice and more flexible time-tabling. Greater personal freedom and being treated like an adult were also very dear to many pupils' hearts, including the removal of what they saw as petty school rules. Many wanted more work experience or lessons related to the real world (e.g. how to secure employment or open a bank account). Lessons in general were seen as largely irrelevant to their adult lives, except Maths, and even there a lot of the work in Geometry and Algebra was viewed as useless. (These issues receive further attention in subsequent chapters.)

Break-time appropriations

It has already been stated that break-times and short gaps between lessons provided other opportunities for pupils to appropriate school facilities to their own ends. In particular, smoking has been referred to as one major way in which less-achieving pupils in particular challenged the school rules and created for themselves a space of their own during breaktimes. Other pursuits included ribbing or ridiculing other pupils, gossiping and playing rough, but Natalie and her friends had another, rather unusual way of passing the time.

One favourite entertainment these girls indulged in at lunch-times was induced fainting in the girls' toilets. A volunteer would stand by the basins enfolded in the arms of a trusted friend standing behind her. She would take a few deep breaths and then be clasped tightly around the chest from behind and tilted backwards off her feet whilst holding her breath, the friend taking her entire body-weight. A few seconds in this position led to loss of consciousness, signalled by a slump of the body and release of the breath whereupon the friend would slowly let the volunteer, still unconscious, sag to the floor and lie down. Those present would watch to see how long it took for the girl to come round. This process was frequently accompanied by involuntary twitching and little unintelligible vocal noises. Details of these would be recounted to the volunteer upon coming round, who would find it fascinating to hear what they had 'been like'. A pounding headache often followed these little escapades and sometimes girls would double check that their mates had aspirins before fainting. Dousing with water was often called for.

The girls treated this activity quite lightly yet there was always an acknowledged element of risk-taking which they seemed to enjoy. Danger was an implicit part of the game, both physically to self and in terms of being 'caught' by a teacher. These fainting exercises can be viewed partly as bravado and testing of one's nerve but also as a direct relief from boredom. There was nowhere to go locally at lunch-time if they left the school premises and nowhere to go on site, except to the main hall which would have been crowded if everyone had done that. These girls felt very strongly that they should have their own common room on site where they could sit and smoke and listen to music. The 6th formers did have such a place including pool tables, music, public telephone (broken by vandals) and coffee machine, but 5th formers and lower age groups were barred and they resented this.

Pupils - an overview

The above incidents highlight a clash of interests between the school institution and the needs of low-achieving pupils. There were many other areas of minor discord but these did not necessarily take the form of any overt challenge to the status quo, rather pupils expressed opinions on things they wanted to see changed and in the meantime, simply 'cut off' from the learning experience to a greater or lesser degree. There were some volatile incidents but in the main pupils either accepted the education on offer or rejected it with passive indifference, creating other moments of excitement in their lives during their spare time. The latter response is reminiscent of Willis' (1977) 'lads' who sought alternative criteria against which to judge themselves rather than the accepted school norm of academic achievement.

However, the way in which pupils were prepared to engage with staff in a constructive way by making suggestions in lessons and querying the way in which things were done was an important factor indicating the possibility of re-engaging such pupils in education by effecting changes in line with their interests. Teachers, however, did not appear to respond to such pleas.

Here it should be borne in mind that the main focus of this study was underachieving pupils and their perspectives of school and work, and that it was, therefore, mostly the company of either CSE or non-exam takers that was being sought. Observations of, and talks with a few top-achieving pupils by way of comparison did take place but the major interest, and hence time spent, was with the lesser-achieving group. These pupils did not live for school but they valued it for the opportunity it provided to meet their friends. They also hoped it might help them in finally securing work.

Regarding friendships, it can be said that these were largely taken for granted. Each pupil had a clique of friends that came together at various parts of the school day. Some teamed up on the way to school, some would wait for each other in the school grounds before first lesson and some would deliberately arrange to meet at a certain favourite spot at break or lunch time. School was therefore a guaranteed meeting point and locus of social contact albeit an enforced one. Friendship groups among the 5th form remained fairly constant with some pupils having 'been mates' since middle school days. Whilst pupils clearly rated school as an opportunity to see their friends daily, they still viewed school itself negatively as boring and irrelevant.

Regarding the later search for work, a great number of pupils already had part time jobs. When asked about these, pupils said that they did it for the money which they then spent on themselves. Clothes, records, saving for a bike at seventeen years of age, 'fags', 'booze' and going out were the main items mentioned in this respect.

Many did Saturday jobs, sometimes combined with a few hours after school during the week (e.g. late-night-shopping Thursdays plus Saturdays in a shop). Many others did evening work waiting at tables at a large residential centre nearby. Others helped out in garages, butchers shops, newsagents, hairdressers, did cleaning or fast food preparation. Apart from waiting, most part-time jobs were gender segregated with girls taking shop work, hairdressing and cleaning, whilst boys worked in garages, butchers shops, fast foods, or small industries. For some, this was creating contacts with employers that led to later offers of full-time employment upon leaving school, but others hated what they were doing and defined it as 'boring'. At Leafield, virtually all pupils not intending to carry on in the 6th form were interested in all forms of work experience. They saw it as valuable and practical and wished they could do more via the school. School work experience schemes were frequently not liked, but still, great emphasis was placed on wanting to try more types of work to see if something 'interesting' could be found. Such issues are mentioned just briefly here in order to set the scene but they receive greater attention in subsequent chapters relating specifically to gender and employment factors. Meanwhile, an overview of the 5th form would not be complete without some information on their teachers. This is the subject of the next section.

The teaching staff

As teachers have been implicated as part of 'the problem' via pupils' criticisms of their lessons, no study of Leafield School would be complete without an introduction to the teachers, their policies and their staffroom.

The teachers in action

From observations, the 60-plus teachers at Leafield led busy, if not hectic lives. The initial week spent following the timetable of one particular teacher led this researcher to wonder how staff could keep up such a pace. Field notes over the first few days contained asides such as 'Phew!' and 'Knackering!' bsed on rushing from lesson to lesson across the school campus, locking and unlocking classrooms, pushing against waves of pupils in corridors to get from A to B and trying to settle down quietly and quickly for some work each period.

A clue to this high speed pace was offered in the staffroom at 8.20am on the researcher's first morning in school. The large, square room could seat some forty people but at this early hour chairs were hardly in use at all. Staff were collecting letters and notes from pigeon holes, dashing out of the little adjacent marking room, double-checking notices of relevance to them on the board and passing hurried messages and up-dates to each other. Often two of these activities would be tackled simultaneously and, with something close to military precision, the room became virtually abandoned about two minutes before class registration began.

The hustle and bustle of the staffroom was very much of a surprise. From this and many later observations it was clear that staff had to do a lot of 'thinking on their feet'. There was very little free time to plan work or mark. At break-times, teachers would catch up on their internal mail, speak to each other about particular pupils (e.g. where a subject tutor had to report some misbehaviour to a form teacher), or rush off to photocopy something necessary for the next lesson that had been prepared the night before at home. At lunchtime, there might be some marking or more lesson preparation and there were after-school curriculum or staff meetings each week, excluding any extramural activities and clubs individual teachers might be involved in. That the teacher's life seemed utterly hectic, offering no time to think and plan ahead is something of an understatement. It was impossible not to have a great deal of sympathy for staff in their efforts to cope with the daily bustle. In addition, simply controlling each class was a major drain on their resources.

The impression time and again in making the transition from staffroom to classroom was one of being wound up like a clockwork machine ready for the next spate of action. The two worlds appeared very distinct, that of staffroom being adult, hectic yet in control, with consultation and fraternisation amongst equals. That of the classroom was one of intended control of pupils, a world of non-equals that threatened to be both hectic and out of control on many occasions. The difference in 'personality' between staffroom and classroom was noticeable with some teachers but not all. Some struggled with their classes, others coped, whilst others thrived. Female more than male teachers failed to cope in the matter of classroom control, a feature of school life which only became apparent through later observations and discussions with informants. This matter is dealt with in more detail in Chapter 3.

In addition, most of the staff's knowledge about pupils came about over coffee or lunch, often in the form of rapidly delivered messages or anecdotes in the staffroom. Hammersley (1981) has indicated the importance of the staffroom for the sharing of ideology and information about pupils whilst Woods (1979) has said of the staffroom:

> This is indeed a haven in stormy seas, and recourse must be had to it at regular intervals (Woods, 1979, pp. 211-2).

Certainly, at Leafield, the staffroom was a place to wind down, a place of comfort and support from colleagues in which opinions and frustrations could be aired.

It was also a place where the researcher could make many fruitful contacts with staff. Teachers, for the most part were keen to provide additional background concerning individual pupils. For example:

> Julia was brain-damaged - hence her abusive behaviour and bad language in class.

> Ian had been fined £300 in the juvenile courts the week before thus explaining his anti-social behaviour.

> Jenny got uptight about finding sufficient library books because she wanted to do well at school, unlike her mother.

> Sonia (a black pupil) had a tragic family background which, for the teachers, explained a lot of her disruptive behaviour in class.

Sometimes teachers would provide snippets about a class as a whole:

> 'They're a strange bunch, nasty with each other. You'll see.'

Another piece of information imparted was that: 'wet days are the worst'.

The most frequent type of information imparted about pupils concerned things which, in the teachers' eyes, served to explain unwanted classroom behaviour. This information was part of the teachers' own elaborated knowledge about pupils (Hargreaves, Hestor and Mellor, 1975) and they were keen that the researcher should also have this insight. Such staffroom news was documented with interest, and it was pleasing that the staff were prepared to confide such information for it signified their acceptance of the researcher. However, it was important to step back from the judgements and connections they made about pupils as a result. In this the researcher was uniquely placed between teachers and pupils due to access to pupils' own explanations and rationales for events that took place. The researcher was privy to both points of view.

Old righties and young lefties?

During one interview with the Head, undertaken to provide background knowledge of the school and the changes that had been implemented since his arrival in 1982, the conversation turned to his analysis of staff attitudes. During his attempts at curriculum reform which included more mixed ability teaching, less demarcation between disciplines and mergers between previously separate departments he had met with opposition from those already polarised politically 'to the right'. He felt that politics lay at the heart of the stance taken by staff on the issue of curriculum reform stating:

> 'All reforms and objections to them are centred on this [politics] .... and age is not a factor'.

The Head thought that there were both 'old righties' and 'young righties', as he termed them, and that these were opposed by both 'young lefties' and older teachers who were prepared to consider reforms out of 'benevolence' and a belief that education should be 'child-centred'.

From observations of staff, both with their colleagues in the staffroom and in lessons, it appeared that age was not necessarily a factor as the Head suggested. Most teachers who prefered the status quo and resisted notions of change were generally the older ones but they were also the ones who had taught for most of their careers in the selective secondary modern/grammar school system. However, there was something of a clearer gender distinction with female teachers of various ages and a smaller number of young male teachers being most likely to entertain curriculum innovation and equal opportunity issues. Indeed, it was discord over equal opportunities that provided the chance of observing what the Head had tried to indicate.

The equal opportunity issue

During the period of this research at Leafield the school had no official, written equal opportunities policy and no specific guidelines for staff to follow. Thus, should staff find themselves witnessing a racist incident or suspect a gender distinction of any kind there was no policy statement or code of practice to refer to as a starting point for action. The only written indication of the schools stance on racial and sexual equality was the broadly worded statement in the school prospectus which read:

> We aim, at Leafield, to provide the best possible secondary education for every one of our students .....[plus] ..... respect for the worth and dignity of all people whatever their race, nationality or creed (A Guide To Parents, Leafield School, 1984).

There was, however, an Equal Opportunities Group at the school, which pre-dated the arrival of the new, reforming Head in 1982. This group consisted of individual members of staff who came together on a voluntary basis in view of their mutual concern about racial and gender inequalities and sexist practices in both education and job opportunities. The group held its meetings after school and whilst all staff were welcome to attend, few did so. The vast majority of teachers were soon off campus after 3.00pm and whilst this could have been attributed to the union industrial action taking place in 1984/1985, a long-standing member of the group indicated that attendance at meetings had been low from the outset, prior to industrial action, with only a few committed teachers participating.

This Equal Opportunities Group was busy compiling an equal opportunities statement with a view to it becoming the school's official policy, subject to discussion among all staff. Their draft statement caused a minor storm among some of the older male teachers, who could be placed in the Head's category of 'old righties', when it was first circulated for discussion.

One afternoon in the staffroom three of these male teachers were observed complaining about its content. The document suggested that there was a need to actively combat discrimination through anti-sexist teaching practices. The following rumblings were overheard somewhat disjointedly as it was difficult to listen overtly at the time:

> First Teacher: 'We've got the royal "we" here but nobody's consulted

me about it.'

Second Teacher: 'Yes, well there's no such thing as democracy here you know,' and again, a few minutes later, 'the girls have had the option of a five-a-side football team for the last four years.'

Third Teacher: '..... it only serves to highlight things.'

The three teachers involved were clearly aggrieved that such a statement could be developed without them being consulted. Yet the draft was being circulated specifically for consultation. As one of the three men involved in complaining was the careers teacher it was, perhaps, surprising that he in particular had not been an active member of the Equal Opportunities Group.

This group of three continued to grumble about the approach suggested in the draft statement and were soon joined by two female members of staff who were similarly unimpressed by the stand advocated. The general feeling of this group was that the extent of sexism in school was overestimated and that direct anti-sexist education was overreacting to the point that it would highlight sex differences and actually create trouble. Giving publicity to sexism was tantamount to encouraging it and they preferred to 'operate in an ordinary way' as one teacher put it. Operating in an ordinary way meant maintaining the status quo which was taken to be neutral action. For these teachers, and others at Leafield, too much fuss was made about sexism and it would be less of a problem if people did not cause trouble by drawing attention to it. Racism, they felt, was also subject to beingoverplayed'.

This example illustrates the diversity (if not polarity) or opinions among staff, opinions which informed attitudes, and affected curriculum content and actions in the classroom.

Wags and drags

In the staffroom it was plain to see the split between the 'old righties' and 'young lefties'. The former were predominantly older male teachers, and a high proportion had taught in secondary modern schools prior to the introduction of the comprehensive education system. A large sub-section of this group was an all-male, smoking fraternity that appeared even more apart and separated from the main body of teachers by their relegation to the 'Smoking Area' of the staffroom. This group had a distinctly 'macho' image with conversation and humour centred around football, pupil anecdotes, their subject areas (technical, scientific and mathematical), and a distinctly male view of the world. Burgess (1983, 1987) remarks upon a similar scenario at Bishop MacGregor School where first gender-segregated seating and later a male sports ethos dominated in the staffroom.

The researcher's presence in their section of the staffroom was made to feel like an unwelcome intrusion into 'their' domain. Conversation would cease and only get going again limply, on new, 'neutral' topics. Alternatively the researcher was set up as a target for their humour or their negative remarks about researchers. For example, one lunch time the greeting was:

> 'I don't know George but these researchers get younger all the time,' (smiling condescendingly). 'Amanda was in my class this morning and it was over half an hour before I realised!'

Such flattery was absurd for a woman in her thirties. Conversations with these teachers revealed that they generally hankered after old principles and values they felt were crumbling (or had crumbled away totally) in schools today. Preferences were stated for school uniform, corporal punishment, 'realism' over academic achievement and job attainment, a return to the basic three Rs and a practical grounding without a lot of 'fancy stuff'.

Problems in education were seen as more created than real with researchers clearly responsible for making much out of small issues. This researcher was challenged (albeit in a polite way) to defend the research being conducted for this study and questioned about its utility in educational terms. This group represented the disbelievers, those who saw little benefit in new ideas on pedagogy or educational reform. They were quite fixed in their ideas, consolidated by their reflections over many years of teaching.

This group of three, aided and abetted by other male members of staff, were also responsible for much of what passed as staffroom humour. They were the 'staffroom wags' who enjoyed jovial criticism of the school's bureaucracy and shared jokes about pupils and classroom anecdotes. Sexism and racism crept into their humour, much of which was gained at the expense of other members of staff whom they had perceived as being humourless and who have termed here as 'drags'.

The 'drags' were the more serious minded 'young lefties' who did not find sexist remarks funny. Here the teachers were mainly younger and female although not exclusively so. To these teachers, pastoral care was important, as was developing good relationships with all pupils and assisting them to reach their full potential. Their opinions on teaching included the following:

> Young male teacher: 'They've got to like you otherwise they won't

listen. Shouting is out, you'll lose their respect. You just have to explain things and make them appeal.'

Young female teacher: 'You've got to really like teaching them otherwise it won't come across properly. I really like my pupils as individuals, it's important.'

Such teachers were also aware of potential sources of racial discrimination, acknowledging the possibility of unintentional and indirect racism in school policies and practices. To the 'wags' of the 'old righties' camp this was 'over the top' and taking life far too seriously.

The 'wags' demonstrated their attitude towards gender and racial issues in what could be termed thoughtless humour and ribbing. For example, in a negative discussion of student teachers currently visiting the school one of these 'wags' said to his colleagues over coffee:

'I hear old Harry had a nice Spanish bit in his class the other day.'

The speaker clearly thought he was being amusing and his colleague smirked over the 'double-entendre' contained within the use of the word 'had'. No-one present, detected the subjugation of both women and other racial groups implicit in this piece of conversation. As Burgess (1987) states:

..... women teachers were not just judged on qualifications but on personal characteristics: age, appearance, marital status, success with their own families and so on - all qualities that would not be used to judge men (Burgess, 1987, p.18).

However, the 'wags' went further by having a running joke about the school's token feminist. Miss Peters, who was a committed member of the Equal Opportunities Group had gained herself the reputation of the 'angry young woman' and arch-feminist because of her tendency to tackle other members of staff about their stereotypes and gender biases. Needless to say, this did not go down well with many male teachers, particularly those in the Head's 'righties' category who were not used to being challenged to explain their views or being tackled over their sexist remarks. As a result, she was frequently alluded to in derisory terms, both inside and outside the staffroom and typical staffroom comments were 'Don't let Miss Peters hear you say that, Tom!' and 'Sally wouldn't like that!'

Both staff and pupils soon picked up on such issues in developing a uniform typification of a teacher. At first it was unclear to this observer, how pupils came to view a teacher in the same light as members of staff because the two settings in which pupil/teacher and teacher/teacher interaction took place were quite separate. Pupils, for example, did not enter the staffroom (they were always spoken to outside in the corridor if necessary) and teachers did not team teach or observe each other's lessons. However, observation revealed that teachers did pass on bits of gossip and news about other members of staff to their pupils in the course of their lessons which led to a common picture of the person concerned. This, plus the openness of most staff with their own form group about issues and incidents they were involved in, provided sufficient 'evidence' for opinions on individual members of staff to be formed with a high degree of overall uniformity. In consequence, Miss Peters gained her label in this way.

Feminism then, was not viewed terribly seriously by many members of staff. The topic was polarised into its extremes and fun was poked at those making a stand within the establishment. Similarly, racial equality issues were not taken as matters of urgent concern. Indeed, the topic hardly ever arose during my period of observation, it being something of a 'non-issue'.

Leafield School Overview

Ethnographic research in general and participant observation in particular, has a tendency to over-emphasise the exotic or aberrant. It is always easier to treat as important the events which were memorable rather than mundane.

This account so far, of corridor chaos and people jams, hassled and polarised teachers, plus a mixture of disruptive, bored and resigned pupils is merely an overview of the main themes which presented themselves to a participant observer in the early days and weeks of research. Recording them is not intended to deny that the school day generally passed off in an effective and efficient way, successfully time-tabling hundreds of pupils for dozens of subjects. Nor is it intended to denigrate the hard work and effort put in by teachers either in their subjects or in the matter of classroom control. Nor should it detract from the many pupils who, by and large, got on with their work and paid attention in a polite way.

The focus of this study, after the initial classroom observations, was in-depth discussions with individual pupils, plus analysis of pupil responses to school as elicited via a questionnaire with the entire 5th form. Many of the comments that arose in initial encounters with the 5th year were to emerge as major themes during later in-depth discussions and through the replies to the questionnaire. In particular, aspects of teacher control, subject choice and vocational training were mentioned repeatedly in the questionnaire returns, whilst in the discussions and observations, aspects of gender, race and class and personal attitudes to the world of work were expressed. These issues are now addressed in turn in the next three chapters.

Notes

1. This thesis cannot be cited in full as it give the proper name of Bridgehurst and would destroy anonymity.

2. As above.

3 Boys and girls - different but equal?

Introduction

The 1980s witnessed an ever-increasing research interest in gender socialisation and gender differences in education. Early feminist writings included a focus on the unequal character of girls' education and life chances vis-á-vis boys (e.g. Sharp 1976, Deem 1978) and these were followed quickly by detailed studies into gender and the 'hidden curriculum', a term coined by Jackson (1968) and narrowed by subsequent authors (e.g. Burgess, H. 1983, Samuel 1981) to refer to the process whereby existing divisions in society are inadvertently communicated to pupils via school organisation and through images and statements presented by teachers and text books.

During the early 1980s such researchers as Delamont (1980), Stanworth (1981) and Measor (1984) added much to our understanding of how gender processes operated to disfavour girls whilst others focussed on girls' own aspirations (e.g. Griffin, 1985) or girls' treatment by boys (e.g. Cowie and Lees, 1981).

In all studies, the whole person was not researched to provide a detailed and integrated account of gender, social class, ethnic origins, school experiences, personally held attitudes, future aspirations and actual destinations.

This study attempts to provide such a perspective for both girls and boys and this chapter begins the process by identifying some of the factors present at Leafield School which created inequality between the sexes before considering the gender-specific interactions and attitudes of the pupils themselves.

In this respect, it should be borne in mind that Leafield was a 'caring' community school whose ethos was to serve all pupils equally. However, the school policy regarding gender issues was well-meaning but loose with no official written guidelines for staff to follow (see p. 22).

Curriculum content and teaching aids

Subject choice and non-choice

There was some evidence of an overt gender divide in the curriculum at Leafield. Two examples of lessons where gender was taken as a determinant were P.E. and Parentcraft. In P.E. boys and girls were taken in separate groups, each with a same-sex teacher, and using separate toilets and changing rooms. Each gender group concentrated mainly on differentiated games (e.g. netball for the girls and football for boys; gym work for girls and outdoor activities for the boys). Delamont (1980) refers to a similar segregation of the sexes in sports in her study of two English middle schools arguing that in conjunction with regulations concerning uniform and gender-divided registers, pupils were constantly reminded of their sex and sex differences.

At Leafield there was no school uniform, although pupils were expected to dress 'neatly', cleanly and appropriately for a day's work in school. There were no gender divisions in registers of any kind to compound gender distinctions fostered through segregated sporting activities. However, there was an additional, and total exclusion of boys in the teaching of Parentcraft, an all-girls subject which covered aspects of pregnancy, birth, infant care and child development, alongside practical project work such as making baby clothes or items for the nursery. This subject was a differentiator not only in terms of gender but also in terms of achievement. Parentcraft was a CSE subject which was not taken by the girls from the O-level group who were taking, on average, five or more O-levels. Thus, it was only less-achieving girls who were overtly prepared for motherhood. Both Griffin (1983) and David (1985) have commented on such courses in schools and colleges plus on YOP and YTS schemes. As Griffin (1983) states:

> It is not simply that young women are being pushed to the more exploited margins of the labour market. They are also being prepared

with renewed vigour for their primary role as moral guardians of home and family life (Griffin, 1983, p. 73).

Indeed, preferred jobs as cited by questionnaire respondents indicated a strong interest in looking after children among 12 per cent of less-achieving girls. In addition, girls actively considered their eventual roles as mothers in thinking about their futures as evidenced by in-depth informants who, without exception, saw having children as distant events (i.e. coming along during their mid or late twenties) but nevertheless as an accepted part of their future lives:

> Vanda (less-achieving black pupil): 'Marriage? Much later on, in my 20s or 30s. Then two children and stay with them all the time 'til they're grown up.'

> Delia (less-achieving black pupil): 'I don't want to get married, not yet anyway ...I would like kids, yeah!'

Girls' perceptions on careers, marriage and children receive further attention in Chapters 6 and 7, but for the present it is important to note that their assumption that children and child-rearing would be an automatic part of their lives in years to come was fuelled, in part, by the biological facts and maternal skills taught only to the less able girls (Skeggs, 1988).

Achieving O-level group girls displayed less traditional expectations in relation to children and child raising:

> Sarah (achieving white pupil): 'I'm definitely not interested in marriage 'til my late 20s. I want to travel and get a job and "do" something. You're restricted by kids and a husband, there's the need for two good wages to support a mortgage. I want to be free of that.'

> Pauline (achieving white pupil): 'I don't know about children. They probably suffer if you dump them on a baby sitter at six months but probably also if you're bored at home with them .... I would want to share looking after them with my husband.'

These two academically achieving girls clearly saw children as a constraint or problem vis-á-vis employment, and were reluctant to relinquish career aspirations in favour of child-raising. Their solutions involved either delaying children or sharing care of them with their partner. Whilst their academic achievement alone could lead these girls, and other like them, towards more career orientated expectations, the school in not offering them a child-care subject was reinforcing the view that their future role lay in something other than looking after children.

Similarly in excluding boys from learning about pregnancy, childbirth and childcare, the school could be assisting a polarisation of interests between the sexes. The boys were not provided the opportunity to reflect upon the world of childraising and so had no knowledge upon which they might judge their future role as prospective parents. Understandably then, from their position of ignorance, it was that a group of boys tittered and joked when the option of 'unmarried mothers' arose as a topic in the non-segregated subject of Social Studies. They were scowled at by some of the girls, but their reactions can be attributed not just to immaturity but also in part to the fact that such things were perceived as nothing to do with them; a world apart. However, both biologically and socially, males are implicated in the theme of 'unmarried mothers' and by excluding boys from Parentcraft, it could be argued that the school was missing an opportunity to widen their understanding and develop notions of equality between the sexes.

However, as Delamont (1980) says:

> ..... organisational segregation would not, in itself, be significant if it were not just the first of many ways in which school life separates and then stereotypes boys and girls (Delamont, 1980, p. 27).

At Leafield, the Parentcraft issue was compounded by the fact that it was timetabled against German, History and Woodwork. Similarly, Needlework, although not solely intended for girls, was timetabled against Woodwork. The result was that pupils who chose a subject traditionally associated with their gender were rendering themselves unable to explore skills usually associated with the opposite sex due to timetable constraints. In consequence just one boy, Will, was taking Needlework in the 5th year and he had a special 'justification' for doing so. He suffered from occasional epilepsy and was being steered away from dangerous machinery in technical lessons towards practical but safer skills that he could cope with.

In a reverse situation, just one girl, Ann, chose Woodwork. She was good at the subject and had been part of the group for two years, but whereas Will had been accommodated readily by the girls in Needlework, Ann had experienced more difficulty in becoming accepted:

Ann (white pupil): 'They [the boys] didn't speak to me at first but they do now. I don't get teased anymore and I may go on into 6th form .... other girls won't join in Woodwork because they know I'm the only one and don't want to be the odd ones.'

Ann, therefore, felt able to be 'the odd one out' but other girls felt the pressure to conform to gender stereotypes and expectation. Boys on the other hand had less inhibitions about entering one particular sphere, namely cookery, which could be taken superficially to be a 'girls' subject. However, there were good local prospects of careers in catering and the school had strong links with the local College of Further Education where additional catering qualifications could be obtained. Boys then, were willing to enter the traditionally female domain when job prospects were involved and this was indicated by the fact that boys were just over half of the pupils attempting catering at CSE level but were hardly represented at all in the more domestically based Home Economics CSE (see Table 3.1).

Table 3.1
Catering subjects, examination entries by gender, summer 1985

Subject	No. of boys	No. of girls	TOTAL
Catering (CSE)	12	10	22
Home Economics (CSE)	2	15	17
Food & Nutrition (O level)	0	5	5
All	14	30	44

Source: *Leafield School Examination Statistics (1985)*

On the more academic plane of O-levels, it would appear that able girls and not able boys were encouraged to enter for Food and Nutrition O-level, for five girls and no boys undertook this subject. This could be taken as an indicator that more able girls were channelled either by teachers or their own interests into a subject linked with the role of 'caring provider'. Griffin (1985), in her discussion of equal opportunities related to 'free' subject choice at school states:

> There is nothing equivalent about boys taking cookery or typing, and that of girls taking metalwork or T.D. ...Male students who took 'girls' subjects were assumed to be learning a skill for future use in the labour market. They were taken more seriously than their female peers in the

same classes, to whom such skills were supposed to come naturally for use in their future roles as wives and mothers (see Dyhouse, 1977). Female students who took 'boys' subjects' were either presumed to be interested solely in flirting with the boys, or discounted as unique exceptions (Griffin, 1985, pp. 78-9).

Griffin's statement would appear to hold true for Leafield pupils for the uptake of Catering CSE by boys was directly in line with the school's strong emphasis on 'good jobs' in catering. Similarly, with one girl undertaking Woodwork, no girls in Metalwork and no specific impetus to encourage girls in these domains, there was no scope for this lone girl to be taken seriously.

In contrast, three times more boys than girls were entered for O-level Physics, a typically 'masculine' area of the sciences.

Table 3.2
Science subjects, O-level entries by gender, summer 1985

O-level subject	Boys	Girls	Total
Physics	22	7	29
Chemistry	4	12	16
Biology	8	14*	22
All	34	33	67

(* = includes 2 girls taking Human Biology)

Source: Leafield School Examination Statistics (1985).

Table 3.2 above, indicates that whilst girls and boys took science subjects in equal numbers, there was a strong bias in favour of boys selecting Physics and girls selecting Biology in line with the findings of the 1985 national School Leavers Survey (DES, 1986), but the entries for Chemistry appear to indicate that girls were in the majority, contrary to larger scale statistics. However, an examination of Chemistry pass rates produced a different picture, for eleven of the twelve girls attempting O-level Chemistry were ungraded whilst all four boys received a graded result.

Curriculum content

Girls' interest in, and success in science subjects has received attention from Measor (1984), who undertook qualitative research to discern the reasons behind girls' failure in comparison with boys. She found girls traditional interests to be unsatisfied by the topics covered in the sciences and that girls tended to be marginalised by teachers in science lessons due to negative statements about their ability. In addition, girls' emerging notions of femininity were found to be at odds with the prevailing 'masculine' image of the sciences.

At Leafield, evidence from classroom observations and pupil accounts would appear to act in support of her findings. For example, one group of girls complained bitterly among themselves, and out loud to the biology teacher, that they found plant reproduction boring:

'Why can't we do something on human birth?' one white girl enquired.

This sentiment was echoed by her friends and repeated again to the teacher later on in the lesson but the teacher made no attempt to explain the rationale of the syllabus and made no offer of human biology topics for future lessons. As a result the girls remained disgruntled and showed signs of 'cutting off' from the lesson by talking among themselves, failing to copy down work and generally not paying attention.

Two other girls who were observed to be heavily outnumbered in a physics lesson (twenty boys and three girls) were similarly unenthusiastic about an experiment involving magnets and a solenoid, despite their success at the work benches. Natalie and her friend were the only two in the class to put six magnets together and obtain a good current. The teacher (male) asked them to demonstrate their success to the rest of the class but both were reluctant, preferring the teacher to do it. Eventually they were coaxed to the front of the class and successfully performed the same experiment again. The boys were very impressed by the amount of power achieved. When the girls sat down they were not concentrating on the ensuing discussion about the implications of their discovery, instead they played with the magnets and appeared to have no interest in the topic whatsoever. As the next stage of the lesson developed they started to talk about their mates, about who was a 'slag' and who had been beaten up. They did not complete their work.

Natalie and her friend were unwilling stars in the above episode. They did not take pride in their achievement nor did it motivate them to pursue their work. This was even more surprising because Natalie's deep desire was to be a vet and she knew she had to obtain Physics O-level along with other science subjects to reach her goal. Measor (1984) has cited pupils' own emerging sexuality and associated role expectations as a major factor in negating girls' interest in science and it could be argued that Natalie was acting deferentially towards the male sphere in recoiling from her success with the magnet experiment, but she was also totally disinterested in the magnets and solenoid. Measor indicates that the 'feminisation' of science subjects (e.g. creating perfumes instead of noxious substances in Chemistry) might assist girls in seeing the relevance of science in their lives and so maintain their interest. In this respect she notes that, in her own study, boys interests were accommodated in Needlework classes where they were allowed to make football scarves.

At Leafield, boys seemed to be similarly accommodated in the Home Economics sphere where most of them took Catering CSE as opposed to Home Economics CSE (see p. 57 and Table 3.1). In Needlework, Will was also accommodated by allowing him to knit a football scarf. In the science sphere, however, Physics and Chemistry seemed to follow the traditional pattern inasmuch as the lesson content had far more relevance to the outside interests of boys than girls. Thus, in the above incident, despite the teacher's encouragement towards Natalie over her success with the magnets and solenoid, he was unable to obtain her genuine involvement in the lesson. Obtaining a high power reading in the experiment simply did not impress her like it impressed the boys and she remained detached from her achievement.

Girls appeared to have similar problems in finding relevance in Computer Studies. The school had a recently-furbished Computer Centre (courtesy of a generous donation by a local company) and some Mathematics lessons involved recourse to this Centre and its facilities. Here again, Natalie's reaction to computers was interesting for her veterinary ambitions required Mathematics as well as science subjects. She was observed in one of her computer studies lessons in which the boys quickly got on with the design task in hand whilst Natalie and her friend could not get started. The teacher eventually worked his way around to their consoles and started off the programme for them, but when he moved on they still did not know how to create the required design pattern on the screen. Instead of asking for additional help they settled down to utilising their limited knowledge to outline a house on the screen and then proceed to write up their names in differently coloured bands. They stayed undisturbed in this way for the remainder of the lesson whilst the teacher attended to other pupils (mostly boys) who were much more involved with the programme.

Culley (1988) notes that in the majority of schools computers are frequently linked to the perceived 'masculine' domain by being housed in Mathematics or Science Departments with male teachers in charge of them. In addition, she argues that the software used relies mostly on mathematical and technical concepts, rarely utilising word games or graphic applications that might create more appeal to the girls. At Leafield there was some evidence to bear out Culley's claim that computers are rendered less attractive to girls than to boys for similar reasons. Natalie's contact with computers was solely through the Mathematics lesson, a subject she detested, and her teacher was male. The Computer Centre was often frequented by older boys on a voluntary basis, giving the place an air of masculinity, and the programme observed was evidently of more interest to the boys than the girls. There appeared to be no way in which Natalie and her friend could use their initial drawing of a house on screen and their interest in writing up words in different colour combinations to develop their skill and knowledge of computers. They, therefore, remained on the periphery of this computerised world and the fact that they were not alone in their disinterest and lack of attention was borne out by subsequent questionnaire data whereby it transpired that only one girl in the 5th form indicated any interest in working with computers.

Teaching aids and the hidden curriculum

A number of observations whilst sitting in lessons led to this researcher's conclusion that Leafield pupils were being presented with a wealth of stereotyped gender images in text books and via teaching aids and teachers' statements. Whilst such images were not intended to convey messages specific to one gender or the other, that they did so by both subtle and not so subtle means. Indeed, in terms of such messages being part of a 'hidden curriculum' it seems necessary to agree with Hargreaves (1978) who asks:

> from whom, one wonders, is the hidden curriculum hidden (Hargreaves, 1978, p. 97).

Some Leafield pupils seemed quick to detect and challenge items or issues that they viewed as sexist.

Female pupils would criticise the use of the word 'he' and 'man' in textbooks, complaining that it could be a 'she' or a woman involved instead, and teachers did not always respond positively to such attention to detail. For example, a male Biology teacher was heard to say the following to a female O-level pupil to pre-empt her anticipated criticism:

'You're OK here Pauline, this is Man with a capital M referring to the whole species, it's not talking about men.'

Deflective action of this kind was only observed in male teachers and the way in which it was done could be termed patronising. Whilst at one level the teacher was noticing and rectifying a possible sexist connotation, he was also trivialising the incident by directing his critique at one known feminist member of the class instead of the whole group, as if the topic was only of interest to her.

This teacher was also observed to single out the girls in another biology lesson as if they formed some separate category of pupil. In giving out instructions about a biology practical that would take place the following week he noticed that four girls at one table looked surprised and ready to query it with him. he pre-empted what they might say with the following:

'Now, there's nothing to worry about. I know you girls tend to worry about tests the most.'

Observing from the same table, the girls' reactions did not seem to indicate concern, rather only that something unexpected had been announced, yet the teacher took it that they were 'worried'.

Stanworth (1981) vividly portrays the ways in which teachers at a College of Further Education had different opinions of their pupils' characters and abilities based on their gender. Important in her study was the fact that the pupils being differentiated were achieving pupils of A-level standard who might expect to be judged by their academic merit. Similarly at Leafield, in the above incident, the teacher was talking to a group of four achieving O-level takers including the two girls expected by the school to gain some of the highest science grades in their year. Gender stereotypes were therefore being utilised and imputed irrespective of ability.

Another challenge over textbook content arose during a Religious Knowledge lesson; a subject taken at CSE level by virtually all pupils. In the key textbook a chapter on 'suffering' read:

'a man might make a stand for what is right .... [and suffer consequences as a result] ... or a girl lose a boyfriend by refusing sex.'

Here, as on many other occasions, it was the pupils who would point out bias to the teacher, the teacher having missed the point or let the issue slide. The ensuing discussion cited below indicates an increasing awareness among pupils of stereotyped images that were suppressed by generalised counter statements:

> Black, female pupil: 'This is a real sexist book. Why couldn't it be a boy who refused sex?'

Reply from her white friend:

> 'Because boys are randier than us and want it before we do'.

The teacher broadly agreed with this last statement saying that he could not think of an occasion on which he would refuse an offer:

> White, male pupil: 'What if Margaret Thatcher fancied you?' (laughter)

Although the issue lost momentum at this point another girl brought the subject up again later in the lesson:

> Pauline (white pupil): 'I think this chapter is too sexist and we shouldn't be reading it.'

The male teacher agreed and said that now he, Pauline and Miss Peters (the 'feminist' teacher) were agreed on this point. Using this as a definitive statement the issue was dropped and the lesson continued.

Teachers clearly used such strategies to pacify or cajole those who might be outspoken in class and in consequence made no attempt to deal actively with the underlying issue. Teachers in general did not take individual action to seek out alternative books and materials nor did they indicate to the class that an important point had been made. Instead each incident as it arose, was dealt with in an ad hoc manner.

Delamont (1980) found that it was in the area of teaching that teachers' sex stereotypes came through most strongly, noting that:

> the more the teachers tried to make the lesson material relevant and immediate to the pupils, the more likely they were to make sexist assumptions and remarks (Delamont, 1980, p. 54).

Certainly the teachers in the Religious Knowledge and Biology incidents cited here, were trying to be affable and involved with their students, yet their relaxed and unguarded comments betrayed some of their own gender-specific assumptions regarding feminism, predisposition to fretting and sexual desire.

Whilst pupil challenges did occur, albeit with little real response, there were many other hidden messages to pupils that passed unnoticed. For example, one girl was reprimanded in a needlework lesson for swearing and belching with the remark:

    Teacher: 'That's not very ladylike, Susan!'

Such instruction was not queried. Similarly, plenty of discriminating images did not attract attention, both in books and other teaching aids such as videos. Men were still predominant as activators in science and mathematics material, for example a maths video depicted only young men involved in an exercise to teach themselves percentages. Similarly, Geography and History textbooks provided images of mostly male contributions towards our own and other societies. Such images, presented as objective facts, offered less scope for girls to challenge the validity of what was conveyed.

Furthermore, 'information' videos prepared by outside industries offered distinct images of a gender divide in paid work. One such 'fill-in' video used to keep a class occupied because their teacher was off sick was about the North Sea industries (fishing and oil platforms). The film focussed entirely on men, as fishermen, oil riggers, divers, technicians and so on. As such it portrayed the working world as a man's domain, devoid of women. The implicit assumptions about women's unsuitability for or lack of interest in such work were unconsciously passed on to pupils. The film provided no hint of job or career relevance for girls. Observing the class as they watched this video, it was apparent that the boys sat quietly and watched with interest whilst the girls began to day dream, fidget, fiddle about and talk to each other. It was one of the few occasions observed when girls were noisier and more disruptive than the boys. This could have been due to their lack of identification with the film's content. Afterwards, two of the girls said it had been 'Dead boring!' but two boys described it as being 'Good' and 'Alright'.

Caring teachers?

Examples have been cited above where teachers acted carelessly concerning their own discourse with pupils or where they did not provide adequate support in championing equality. However, some teachers, all of whom could be included in the Head's 'young lefties' category, took great pains to redress the balance between the sexes. This they did without 'making waves', preferring instead to gently encourage more open attitudes on gender issues among pupils. For example, in Social Studies one female teacher had the following to say in response to a pupil referring to an electrician as 'he':

> 'Yes, but is it always a man who's an electrician, Tina?' (pause) 'No, sometimes it's a woman isn't it?'

One male science teacher at Leafield expressed his active intention to encourage the girls in Physics and Chemistry as much as possible in order to promote equal opportunities and he was observed to assist girls sympathetically during lessons, making sure that they had a voice in class and were involved in discussions and practical experiments.

One of his colleagues made similar efforts to encourage the girls and Natalie (a white pupil) proudly said of him:

> 'Sometimes he lets us work in the corridor to get some peace and quiet'.

Whilst this girl clearly saw her teacher's action as a favour designed to help her accomplish her tasks, there was another side to it inasmuch as her removal from the mainstream classroom could be regarded as an exclusion and marginalisation of girls in science as Delamont (1980) and Measor (1984) have argued. Indeed, the need for her and her female peers to be offered an alternative quiet spot in which to work, indicated that boys were 'taking over' in the laboratory, steering the lessons towards their interests, with their preferred noise levels and work strategies allowed to operate. Certainly from observations in science lessons, it was the boys who appeared to be 'at home' at the benches, commandeering whole blocks of stools at the benches, grabbing the available equipment first and operating a noisy cameraderie with their 'mates'. In such circumstances, the solution of removing the girls to work elsewhere in peace may well have been the most practical, but the larger issue of whether boys should be allowed to dominate the laboratory space in this way did not seem to attract attention.

Ironically, whilst the boys could be said to have the 'upper hand' in the laboratory situation described above, it was they who complained about favouritism being displayed towards the girls in allowing them to work unsupervised in the corridor. This researcher's suspicions (which could not be proved) were that the boys wanted to work in the corridor in order to muck about, out of earshot and out of sight of the teacher, but this grievance that girls received preferential treatment from teachers recurred in other lessons, especially over privileged access to the library.

In one Social Studies class the female teacher was having difficulty controlling an unruly group of 15 boys and 8 girls. In order to thin out the class and make it more manageable the teacher asked for 6 volunteers to work in the library. Virtually every hand shot up and the teacher selected a disproportionate number of girls (2 boys and 5 girls) for the privilege of working in the library. 'That's not fair, Miss', shouted a few boys almost in unison. 'You always let the girls go!'

Afterwards, the teacher explained why so many of the boys had been refused a turn in the library. She was quite clear that the issue was one of control and that boys were definitely more unruly and could not be trusted to work quietly without supervision whereas the girls (and a few studious boys) could. As a result the library could provide peace for those who wanted to get on with their work away from the disruptions usually present in her lessons, a feature which was borne out by the statements of some of the girls sent to work in the library (see p. 40).

In this example too, boys were creating a classroom scenario of their own and studious girls who objected to their behaviour found it impossible to concentrate in their presence. The girls were 'accommodated' by a teacher who cared about their progress, and a decision was taken to offer them removal (and possible marginalisation), from the mainstream because of the disruptive behaviour of boys. Girls, once again, in being offered the favour of an alternative place to work were nevertheless implicitly being treated as secondary to the boys, for the latter were not controlled in order to provide an atmosphere conducive for all to learn within the classroom. These boys, however, did not see that they had 'won' classroom space for their own purposes and complained that favouritism had been shown towards the girls.

Boys often indicated that they thought teachers were softer on girls, seeing themselves as hard-done-by in comparison. This antagonism between the sexes was also expressed in other ways both amongst the pupils and between pupils and teachers. The remaining sections of this chapter now turn away from curricular and teaching issues in order to examine the gender perspectives and dynamics that prevailed amongst the pupils themselves.

Pupil's action and reactions

Pupils' own perspectives on gender related issues cannot be judged solely by public incidents in the classroom. However, from school observations, comments overheard and viewpoints expressed in one-to-one interviews, gender was demonstrated to play a very important part in shaping their lives. Gender shaped school-related actions and reactions, but it also shaped other private and public aspects of their lives, both present and future.

Segregated seating

The most startlingly obvious evidence of gender differentiation displayed by pupils lay in their preferred classroom seating arrangements. Almost without exception, girls would occupy one table whilst boys occupied another. Such mixing of the sexes as there was could usually be attributed to the last people entering the room being forced to sit at whatever table remained available, or to the deliberate actions of teachers in splitting up groups of boys or girls to stop them messing with their friends.

In the main, both girls and boys preferred to 'sit with their mates' and these 'mates' were always of the same gender. Initially this surprising, especially among 15-16 year olds, some of whom were physically mature. Such 'perfect' gender clustering had not been anticipated, especially among post-pubescent pupils, some of whom were dating. Yet, during lessons the preference was always to sit with friends of the same sex. Observations, even during a week spent in the library administering a questionnaire to the whole 5th form year (who arrived in form groups for their career interviews with the Head) showed that pupils still group themselves informally at tables with something close to a perfect gender split. Delamont (1980) records her similar findings in two schools as follows:

> This most noticeable pupil behaviour in the two schools ... was their physical sex segregation, which occurred in lesson after lesson (Delamont, 1980, p. 58).

Delamont goes on to demonstrate from fieldnotes that girls simply would not settle until they had organised seating for themselves away from the boys and she indicates an atmosphere of non-co-operation and banter between the sexes. Observations at Leafield serve to corroborate her statements. Not only did girls and boys actively try to avoid sitting together in class but much classroom banter consisted of boys versus girls, usually with the boys starting the process. In classroom tests, boys and girls would compare their marks with their same-sex friends in an interested and sharing way, but would establish the marks of other opposite sex members of the class in order to boast or sneer at each other. In this context, it should also be borne in mind that Natalie and her girlfriend worked alone together on their solenoid experiment in a classroom full of boys and were not at all keen to share their success with the rest of the class (see p. 59).

Teachers and pupils offered different explanations for segrated seating. Their reasons were not necessarily mutually exclusive, rather, both could hold true simultaneously. For their part teachers put this differential seating down to the fact that boys and girls did not have a lot in common in teenage years. Girls were seen as maturing earlier than boys and having little physical attraction to boys of their own chronological age. Similarly, their interests were seen as polarised with both girls talk and boys talk being of little consequence to the opposite sex.

Pupils themselves explained the phenomenon somewhat differently with girls being better able to articulate their reasons. For them, seating patterns reflected friendship patterns and it was always preferable to 'sit with your mates' in lessons. Girls in particular placed a high value on their friends and spoke of school as an opportunity to be with them:

> Angie (white pupil talking about her girlfriends): 'We usually sit together, 'cos it's more interesting like.'
>
> Danielle (white pupil): 'We go around together and we like to sit with our mates so we can have a chat and that. Some of us go back to [Middle School] days.'

The social aspect of school was very important to pupils, especially the girls, and later this proved to be something the school leavers sadly missed and envied the 6th formers for. As one girl said ruefully:

> White, female pupil: 'You don't find out 'til after you've left.'

Seating patterns, therefore, reflected friendship patterns and the fact that these friends were same-gender friends seemed altogether too automatic and obvious for most informants to explain. Friendships centred on things shared in common; likes and dislikes, music tastes, interest in sports, clothes, etc. and in general these things were found with others of the same sex.

To corroborate the explanation of both teachers and pupils, fieldwork threw up only one noticeable boyfriend/girlfriend relationship among the 5th formers and here this couple's attraction to each other did lead them to sit together whenever possible. The only other evidence found of a cross-gender friendship, leading to the two pupils concerned deliberately sitting with each other, was the case of a boy and girl who were both keen on motorbikes. The girl was very masculine in her self-presentation with very short hair, a man's cap, jeans, lace-up boots and a bomber jacket. The pair of them would sit together in class to talk about bikes and how they were going to get a particular one on the road. This girl had crossed the boundary into 'boys' interests' and taken on a 'boy's image' and was accepted for these interests rather than her sexuality.

Gender-based tensions and sexuality

In the main though, girls and boys preferred to remain separate from each other in class and there was evidence of a divide based on a belief in polarised sexual differences. The Religious Knowledge incident cited on pp. 62-3 had important overtones of this, presenting a double edge to the issue of sexism raised by a pupil, for it was the boys who guffawed and jeered when Colette queried a sexist connotation in a book, implying she was out of step not the statement in the book. In addition, it was a girl who offered the explanation that boys 'are randier than we are'. Thus stereotyped assumptions about the sexuality of the opposite sex were already incorporated into the everyday understandings of these pupils.

Barnes and Todd (1977) noted a lack of co-operation between the sexes in their study of young teenagers concluding that the two sex groups may even polarise. Certainly an atmosphere of vying with the opposite sex was apparent in Leafield classrooms and this became more noticeable during break times when pupils were more free to act as they wanted. Indeed, break times revealed aspects of polarisation that involved boys' sexual domination of girls with girls being either unable or unwilling to 'give as good as they got'. This aspect of gender relations is explored later in this chapter.

From discussions it was clear that boys and girls had little direct sexual contact with each other. Whilst no-one was asked directly about their sex lives many volunteered information. Girls in particular were more forthcoming in this respect and here the gender of the researcher must be taken into account in understanding their openness.

For most girls sex was something to get involved with when they were serious with a boy and they felt this had not happened to them yet. Those with boyfriends said the boys were older than themselves and not connected with the school. School was therefore fairly free of romance and sexual activity. But sexuality was raised at school by virtue of remarks, reputations and mucking about.

Sexual insults

Concerning remarks and reputations, broad gender stereotypes were employed by the pupils in classifying each other. Girls were referred to by both boys and other girls as 'slag' and 'cow'. Such a label could be earned by actually being promiscuous or simply by seeming to be so. Such detail as wearing a lot of make-up, or very tight, short skirts and 'chatting-up' lots of boys was taken as 'evidence' of sexual promiscuity. That reputations far exceeded reality was indicated by the fact that my female informants knew only one girl who boasted openly about her sexual activities (e.g. would enthuse about how many times she had 'had it' the night before) and even she could well have been exaggerating. In addition, as previously stated, there were virtually no overt signs of boy/girl relationships at 5th form level.

Cowie and Lees (1981) indicate that the label 'slag' is easy to earn and difficult to dislodge because it is hard for any girl to 'prove' she had not done something she is accused of doing. Certainly at Leafield, the label 'slag' was very easy to earn, not just through behaviour connected with boys but also through individuality in fashion, and rudeness or 'bitchiness' towards other girls. Cowie and Lees note that girls as well as boys apply the derogatory 'slag' label to other girls suggesting that this indicates that girls are prepared to accept and operate male values of female sexuality. However, the girls' usage of the term 'slag' at Leafield appeared to differ from boys' usage. Girls used it more as a general insult for girls they found unpleasant, but boys used it more in the narrower sense of sexual looseness based on their knowledge of how many boys a particular girl had gone out with and the outcomes (real or assumed) of those liaisons.

Boys at Leafield were seemingly attempting to sanction and control girls' sexuality by their definitions of them, and the power that this had to discriminate against girls was all the more powerful because there was no equivalent pressure girls could exert upon boys in linguistic terms. Spender (1980) argues that there are far more derogatory adjectives for women than there are for men, whilst Cowie and Lees argue that most of these rely on a sexual double standard whereby boys' libido is seen as legitimate but girls' as illegitimate. Certainly Leafield girls seemed powerless to counteract boys' insults with anything like similar potency. Boys were cajoled as being 'randy' or 'a ram' but as Spender says, such terms were more flattering than insulting to the boys for they smacked of virility, something the boys prized.

Another separate aspect of language was the fact that boys' talk was punctuated, almost as a matter of course, by various profanities. Key words involved were 'fuck' and 'cunt', used mostly as adjectives to add emphasis to the discourse and seemingly to provide an air of maturity for the speaker. These words were also used by boys to describe other boys, and common usage included such items as 'You stupid fucker' and 'He's a silly cunt'.

In this way, boys seemed to be using words with a sexual connotation in a broader way as all-encompassing insults and in this, their usage of such words had parallels to the ways in which girls would apply the terms 'slag' and 'cow' to each other. In addition, for both sexes, these words could be used softly towards ones 'mates' as if to indicate that the friendship was strong enough to cope with such words used as gentle chiding.

Sexual innuendo and jokes

Apart from the overt use of sexual insults described above, sexual innuendo and explicit sexual remarks or actions played an important part in banter and humour between the sexes. The scope for this was enormous ranging from graffiti to dirty jokes and from taunts to classroom quips.

In general, Leafield was remarkably free of graffiti. One exception to this was a somewhat splendid cariacature of the Head drawn by an anonymous artist behind the bicycle sheds and even the Head thought that this was 'a rather good likeness'.

Apart from this there was little evidence of illicit spray painting or carving, but the occasional erect penis or 'tits and bum' type of sketch would appear chalked on a wall or drawn in a book. One Religious Knowledge textbook observed contained a picture of a woman looking upwards (as if to heaven). A balloon from her mouth sketched in by a pupil read 'Give us a fuck!'.

In class, opportunities to rib members of the opposite sex were not often missed and in the protected environment of the teacher's presence, girls were as good as boys at 'dishing out the treatment'. For example, in one lesson Nigel was falling asleep over the desk. A girl nearby noticed and said:

> White female pupil: 'You're knackered I expect from what I heard you were doing last night.'
>
> 'You're only jealous!' came the reply.

Broader stereotypes of the opposite sex were also aired in the classroom and for the most part, these were given credence by the lack of any reaction from the teacher. In one lesson, a girl pupil became irritated by her nearby male companions who were messing about. She muttered about them and gave them some dirty looks which the boys noticed. Said one of them:

> White, male pupil: 'What's up Tracy? Wrong time of the month is it?'

Neither she, nor the teacher challenged this comment although it had been plain to hear. Thus, classroom barracking based on accepted 'differences' served to polarise pupils into a 'them and us' situation along gender lines. Sexual taunts were also a favourite breaktime occupation at Leafield that were indulged in primarily by boys at girls' expense. Taunts included:

- name-calling (designed to embarrass the girl concerned),

- walking close behind a girl using thrusting movements of the hips (designed to embarrass the girl and cause amusement to male friends watching),

- bumping into girls to rub up against them, and

- overt sexual offers,

Girls were less explicit in their pranks on boys. Comments and 'come-on' looks were two methods employed but mostly there were just verbal protests or reproachful looks in retaliation for offences committed by the boys. For example, crossing the courtyard late one breaktime, Natalie, who was behind her friends squealed:

> Natalie (white pupil): 'Quick! Look! Do something Mandy, he's groping my titties.'

A teenage boy had lunged at her and grasped her from behind with his hands full over her breasts. She wrested herself free and gave him a disapproving look combined with a broad beam. His actions were brushed aside and treated with amusement.

In contrast, the most daring escapade involving girls against the boys was one related by Natalie. She explained how she and two other girls had peered over the wall of the boys' toilet to watch a boy they fancied 'having a pee'. Girls' pranks against boys were, therefore, far more mild and conducted more at a distance than were boys' pranks aimed at the girls. The latter did not seem to see anything wrong in forcing themselves upon girls via direct physical contact. In this they displayed an implicit belief in their right to women's bodies, a point argued by Hamblin (1983) in her discussion of a questionnaire into male/female relationships conducted with readers of

Spare Rib. In additions, this type of action could be described as sexual harassment in line with Mahony (1985) and Jones (1985) who found similar examples of physical molestation and sexual graffiti in mixed schools.

The tip of the iceberg?

One disturbing feature of research at Leafield was the fact that for some of the female informants, what happened to them at school at the hands of the boys was mild in comparison to what happened beyond the school gates.

A popular activity among the girls was babysitting. It provided pocket money and the chance to get out of the house without having to spend money. However, two girls told me that they had had problems with the fathers of 'their babies'.

> Natalie (white pupil): 'He'd go upstairs for a shower and come down again in the nude, it was embarrassing.'
>
> Tessa (white pupil): 'Yes, mine used to put his arms round me for a kiss. I told him I'd tell his wife and he stopped doing it.'

These girls saw 'the fathers' as a perpetual problem in babysitting. They despised them rather than feared them but never complained openly to their families or the wife involved. Their reasons for keeping quiet were that they loved 'their babies' and would miss them badly if they had to stop babysitting. However, their silence could also be taken as an indicator that these young women 'expected' to be troubled in this way. As Mahony states:

> [girls] regard sexual harassment as a normal part of daily life (Mahony, p. 49).

It was this type of experience, combined with the breast-grabbing episode mentioned above that led Natalie to form a very negative view of men altogether.

> Natalie: 'They only want one thing from you!' she averred.

It is not surprising then, that girls like Natalie sought out and valued the friendship of their own sex and claimed to have little interest in boyfriends and marriage, at least for the time being.

Attitudes to school

Returning to issues associated with schooling, a gender divide was apparent in pupils' attitudes to school and aspects of deviance. From the questionnaire conducted with the entire 5th form it was evident that girls and boys had different priorities in their reasons for liking school.

On friendships

The single, most quoted reason from girls for liking school was the opportunity to meet and socialise with friends (44 per cent), closely followed by enjoyment for certain lessons (39 per cent). Most girls had a whole cluster of girlfriends and, as mentioned earlier in this chapter, they made sure they sat with 'their mates' in class whenever they could. This was particularly true of less-achieving girls (CSE and non-exam takers) and formed a contrast to the pupils studied by Llewellyn (1980) for whom 'friendship and loyalty links were virtually non-existent' (p. 47).

Leafield girls at all ability levels valued their friends, and less-achieving girls looked back fondly upon their escapades after leaving:

> Shirley (white pupil, 8 months after leaving): 'I already miss school ... not exactly to learn again but [to see] my friends and to have a laugh; hiding in the toilets to have a fag. Nothing like that at work, not at all.'

The tendency among girls to mention missing their school friends many months after leaving indicated how important the issue of friendship was to them, although they had not realised this whilst still at school:

> Tessa (white pupil, also 8 months after leaving): 'I miss school, didn't think I would but I do. I miss my friends .... you don't find out until you leave.'

Other researchers (e.g. Meyenn 1980, Delamont 1980) have acknowledged the importance of female friendship groups and Griffin (1985) has stressed the importance of their own space within mixed schools such that:

> the girls' toilets or cloakrooms provided an ideal refuge from teachers and the boys .... the toilets were a favourite place for skiving off lessons (Griffin, 1985, p. 20).

It has already been indicated in Chapter 2 that all pupils appropriated school facilities for their own purposes, but the girls' toilets were a particular focal point. As Shirley explained, they were a place to 'have a fag', or to indulge in fainting sessions or gossip. This location (as opposed to the bicycle sheds or playing fields) was no accident in that it was a special 'girls only' space. Griffin is correct in suggesting that the toilets can be a refuge from boys and that female friendship groups can be an important demonstration of solidarity and withdrawal from male-dominated domains within the school grounds. Girls could have avoided teachers at one of many venues on site but they would have been in the company of boys doing precisely the same thing. At Leafield, girls found it preferable to be by themselves away from the barracking and taunting of boys and the girls' toilets provided a 'haven in horny seas'. In addition, the asexual and non-threatening friendship of other females was in itself an important mechanism for mutual support among the girls. Comradeship and solidarity were important in a social setting where boys' actions at girls' expense could be regarded as intrusive.

That girls' friendships served this specific purpose at Leafield was perhaps indicated by the fact that, almost without exception, female in-depth informants lost contact with their friends after leaving school. Many of these girls lived literally around the corner from each other yet they did not take steps to keep in contact, even though many found their new lives and work boring. Girls' friendships were, therefore, important within the context of school and the events experienced there. For girls, school involved a double impact from both teachers and the boys; for boys it meant an impact from teachers only. This could account for the fact that only 26 per cent of boys cited friendships as their main reason for liking school in the questionnaire. Instead their highest priority for liking school was the lessons, with 47 per cent putting this first on the list. It could be argued that boys had less need for the support of same-sex friends at school, as they were not subjected to the type of harassment from the opposite sex that they themselves initiated. Their ability to list lessons/subjects as their main reason for liking school was precisely because they were free to enjoy them if motivated to do so, with no direct impediments from the girls.

On teachers

Whatever the discord between the sexes at Leafield and despite different main reasons for liking school, girls and boys were unanimous in their prime reason for disliking school. The most frequently cited reason, reported by 38 per cent of both girls and boys, was 'the teachers'. By this was meant teachers' attitudes towards them, and pupils were unequivocal in down-rating teachers who were unfair or who talked down to them and who treated them like children. Rosser and Harre (1976) state that pupils deem it very important that teachers should be fair and that being too strict or unfair was one of the major 'crimes' teachers could commit. Leafield pupils certainly operated the same ground rules and in consequence teachers who violated their 'human rights' gained the dubious distinction of being the major cause of making school an unpleasant experience. To illustrate this point, in-depth informants complained about the attitudes of teachers, especially where they felt that teachers 'put them down':

> Vanda (black pupil): 'Their attitude I suppose .... some could be very snobby. Some people think we're like little kids and need a proper telling off .... I rebelled most probably, so talked and messed about. I would have been different if treated differently, I'm positive.'

> Shirley (white pupil): 'Some teachers attitude was helpful, for example Mrs Henderson gave you more equal treatment, really nice. But others, like Mr Kelly, if you were just a couple of minutes late he wouldn't wait for you to explain, stand there and shame you up in front of the class.'

Pupils hated being told off or being made to look small. They wanted to be treated as equals and rejected child status (see also Griffin,1985). Having a laugh with teachers was also valued as an indicator of a good working relationship and this was taken as proof that they were accepted on equal terms by teachers. As one boy explained:

> Eddie (black pupil): 'Some teachers were alright, you could have a good laugh and they'd talk to you normally .... didn't talk down to you or nothing.'

Both Woods (1979) and Willis (1977) have stressed the importance of teachers' ability to 'have a laugh' in forming good pupil relationships. As Woods (1983) states:

> Humour eases interaction when it has got into embarrassing or otherwise difficult situations. It is a great leveller, for though the teacher is in authority over them, it shows that basically he or she is one of them (Woods, 1983, p. 56).

Whilst pupils valued 'having a laugh' and wanted teachers to be able to respond in this way, the more common occurrence was that teachers were viewed negatively for not being able to match up to this standard. The net result of this was that pupils distanced themselves from the learning process if they perceived their teachers as being unjust.

Other complaints levelled at teachers are discussed in Chapter 5 in relation to social class interests, but the criticisms raised so far have been mentioned at length here for two main reasons. Firstly, because despite any polarisation of the sexes, both girls and boys were united by the fact that these teacher 'failings' formed the key to dissatisfaction with school, and secondly, because these complaints about teachers' actions interlinked with another aspect of schooling, namely discipline, upon which pupils had differing and gender-specific opinions.

On discipline

The questionnaire with the 5th form included an opportunity for pupils to list their suggestions for improving school. 'Better teachers' was the inevitable response of many pupils given their feelings illustrated above. Some also cited more interesting subjects, rearrangement of school hours and better equipment/funding. On these issues boys and girls could not be distinguished, giving their replies in similar proportions. However, 13 per cent of girls requested stricter discipline in school, whilst only 7 per cent of boys mentioned this. This faithfully reflected the complaints about discipline raised by in-depth informants. Virtually all the girls felt they could have done better at school and most blamed classroom noise and disorder as major reasons for failing to do so, as with Griffin's girls (1985) who also bemoaned teachers' lack of control. However, they acknowledged that if others were mucking about they found it hard not to get involved themselves. Consequently there was a recognised lack of self-discipline which they found difficult to control. Nevertheless, girls felt that teachers should have stopped classroom disruptions in order to create an atmosphere conducive to work. Tessa's complaint below was typical of many less-achieving girls:

> Tessa (white less-achiever): 'I went downhill in the last year. Originally I was in for O-levels but I messed about with Natalie and got put in for CSEs instead .... I think teachers should have been harder.'

Marsh, Rosser and Harre (1978) in researching classroom disorder, noted a similar desire for control among their pupils who wanted teachers to be firm.

Pupils like Tessa expected teachers to successfully tread a very fine line between being too hard and too soft. They despised authoritarian control, hated being 'shamed up' or 'put down', and rejected being treated 'like little kids'. On the other had 'soft' teachers were almost equally despised and were played up in lessons. As March, Rosser and Harre (1978) state, pupils were:

> Insulted by weakness on the part of those in authority who they expected to be strong, and this weakness, once established, provokes more playing up (March, Rosser and Harre, 1978, p. 38).

Somewhere between the two, teachers were expected to strike an effective balance, keeping classroom order without making any enemies.

The most striking feature about pupil complaints concerning lack of discipline was not, however, that girls mentioned it more times than boys, but that women teachers were criticised more often than men for their weakness and lack of control. Thus, although in the questionnaires, twice as many girls wanted extra discipline from teachers, in the in-depth interviews equal numbers of both boys and girls could see that it was often lacking and blamed women teachers far more than men for this state of affairs:

> Duncan (white less-achiever): 'Men hold the class together better, women are OK but they can be a bit bitchy.'

Intertwined with criticisms of female teachers lay acknowledgements that pupils played up the women more than the men. Pupils could articulate a cycle of events involving their negative perceptions of female teacher control and their responses to that, leading to chaos:

> Peter (white achiever): 'Mr Lukes was the best, harsh but fair. Social Studies, Mrs Cornforth was one of the greatest tits in the world. She'd promise things and not do them so then we played her up .... Definitely boys played women teachers up more than men. They fear men more .... The more women tell you off the more you resist them. Men stamp their authority on you more than women.'

Beynon and Atkinson (1984) discuss the way in which pupils can actively combine in the classroom to 'suss-out' teachers, indicating a particular tendency to challenge women teachers who are suspected of being 'weak'. Leafield pupils were very good at this, utilising techniques that ranged from using four-letter words to creating disturbances and making provocative statements like 'Miss can't teach'.

When probing into the clear distinctions that pupils made between male and female teachers' ability to control the class, most could think of individual teachers who did not fit the stereotype. Some men were said to be too 'soft' and some women were said to be 'OK' or 'alright' but only one informant gave women teachers the credit for controlling the class through different means than men and even he saw women opting out at the higher levels of disciplinary action:

> Eric (black less-achiever): 'Women handle trouble more psychologically but I was struck that it was always men at the top. Miss Baverstock used to use men to handle trouble.'

Overall then, many pupils operated under the assumption that women teachers had less control over the class than men. They were seen as less forceful, easier to 'play up' and as operating differently from men. Both boys and girls shared this perception of women teachers, although girls were more likely to make reference to specific women teachers whom they had found very helpful. Pupils were, therefore, stereotyping their teachers by utilising broader societal assumptions concerning female characteristics and then reinforcing that stereotype by virtue of their own response in the classroom.

On classroom behaviour

In the foregoing discussion, pupils admitted to playing up teachers if they were too 'soft' and to rebelling against them if they were too 'hard'. However, the way in which pupils did so was largely gender-specific. One boy summed it up nicely:

> Peter (white less-achiever): 'Boys are more boisterous than girls at school, you can see that straight off.'

Peter's statement appeared to be quite accurate from observations in class. Both boys and girls would talk, fidget, waste time and so on, but boys were decidedly more noisy in doing so, thereby gaining increased teacher attention. It was the boys who would enter the classroom banging bags down on the desks and scraping chair legs on the floor. It was boys tho would lob bags across the room when the teacher was out, and it was boys who made a nuisance of themselves shouting out answers or demanding to be dealt with.

Boys' behaviour in this respect did not pass unnoticed by the girls:

> Vanda (black less-achiever): 'Boys - they could do what they wanted, and girls - they were under there!' [pressing her thumb on the table].

Spender (1982) has highlighted this more 'pushy' element in boys, claiming that it provides boys with the opportunity to claim more of the teachers' time which was, in consequence, shared out unequally between the girls and the boys. At Leafield, it was invariably the boys whose noise levels and antics caused actual classroom disruption, for girls misbehaved in a different way.

For girls, misbehaving usually took on a much quieter form. Girls would whisper to each other incessantly and carry on quit conversations that did not attract teacher attention. They would also doodle in their note books, manicure their nails, sort and re-sort their pencil cases, and resort to daydreaming.

All this meant that girls were less 'trouble' than the boys, but it also made them what Stanworth (1981) describes as the 'faceless bunch'. Girls could, therefore, slope through their lessons doing very little work yet escape the notice of the teacher.

Anyon (1983) argues that this type of turning away or withdrawal from lessons constitutes an action in its own right and that in consequence such girls can be considered as deviant and resisting school processes. Stanley (1986) argues that the quiet passivity of girls can also be attributed to behaviour expected of them by teachers and society, seeing it as:

> a successful adaptation to the situation of girls in school (Stanley, 1986, p. 275).

Both these aspects of girls' classroom behaviour were present at Leafield and girls did not recognise that their actions rendered them 'invisible' in comparison to the boys and might affect the help they received and their levels of achievement.

Battle of the sexes?

To summarise, there was evidence of polarisation between the sexes at Leafield and that this divide was applied by pupils not only to themselves, but also to their teachers.

A powerful part of this polarisation was the stereotypical attitudes pupils held about their opposite sex peers, especially on matters of sexuality. Perceived 'feminine' or 'masculine' attributes were also transferred onto members of staff such that women teachers were perceived as 'weak' or 'bitchy', whilst men were seen as 'hard' or having authority.

However, apart from any preconceived ideas about masculine and feminine behaviour the pupils may have held, they also observed actual differences in boys' and girls' behaviour in class and acknowledged that those differences existed. Boys and girls reacted differently to staff. They also barracked each other in lessons and vied with each other for the upper-hand in classroom banter. Boys harassed girls both directly and indirectly and girls gave them the 'cold shoulder'. Here then, was a subtle yet truly comprehensive battle between the sexes.

Thus a combination of broader beliefs and attitudes plus first hand experience formed the stock knowledge about each other. Feeding this knowledge was the response of teachers in interacting with pupils together with the content of teaching aids and issues related to organisation of the curriculum. These three features of schooling combined to fuel pupils' existing gender-divided attitudes. Only a few brave and persistent girls challenged these classroom messages and their viewpoint was marginalised via teacher strategies of placation instead of action.

Girls wanted extra discipline at school in order to control the noise and disorder that was more often than not created by boys, and female friendship groups were an important and pleasurable feature of daily life for them. The realities of boys' behaviour towards girls made for the efficacy of such groups as a sanctuary, away from the world of the boys.

Such then, were the aspects of gender that were observed being played out at Leafield and that were recounted by the pupils in both discussions and questionnaire replies. The school's lack of any guide-lines to staff on how to guard against sexism in the class-room contributed towards this. A lack of policy on combating sexism among pupils also led to the unchecked formation of a highly polarised set of gender-related attitudes that boys and girls held about each other and about themselves. On this evidence gender inequality existed at Leafield to disfavour girls at a variety of levels within the school. As Griffin (1983) states:

> Those working in the area of young people's education .... need to think long and hard about the relevance of their work to the female half of the population (Griffin, 1983, p. 75).

4 Black and white - unite or fight?

Introduction

Leafield School was located within a Local Education Authority that had no written policy on either equal opportunities or multi-cultural education. The Chief Education Officer in addressing a conference said that schools should anticipate 'the inexorable march of events' in our society and 'better equip their pupils for such a future', but this philosophy did not encourage him to see the benefits of a written policy.

The Local Authority, which claimed on all its vacancy advertisements to be 'an equal opportunity employer', provided support for a Multi-Cultural Education Centre set up in 1978. This support included the provision of premises, materials and a small staff to whom schools could turn in search of multicultural literature and teaching packs, and from whom advice on teaching methods, classroom materials and mother-tongue support teaching could be obtained. This Centre developed slowly, able only to engage actively with schools who were willing to utilise its resources and having little or no power to engage other less willing schools in multi-cultural initiatives. Troyna and Ball (1985) studied schools' usage of the LEA's Multicultural Education Unit at Milltown with similar conclusions. In Bridgehurst, it was not until 1986/87 (after the research period at Leafield) that the LEA produced a prejudice and equality document which became something of a catalyst for discussion among teachers.

It is widely assumed (e.g. Little & Willey 1981, Swann 1985) that the development of a written LEA policy is of crucial importance in involving schools actively in combatting racial inequalities that occur within school walls, be they direct racism (e.g. pupil attacks and insults) or unintentional prejudice (e.g. in stereotyped textbook images or discriminatory practices). Also, as Troyna and Ball (1985) state:

> the absence of an Authority-wide policy is said to have the potential to inhibit developments at the 'chalk face' (Troyna and Ball, 1985, p. 26).

It is against such a background of no written LEA policy, that research into race and its effect on interactions at Leafield took place. The racial dimension was considered in both teacher and pupil interactions and this chapter will argue that the lack of an LEA policy assisted the perpetuation of unchallenged racism that occurred in both blatant and subtle ways.

Multiculturalism and antiracism at Leafield School

Leafield's school policy was stressed as being one of equality of opportunity although it did not have a written anti-racist or anti-sexist policy and there were no written guidelines or procedures for teachers in dealing with racist or sexist events. It followed then that in the absence of clearly defined guidelines for combatting racism any such incidents that arose were dealt with individualistically 'on the spot', if at all, with no system of recourse to a disciplinary procedure or for feedback and discussion with colleagues. In practice what happened in classrooms and staffrooms was distinctly influenced by the perspective of the individual teacher or teachers involved and, as indicated in Chapter 2, some members of staff were not averse to resorting to racist humour in the staffrooms. In addition, Chapter 2 also describes the furore that was created over the suggested policy statement by the school's Equal Opportunity Group, the reaction among some staff being that overt stands against racism (and sexism) were uncalled for and in fact only served to exacerbate 'problems'.

In the absence of a strong anti-racist policy, Leafield might still have had a substantial multicultural curriculum but it did not, and here again research had indicated that few predominantly white schools take multiculturalism seriously (e.g. Troyna and Ball, 1985). In this respect it should be stated that the school's intake included only 5 per cent ethnic minority pupils, the vast majority of whom were children of West Indian origin. During the period of research at Leafield there were only 10 pupils of Asian or Eastern origin in the entire school, the remaining non-white pupils being solely of West

Indian/Afro-Caribbean origin.

Leafield had, indeed, made changes in the curriculum since the appointment of a more progressive Head in 1982. For example the humanities had been broadened to include topical issues of racial and sexual equality both at home and abroad. Religious education had been broadened also, and the school boasted a newly acquired Section 11 teacher whose duties lay in the Humanities and TVEI training.

The school had also forged a link with a black school in a third World country and this incorporated project work, pen friends and an ambitious school trip to visit the other school during the summer vacations.

However, for one reason or another, these genuine efforts to raise awareness and broaden the horizons of the pupils often failed to reach their objectives. For example, the Section 11 teacher was used primarily as a means of spreading the general teaching load rather than as a way to focus on ethnic minority needs and this teacher's classes included general lessons in Mathematics, Parentcraft, Community Studies and History. Her timetable was quite full and her support for ethnic minority pupils was, from observations, primarily conducted through lunch break caring contacts with any minority pupil who had a personal problem at the time. She did do some work on racism and prejudice within the curriculum, utilising materials from the local Centre for Multicultural Education but this was a small part of her teaching load. The local Multicultural Education Adviser indicated that 'Section 11 funding is commonly used to supplement teaching in this way' and this falls in line with the findings of other researchers (e.g. Dorn and Hibbert, 1987) who have commented that Section 11 teachers are often used to improve general pupil/teacher ratios.

Regarding the school trip to the Third World school, the cost of this trip to parents was over £600, immediately excluding a number of pupils whose families could not afford such a sum. Similarly, it proved difficult to raise interest in the pupils when important international issues were introduced into classroom discussions. An example from fieldnotes is as follows:

History lesson with Mr Lukes (11 December 1984)

The class contains 15 pupils; 12 boys and 3 girls. Three are of West Indian origin; two boys and a girl. The class has been working on Apartheid in South Africa finishing off today with Ron Pickering's film on sport in South Africa. The teacher re-capped on earlier lessons and asked why South Africa was prepared to spend £33,000 on assisting international sports events. After a lot of delays and non-commital activity, Sonia, a West Indian informant, suggests it is to make it look as if the races can mix. The film is then shown with much fidgeting and noise from the pupils, used deliberately to indicate their boredom. Afterwards in question time, two pupils state that the film advocates an end to the sports boycott when in fact it suggests the opposite. All three West Indian pupils are among those not really paying attention to the film. Winston, a West Indian boy in the class, is then sent out for fiddling with a pair of clippers from his metalwork class and saying 'Yeah - my tongue!' in answer to a question about whether he had anything in his mouth. The lesson struggles on.

Other multicultural initiatives were also taken by staff with an emphasis on West Indian culture in order to reflect the intake of the school. These included the incorporation of reggae in Music, Drama and dancing classes and a steel band that met to practice after school. The steel band consisted of five West Indian-origin boys of various ages. One teacher in particular, did a lot to keep this band together by constantly encouraging its participants, staying late to help them practice and finding them local community bookings. She later stated that it was a problem trying to get all band members to stay behind after school for practices and a constant worry that they would not show up at booked events.

Beyond this, some members of the school's Equal Opportunities Group actively tried to use non-racist and non-sexist resources and topics in their teaching, but these were highly personalised initiatives. The group, per se, did not make any great impact on either policy or practice at the school during the period of this research, save to aggravate some of the 'rear guard' teachers of the Head's 'old righties' category.

From the foregoing examples of multicultural inputs at Leafield it can be seen that they were largely 'ad hoc' and initiated by individual teachers with a desire to promote multicultural perspectives. This is an experience shared by many schools, with or without a written policy (Troyna and Ball, 1985). The additional absence of an anti-racist policy, however, meant that there was no concerted attack on racism, no common stand displayed by staff to pupils. This was to have repercussions on interactions in the classroom.

Teachers' actions

It has already been indicated that some teachers from the Head's 'old righties' category were not averse to racial overtones in staffroom humour (see p. 50) but did their attitudes spill over into the classroom? Research at Leafield suggested that they did.

Two male teachers who formed part of the smoking fraternity in the 'old righties' section of the staffroom were observed engaging in racist humour in the classroom. One of these, a metalwork teacher, made considerable play, when talking to an Asian pupil, of exhorting 'Mohammed - son of the prophet', to perform some activity or other. The same turn of phrase was used when addressing the boy concerned on a more one-to-one basis, again loud enough for all, in a fairly noisy machine room, to hear. This boy was the only Asian-origin boy in the class and the teacher clearly thought he was being witty and 'pally' by addressing the boy in this way. The boy concerned received such salutations passively but there was no doubt that he was singled out by the teacher because of a perceived ethnic difference.

Wright (1986) reports very similar behaviour from a male metalwork teacher who could not understand why his comments about being 'sent back to the chocolate factory' were received so negatively, stating that it 'was only said in good fun'. (Wright, 1986, p. 131). Her observations, contained in the research of Eggleston et al. (1986), are completely consistent with observations of this teacher who, in common with his male staff room colleagues saw no harm in humour of this type and felt that 'too much was read into things'.

The common belief among the 'smoking fraternity' to which he was a party was that researchers simply caused trouble and made things worse than they really were by placing the spotlight on race. Cohn (1987) found similar attitudes among teachers in Manchester schools quoting one teacher's comment as follows:

> As soon as you institutionalize something it becomes more obvious (Cohn, 1987, p. 10).

The above classroom example was observed directly but pupils also related other, similar things they had witnessed:

> Tessa (white less-achiever): 'In Mr Harper's class a boy made a joke about Mohammed and everybody laughed and the teacher laughed too.'

and:

> Shirley (white less-achiever): 'Mr Dixon used to say something about chappatis and everyone would laugh. He told Pakistani jokes and Irish

jokes and we were all generally treated the same.'

In the latter example it is interesting to note that a white pupil took the teacher's usage of both Pakistani and Irish jokes as proof that he was not racist and treated all pupils the same. Yet as Curtis (1984) states, jokes against the Irish are as racist as jokes against Pakistanis for both serve to denigrate a population considered inferior to the British. Leafield pupils did not perceive that the Irish were being ridiculed in jokes as an ethnic minority, rather they saw the Irish as white and the jokes as a signal that their teachers were 'OK', could have a laugh and treated everyone the same. It would appear therefore that both status and a reputation for fairness in white pupils' eyes was built upon a teacher's willingness to have a laugh (see Woods, 1979) enhanced by their willingness to include racial humour of various origins in their repertoire. It can be debated whether cross-cultural and trans-racial jokes in mixed company are or are not signs of true racial harmony. Certainly the ability to laugh at oneself and one's own group is considered beneficial in our society. When white British people can identify so clearly with black people or Irish people as to laugh with them rather than at them it may be that whites have reached an important stage in the process of anti-racialism, but it is not clear that the incidents cited here correspond to that ideal. The jokes referred to were clearly at the expense of black and Irish people.

As a result, it is not surprising that some of this researchers' black informants picked up on this and presented it as a criticism of their teachers. They were affronted by such humour and in consequence dubbed offending teachers 'racist'. Whilst this did not lead to overt classroom antagonisms or to 'them and us' situations of the kind described by Wright (1986) in her ethnographic study of a mixed comprehensive, there was a clear gulf between both white teachers and pupils and black pupils on this point.

There is a lack of evidence on whether schools with no specific anti-racist policy fare worse in terms of race relations and racism than those which do have one. However staff are more likely to 'fall into the trap' of racist banter in their classrooms if they have not been involved in discussions or training designed to combat prejudice and increase racism awareness.

As indicated above, teachers were not challenged over racist jokes. This was in direct contrast to sexist remarks and offending text books which evoked a response from both white and black girls (see p. 62-3). On gender issues, both black and white girls could unite to defend things female presenting a united front on behalf of half of the school population. It would apear though, that it was more problematic for pupils to challenge racism in the form of jokes precisely because teachers were trying to be affable and because the view of the white majority was that such ribbing was 'fair play'. In addition, it would seem that the subtleties of negative stereotypes and non-existent black faces in text books were not readily identified by white pupils. As a result, black pupils were a minority who did not wish to make a stand alone.

Black pupils reactions to teachers' attitudes

It has been indicated above that racist jokes were not challenged in the classroom and in general black informants (who constituted the entire complement of West Indian-origin pupils in the 5th form) had little to say on this front. However, sensitivity towards race was conveyed via two separate episodes concerning individual teachers.

In one observed incident, the history teacher, Mr Lukes, fell foul of Sonia, a West Indian pupil. Admiring her newly corn-rowed hairstyle he engaged her in casual conversation about it:

> Mr Lukes: 'How long can you keep it in before having to wash it?'
>
> Sonia (indignantly): 'I can wash it while they're still in: I'm not that dirty!'

Sonia clearly thought he was being rude and personal and she separately described him to me as being 'racist'. She based her analysis both on his comment about her hair and on his behaviour in the history lesson on Apartheid (see p. 84-5). In that lesson, Mr Lukes had become exasperated with the disinterest of the class and castigated them saying:

> 'If you can't get interested in that then I'm afraid most of you are going to be bored for the rest of your lives!'

Whilst this had been aimed at the class as a whole, Sonia took a special dislike to it, treating it as a personal criticism. In this case, the topics in hand, namely her corn-rowed hair and South Africa included sufficient ethnic/racial content for her to be on the defensive, indicating the presence of sensitive 'triggers' that could be inadvertently 'set off' by the teacher.

Sonia's response to her teacher can be seen as particularly problematic because in both events in which he gained her disdain, he was trying to be open and non-racist. Subsequent knowledge of this teacher made it clear that his teaching philosophy and political ideology was such that racism was anathema to him. Nevertheless, he inadvertently earned for himself a reputation in Sonia's eyes of being a 'racist'.

A second example of a black pupil's complaint against a teacher came from Delia. She explained things this way:

> Delia (black less-achiever): 'Sometimes, when you'd go to the class there'd be five of us, three black and two half-caste, and one teacher; he only took it out on us, everytime .... It would be nice to see a few black teachers.'

Clearly for Delia, her colour represented a 'separateness' which the white teacher utilised in a way she thought a black teacher would not have done, but there was an alternative explanation which another white pupil articulated well:

> White, male pupil: 'Black people think they're getting into trouble because they're black but it's not. Take Bedford for example, he messes about in class and then gets into trouble for it, not his colour.'

Indeed, classroom observations appeared to bear out this point. Teachers who did not tolerate a lot of messing about in class would sanction offenders whoever they were, but both Delia and Sonia were quick to place a racist connotation on any sanctions they received.

These teachers were, in the main, misunderstood in their motives. They misjudged the reception that their open, jovial or disciplinary remarks would receive and were perhaps naive in thinking that old wounds in the ethnic minority community were sufficiently healed for their banter and sanctions to be accepted as being neutral. Underlying expectations of prejudice still led black pupils to assume the worst.

Teachers' typifications

To be fair to teachers, no-one was observed to overtly discriminate between their pupils but some teachers' typifications led to them hold stereotypical views about West Indian-origin pupils, seeing them as disruptive and boisterous. (see also Brittan, 1976).

One teacher who was involved in equal opportunities work confided in this researcher that Sonia was 'interesting' because she was talkative and exuberant in class. A warning was also provided about her alarming temper.

Wright (1986) also refers to the fact that West Indian girls in her study were seen as 'unpredictable'. Sonia was, indeed, as described in a number of lessons but so were many other white pupils in whom this tendency passed without remark. It was evident that black pupils still stood out in the minds of some teachers and that their behaviour was easier to remember.

Teachers' opinions of black pupils also contained implicit meanings gleaned from information about the home background. One teacher described three of her West Indian-origin pupils as follows:

(about Diane): 'Came middle of the 4th year. A loud, noisy, uncontrolled extrovert. Lives with her mum, a smashing lady. Her mother is supportive [of the school] but can't really do anything.'

(about Vanda): 'Excellent attendance, fair group of friends, cheerful and outgoing. She's doing CSEs, average ability. Lives with her mum, only came to the school once but no problems. Not sure about her hobbies but I think she does lots of babysitting.'

(about Sheilah): 'Lives with her mum, part of West Indian culture. A well-rounded, mature, intelligent girl, gifted in O-level subjects and sport. She's got a pleasant personality, possibly not aiming high enough, she wants to be a travel agent ... her friends are mostly academic but there are some younger black ones who hang around.'

This teacher's perception of these three black girls focussed not only on their academic ability, but also on the nature of their home life, part of which (living with a single parent mother) was seen as 'part of West Indian culture'. In addition, references were made to the control of the parent and involvement with the school, as well as to the type of company the girls kept and their outside interests. Distinction was made between Vanda and Diane, both of whom were classified as of average ability, but viewed either positively or negatively according to other aspects of their home life and personality (see Wright, 1986).

Whilst this well-meaning teacher may have considered these descriptions of her pupils to be objective, there is a wealth of research evidence to suggest that negative and positive stereotypes can be transmitted to pupils via the teacher's attitude thus promoting or inhibiting their academic performance, causing the pupil to become like their label (e.g. Rosenthal and Jacobsen, 1968). This particular teacher could be classified as one of the Head's 'young lefties' but this did not stop her from forming either positive or negative images of black pupils based on factors other than purely educational ones. Her 'progressive' attitudes did not help her to avoid stereotypes in assessing black pupils.

Similarly, one lesson observed passed with the usual range of banter, minor complaints and periods of peaceful work until a West Indian-origin boy was asked to collect up the books and put them in the cupboard. He began to gather them in, in a hit-and-miss fashion. 'All of the books, please' the teacher reminded him. 'Fuck off!' he was then heard to say, but it was not clear to whom or why it was said. The teacher, however, took it to be aimed at her and placed him on a disciplinary referral to another tutor. The final outcome was a later apology from the boy but other white boys had sworn during the lesson and their verbal abuses had attracted no sanctions.

Again, the absence of guidelines in the area of multiculturalism, anti-racism and equal opportunities served to weaken any control the school might have exercised to counter such prejudices forming a regular part of school life.

Teachers' inertia

So far, the attention had been focussed on what teachers did at Leafield that could be construed as racist or prejudiced, but of equal importance is what teachers did not do, in terms of their omissions, that contributed towards the perpetuation of racist values and attitudes in the classroom.

Leaving aside the fact that many teachers did not deliberately try to tackle racism via lesson content and materials, classroom observations led to the detection of one particular issue that seemed of paramount importance, namely that of ignoring racist incidents in the classroom.

In one history lesson a particular white boy sat alone at the back of the class saying intermittently in a loud voice:

'I'm bored ..... It's so boring!'

He was asked by the researcher what he would rather do. Within earshot of a Bangladeshi classmate the reply was:

'Gun down thousands of innocent Pakis.'

Asked why, the provocative reply was:

'Well, it would get rid of them wouldn't it?'

The teacher could not have avoided hearing this. Later, this teacher confided that the boy in question had been fined in the juvenile court that same week and had a 'bad home background'. This knowledge allowed her to consider him unreachable and beyond redemption and so to discount and not sanction his actions. Whilst his internally held attitudes may well have been impossible to shift by school influences alone, observations suggested that they would at least remain hidden and not be expressed in the presence of a teacher who would not tolerate such behaviour. However, this particular teacher lacked classroom control. She was despised and considered 'hopeless' by her work-orientated pupils whilst being totally 'sent-up', taunted or ignored by the rest of the class. Lessons observed with her ended in chaos and one side effect of her lack of control was that pupils such as the one described could get away with unacceptable behaviour.

In a biology lesson a similar incident occurred. The male teacher was discussing the difficulty of genetic experimentation on humans because of their 'dislike for having hundreds of children'. A white boy from the back of the class distinctly interjected:

'but the Russians do.'

Another white boy supplemented this with:

'and Pakis.'

Plenty of pupils heard these remarks and some sniggered but the teacher showed no sign of having heard it. The point having been registered to the satisfaction of the pupils concerned, the lesson continued in the normal way.

In the second incident cited here, it was unclear whether the teacher heard the comment or not, but in other lessons he had been seen to counteract complaints of sexism via anticipatory placation (see p. 62). However, from informal discussions with various teachers it appeared that the absence of challenges to such classroom barracking was due mainly to one of three factors. Either:

(a) teachers valued the peaceful cohesion of the lesson as a whole too much to interrupt the flow by following up provocative pupil remarks, or

(b) they wished to avoid confrontation on racist (or sexist) incidents because they did not feel equipped to handle them, or

(c) they simply did not see the issue as being sufficiently important to warrant attention.

Irrespective of individual teachers' rationales for non-action, all of which were identified by Figueroa and Swart (1986) in their study of racist comment among pupils and teachers, it was clear from observations that this type of incident only occurred in lessons where the teacher was perceived as 'soft'. Most teachers in this category were women, but not exclusively so. This type of racist banter was not witnessed in the lessons of 'no-nonsense' teachers who could maintain discipline. Teachers could, therefore, be instrumental in eradicating overt signs of racism in their classrooms if they were prepared, or felt able, to 'grasp the nettle'. Once again, the absence of school directives on how to handle racist incidents no doubt played a part in teachers' failure to address racist incidents.

Black pupils' perspectives

The issue of white middle class researchers studying aspects of black people's lives is a sensitive one. It could be argued that coming from this group, this researcher could never be accepted sufficiently for black pupils to truly divulge their experiences of racism. However, as discussed in Chapter 1, through a process of giving of self and demonstrating solidarity it was possible for black pupils to accept the researcher as a friend and confidante and to be genuinely open in their discussions. Only one quiet boy, Bedford, indicated that there were things he could say which he preferred not to discuss. In this instance his silence spoke volumes about the emotional pain that experiencing racism inflicts.

It should also be borne in mind that this research was conducted in a part of Britain not noted for high levels of unemployment, high proportions of ethnic minorities or racial tensions. Indeed, OPCS Census Data for 1981 indicated some 1.2 per cent West Indian-born residents in the area leading to an estimated 3 per cent West Indian-origin residents including those born in the U.K. With such low percentages and only 4 per cent of school leavers registered as unemployed at the local Careers Office the future for young, black people did not look bleak. Such factors should also be taken into account in understanding why a white researcher was not perceived as an outsider or intruder, and why black pupils felt able to share their thoughts and experiences.

Having an on-going rapport with all black pupils in the 5th year did not, however, mean that most evidence of racism at Leafield came from them. Indeed, things were quite to the contrary. At the outset it had been anticipated that black pupils would be a major source of evidence for racist behaviour received from their white peers, but in the event, few could relate specific school incidents they found racist, disturbing or insulting.

Black pupils did classify some of their teachers as 'racist' (see p. 88-9) and they firmly believed that there was discrimination in the world of work (this issue is addressed later in Chapter 7) but they were less sure that they experienced discrimination at the hands of their peers. Instead, pupil racism was broadly denied but with some provisos that are worthy of discussion. A sample of statements from black pupils is as follows:

> Vanda (said about school after leaving): 'I never saw any racial signs or insults.'
>
> Delia (on the subject of name-calling) 'Not at all, not at school, but I don't listen to things like that. To me everyone's the same.'
>
> Sheilah: 'Infant and Middle School were worse for racial jokes, but it's much less in Senior School. Just comments about Pakis in shops and "Go back to your own country".'

There was an implicit acknowledgement in Delia's and Sheilah's remarks that some degree of both name-calling and racist humour was occurring at Leafield, but that they preferred to ignore it. Delia's approach was to pay no attention to things she heard whilst Sheilah's was to 'play it down' in comparison with worse things she had heard in earlier schools. From observations this 'low-key' response was typical of black pupils' reactions to any incident that had racial overtones to it. They did not openly challenge teachers they saw as racist, and did not respond in a volatile way to pupils' jibes and taunts. A typical example of how black pupils dealt with little incidents was the way in which three West Indian-origin girls reacted to an immense golliwog on the front of a hand-knitted jumper worn by a white 3rd year pupil. Finding themselves opposite this girl and this jumper at a lunch table they did not openly refer to it in any way but simply pointed and leant over the table for a closer look and giggled about it in a mocking way. The girl concerned seemed to have no conception of what they found so entertaining but seemed instead simply embarrassed by their 'inexplicable' behaviour - another example of a gulf in understanding.

Name-calling and taunts

The issue of name-calling has received attention from such researchers as Figueroa and Swart (1986), Cohn (1987 and 1988) and Kelly (1988). Cohn (1987), using data from Outer London schools, found that over 50 per cent of name-calling reported by senior school pupils involved the use of racist names. She also found that the recipients of this name-calling found it very hurtful, although many found this difficult to admit. At Leafield, black pupils frequently experienced jibes in the playgrounds and open spaces during breaktimes. These jibes were frequently one word slights such as 'choc drop!', 'Paki!', or impromptu attempts at foreign accents and animal grunts as the targetted person walked past. The usual response was to ignore such incidents although occasionally the perpetrator would receive 'an earful'. Pupils certainly did not bother to report such incidents to teachers. Indeed, black pupils did not see all teachers as entirely blameless, and they saw little sense in bothering to tell someone in authority after the event. As one black pupil said:

> Delia: 'What could they do about it anyway? Some of them are just as bad'.

Kelly (1988) found similar mistrust of teachers in her study, and a similar reticence in reporting incidents of name-calling.

However, another avenue for taunting black pupils was through having a laugh at their expense during a lesson, and here it proved problematic to differentiate between the general amusement caused by sending someone up (and the disruption of the lesson that usually ensued) and the added satisfaction that might be gained by aiming the humour at a black pupil. For example, in one of Sonia's History lessons a white boy in front of her was making a good job of forcing her to laugh. He was amazingly inventive in how he could attach a piece of sticking plaster to his face, turning round to demonstrate a variety of permutations to her. It is problematic to assess such interaction as racist for the actor's motives were not clear. Did he want to get Sonia into trouble for laughing or were his antics a spontaneous extention of his chosen role of 'mucker'? (Beynon and Atkinson, 1984). In this instance the latter was suggested for he was being equally silly and irritating towards other white pupils by virtue of such devices as making noises and flicking balls of paper.

However, in another of Sonia's History lessons the same boy was seen to act in a rather different way. As part of many other tricks and ploys to waste time he took a whole piece of plain paper from his notebook, folded it in half and held it in his mouth, opening and closing the flaps like a massive pair of lips. 'Hey, Sonia!' he called to her, making the big paper lips move together and apart again. She gave him a withering look and he collapsed in laughter. The incident was genuinely not noticed by the teacher who was writing on the board at the time.

The dividing lines between humour, cruel humour and racist humour are hard to define but attempts have been made to differentiate between them in the area of name-calling by such authors as Goffman (1963), Cameron (1985) and Cohn (1988). In addition, Kelly (1988) writes:

> .... who would have thought that 'specky-four-eyes' as a name .... could have any connections with racial fights? The answer is that it should not and need not .... but, as we have seen, it is part of the same vocabulary .... as 'Paki' and 'Nigger' which are not only personally insulting, but which can also be used to excite racial tensions (Kelly, 1988, p. 27).

In the two examples of 'mucking' cited above a similar connection can be made, for at some point along the line, racist intent in the activity should be considered. As Kelly goes on to say:

> Until and unless pupils and teachers draw some lines of demarcation between the two kinds of name-calling, the vocabulary of racial names will continue to be prominent in schools and will feed into dynamics of relations between the racial groups (Kelly, 1988, p. 27).

Similarly, it could be argued that both pupils and teachers need to decide just what will and will not be tolerated in pranks played upon black pupils, but as demonstrated in this chapter, both black pupils and teachers appeared loathe to make a stand. The difficulty in pinning down the exact intention behind an incident is a major factor in this respect, but here, once again, the absence of a strong written policy advocating vigilance against such episodes was in part responsible for teachers non-action and white pupils' persistence in indulging in such behaviour.

White attitudes

If black pupils saw little in the way of racial incidents at school, and played down taunts and jokes, then it might seem fair to assume that little or no serious racial discord existed at Leafield. Indeed, blatant examples of racism as cited earlier were indeed the exception, and there were no incidents of fighting breaking out between ethnic groups, and no directly provoked attacks of any description during the period of this research. In addition, staff confirmed there had been no serious racial incidents recorded for disciplinary action for at least the last year. However, listening to the views of white pupils indicated that such an impression of racial tolerance at Leafield would be a false one.

By far the most powerful evidence of racism came directly from white pupils themselves, it being deeply ingrained in their attitudes. The assumptions and beliefs about both immigrants and black British-born individuals shared by many white informants informed their name-calling and teasing in the classroom. The racism expressed in discussions with them came from pupils totally unashamed of their attitudes and therefore in no way inhibited in expressing their opinions. Both achievers and less-achievers were capable of holding racist beliefs and their racism similarly crossed the class divide. Below, Paul is quoted at length. He was a farmer's son and member of the Young Farmer's Association who sat and obtained eight O-level passes and then entered the 6th form:

> Paul (white pupil): 'I'm very racist, it runs in the family. I realise they've got a right to be here but I'm not inclined to have them as my friends. I would rather not mix with black people. Au pairs from Switzerland are OK but they're girls and white anyway .... A bloke from Pakistan gets given a house for nothing and a bloke here has to work for it. Get too many benefits for a start .... If they are no different why do they get the benefits and we don't? .... I can't call them British if they're born here, still got the accent and the colour .... You don't swear at one because you know what's going to happen, there'll be five of them on you, gang warfare!'

Paul's comments indicated a dislike of racial mixing, a belief in black 'gangs' and a particular resentment towards Pakistani immigrants. He was not alone in holding such views which were repeated time and again by white pupils:

> Peter (white less-achiever): 'Blacks always stick together in a fight because they think everyone picks on them because they're black. That Eddie, he's like that, the older they get the worse they get.'

The most powerful message of all, however, was their overriding hatred of the Asian (so-called 'Paki') community:

> Duncan (white less-achiever): 'I don't like Pakis meself. Too many spreading up the Woodlands Road to Hillrise .... I've got some sympathy with the National Front over numbers, colour does set people off.'

An interesting feature of Duncan's racism was the fact that he did have black (West Indian-origin) friends. For him and many others, Pakistani immigrants represented a threat, an invasion, but West Indians were more taken for granted as a feature of British life. Duncan, in common with other informants, operated a double standard in his racism with personal black acquaintances lying outside the scope of his definition of 'the colour problem'. For him, it was the 'Pakis' who were the problem, not non-whites in general, and not his own friends.

Although more boys than girls expressed overtly racist sentiments it was not their sole domain and girls were similarly more hostile towards people of Asian origin:

> Sarah (white achiever): 'There's no Pakistanis in school so there's no real problem. Coloureds [West Indians] mix in but Pakistanis don't, they're more separate in their dress and ways. I think there would be more going on at [two other schools mentioned] where they do go. I think people should act the same as us if they come over here and coloureds do dress the same and so on.'

Sarah's concern was that Asians did not assimilate and absorb British language and culture as readily as West Indian people did. For her, perceived cultural distance correlated with the level of her hostility and negative attitudes.

The extent of anti-Pakistani feeling in the school was such that the few white pupils who condemned racism felt particularly sorry for the school's small Asian population:

> Tessa (white less-achiever): 'Pupils used to say 'choc-drop' and I hated that because they're just the same really, just a different colour. Especially Pakistanis, everybody at the school hates them, I always felt sorry for them.'

Occasionally, a desire was shown to demonstrate greater solidarity with those suffering the effects of racism:

> Derek (white pupil): 'I saw a kid once, a bully, in a gang of kids, come up to this coloured [Asian] guy and call him names galore. If I 'ad the strength of all those guys I'd 'av ... well, you know.'

In discussing 'Pakistanis' at Leafield it was clear that all pupils (including those of West Indian-origin) lumped all Asian-origin people together as 'Pakis'. Pakistani was used as the blanket term irrespective of actual origins. The word 'Paki' was used as a derogatory term in its own right and West Indian-origin pupils also referred to Asians in this way, seeing them as a distinctly different group and usually with similar negative connotations. Thus, just as some white pupils felt that West Indian-origin people had more of a right to be here than Asians, so did some West Indians. In terms of a hierarchy, both groups saw Asians as being at the 'bottom of the pile'. As a result the ten Asian pupils at the school had to survive an enormous amount of prejudice and they too, mostly 'kept their heads down'. This Asian experience was in stark contrast to that of a Vietnamese boy in the 5th year. This boy seemed fully integrated within mainstream school culture. He was popular and frequently seen happily in the company of predominantly white friends. Observation either seen or heard, revealed nothing negative towards him. He was liked by his teachers and praised by them for his above-average academic achievement.

Apart from exploring directly racist attitudes among informants the opportunity was also taken to investigate how these pupils felt about racially mixed friendships and to what extent these actually developed at Leafield. On the theme of racial mixing, all pupils with racist tendencies vouched for the fact that mixed friendships were uncommon:

> Peter: 'Black and white boys don't mix after school. I'm not a racialist, but I don't know why, I don't like to see a black boy with a white girl.'

That aspects of sexual as well as racial dominance were involved here was apparent from the ensuing discussion when he was asked to consider how he would feel if the genders were round the other way:

> Peter: 'Oh no, I wouldn't worry if I saw a white boy with a black girl, but I always say 'Look at her mother though .... in forty years time ....' (shaking his head at the prospect).

If friendships could not be promoted between black boys and white boys of Peter's persuasion, it was possible to gain their distant admiration, based on a respect for 'hardness':

> Peter: 'The only black boy I liked who was hard but kept it quiet was Bedford.'

In this connection the 'hardness' Peter respected was not the 'hardness' defined by Furlong (1984) which related to West Indian boys' 'style', but to an anglocentric notion of 'hardness' which stood for masculinity and strength.

Bedford was indeed quiet as Peter suggested, he was also gentle in his manner, but he was tall, broad and strong. As such, his build with its attendant promise of being able to flatten anyone who stood in his way or abused him, was instrumental in Peter treating him with respect.

The view expressed above, that mixed race friendships were not common, was not in fact borne out by reality. White boys with racist inclinations preferred to believe this, but black boys were mostly to be seen in the company of white male friends and black girls. Hanging around with these girls at break-times did not mean that black girls exclusively spent their free time with the black boys, for they also had many white female friends. White girls, far more than white boys reported having black friends, and for these pupils racism was something that other people felt or practised, not themselves:

> Lynn (white achiever): 'I haven't seen any racism at school, I've got friends according to their personality. My mum and dad are, very, [racist] but I'm not at all. Some blacks have a chip on their shoulder though.'

Ironically, white pupils with black friends could express something of a 'double standard' in their thinking, akin to Duncan's racism (see p. 98), which succeeded in conveying a prejudice held whilst excluding their own friends from the judgements they were making. There were other incidents where white pupils provided evidence of their thinking along racial lines despite accepting black friends as individuals. Lynn's statement above is one example but taking another, entering Wendy's home one day with Sonia (a West Indian-origin pupil) and two other white friends, Wendy's pet dog allowed us all to enter the room peacefully but snapped at Sonia:

> 'See, I told you!' Wendy confirmed to me gleefully. 'I told you our dog doesn't like black people.'

Despite this categorisation along designated lines of colour, Wendy was friendly with other black girls and emphasised the humorous banter which existed between her and them, which in her view demonstrated their complete acceptance of each other and lack of racial prejudice:

> Wendy (white pupil): 'There's a lot of black prejudice and a lot of white prejudice. I'm not prejudiced. In fun Diane will say, "Shut up you white bitch!" and I will say, "Shut up you black cow!" and we'll have a laugh about it. But it can get serious with some people.'

This open usage of 'colour' (as most Leafield pupils would call it) in two-way humour was seen by her as proof of liberation from racial prejudice. Many white pupils expressed sentiments to the effect that they 'treated all their mates the same' and teachers were widely acknowledged by white pupils to do the same. What white pupils perceived as equal treatment to all, however, was not always seen in the same light by black pupils, as already indicated (see p. 87).

Overall, it was noticeable that more boys than girls displayed racism towards black people and more girls than boys spoke supportively about them and reported having black friends. Verma and Bagley (1975) also found English girls to be less prejudiced than English boys. This can be viewed as an important indicator of socialisation processes whereby boys concern themselves more with fears regarding competition from blacks (e.g. for jobs) whilst girls relate their observations of black people more to the nurturing and caring role expected of them by society. Allport (1954) and Abrahams (1972) offer a more psychological explanation for boys' racism in that it helps them to deal with their anxieties and stress in striving for 'success' as part of the masculine role. By extension, girls' tendency to feel sorry for black people, and their greater readiness to take the part of the other and sympathise with their lot, can be seen as being part of the deeply ingrained caring roles internalised by girls, so acutely displayed by Leafield girls in their ideal job choices. Such choices are the subject of chapter 6, but the point can perhaps best be illustrated by one final comment from Wendy in talking about her mother:

> Wendy: 'I'm not prejudiced and neither is my mum. She's thought of adopting one, a black baby. I think that would be nice don't you?'

No problem here?

Leafield saw itself as a community school, but did this mean that all members of that community were receiving equal treatment and respect at the school? The main points in this chapter would seem to indicate that they were not and that whereas girls received a qualitatively different experience of school than boys, so black pupils received a qualitatively different experience than white pupils.

To begin with, neither the LEA nor the school had a written anti-racist or multicultural policy. As such, there was nothing upon which to build guidelines for good classroom practice. This left teachers free to interpret their role with black pupils according to their own personal beliefs and philosophies. As has been indicated in this chapter, this provided scope for some teachers to indulge in racist humour and for others to be misinterpreted in their naive (and sometimes genuine) attempts to involve black pupils. White pupils were also free to poke fun at black pupils.

Black pupils were largely tolerant of this situation, they were neither volatile nor vociferous, but there were indications that their passive acceptance was due partly to a desire to underplay issues which they found hurtful and partly to a lack of faith in teachers' willingness or ability to do anything about their experiences. Some teachers of the 'young lefties' type also doubted their ability to combat racism whilst others more aligned with the 'old righties', saw no need to address the issue at all, again symptoms of a laissez-faire situation and failure to make a policy stand.

Finally, but perhaps most importantly, white pupils were relatively free to make racist comments at Leafield - free from both teachers sanctions and a black backlash. The racist attitudes of many white informants were quite keenly felt and there was evidence of many more negative attitudes and racial tensions lying under the surface than were actually expressed publicly. The failure of this racism to surface in direct action can perhaps be explained by the fact that most hatred was expressed towards Asians, and the majority of non-whites in the 5th form were West Indian in origin.

Overall, the main thrust of education provided at Leafield did nothing to combat the deeply ingrained racist attitudes of some white pupils who remained unchallenged and carried their stereotypical views of black people out into the workplace. The inevitability of this process might have been checked by a positive set of anti-racist policies at the level of the school, although it is accepted that policies are not necessarily put into practice and that the commitment of staff to make concerted efforts in effecting policy is also required. At Leafield, neither was the order of the day.

5 Classes within classes

Introduction

Gender, race and class are commonly taken to be three major variables in the process of social differentiation in schools (Burgess 1986, Blackledge and Hunt 1985). So far, this study has focussed on both gender and race and how these two factors affected the school experiences of Leafield pupils. Findings illustrate how gender had a subtle effect on the formal and hidden curriculum and that it also had a profound effect on the relationships between male and female pupils themselves. Gender also played a powerful part in career choices which are still to be discussed (see Chapter 6).

Similarly, race also affected pupils' interactions with both staff and peers. Race provided opportunities for misrepresentations and misinterpretations between staff and pupils and there was a distinctly racist element in the attitudes some white pupils held about black people which affected the extent of their interactions with black pupils. It has been argued that both gender and racial biases were able to take hold more readily because of the school's lack of a written and conserted policy designed to tackle discrimination.

Turning now to class, the data from Leafield School suggest that the impact of this factor was also two-fold. That is to say, that both pupils' perceptions and actions plus school responses were involved in creating a situation where class 'mattered' and made a material difference to how schooling was perceived and received.

A definition of class

The term 'class' is itself problematic. Firstly, precisely what is meant by class? Secondly, how is it to be measured, if at all, especially in terms of delineating between groups? Both Marx and Engels (1965) and Weber (1968) utilise economic criteria in evaluating class position, and likewise, Giddens (1973) identifies three major classes present in modern Britain:

- the upper class (based on the power of ownership of wealth, property or the means of production);

- the middle class (based on the possession of educational or technical qualifications which create differential bargaining power); and

- the working class (based on the possession of manual labour power).

In measuring occupational status for the purpose of sociological enquiry, such researchers as Glass (1954) have utilised a hierarchical scale by which to grade occupations according to the degree of control they afford over people or resources plus the academic qualifications and/or technical skills required. In particular, a divide has been created between 'white collar' clerical work and 'blue collar' manual work as in Goldthorpe's scale whereby the former is regarded as middle class and the latter as working class (Goldthorpe and Hope 1974, Goldthorpe 1983). Such scales rely solely on male occupations in households and have been criticised by Garnsey (1978) who argues for women's (and especially wives') occupations to be taken into account. In addition, Crompton (1976, 1979) has added another dimension to the debate on the validity of such measures via her arguments concerning the de-skilling of many 'white collar' clerical jobs to the point where they become routine, manually-operated exercises creating a white collar proletariat.

Precise definitions and boundaries in discussing class, are therefore problematic. As Bordieu (1987) states:

> In the reality of the social world, there are no clear-cut boundaries, no more absolute breaks, than there are in the physical world. The boundaries between theoretical classes which scientific investigation allows us to construct on the basis of a plurality of criteria are similar, to use Rapoport's metaphor, to the boundaries of a cloud or a forest (Bordieu, 1987, p. 1).

However, class is experienced, irrespective of precise definitions, just as race and gender are experienced, irrespective of uncertainty about where the boundaries lie in terms of ethnicity or gender orientations. For this reason it is important to consider class as a possible determining factor in the lives of pupils at school.

Class factors in education

The way in which class operates in differentiating between pupils has been researched from a variety of standpoints. The large-scale, quantitative survey by Glass (1954) and the subsequent Oxford Mobility Study by Halsey, Heath and Ridge (1980) serve to provide statistically significant evidence that social class (and the type of schooling that money can buy) does make a difference in terms of educational and occupational outcome, whilst also demonstrating a large amount of inter-generational class reproduction. By means of classifying fathers' and sons' occupations hierarchically along professional, white collar, skilled manual and unskilled manual lines, the latter study was able to demonstrate great fixity at both the top and bottom of the occupational structure and that there was little movement (after controlling for economic expansion) across the so-called white collar/blue collar barrier which is commonly taken to be the divide between the middle and working class (see for example, Goldthorpe, 1980). Such studies have provided a useful 'macro' view of the importance of family origins and schooling on eventual occupational attainment but do not provide explanations as to how class operates in affecting school entry, school performance and informing the attitudes of both pupils and their parents.

Some theoretical writings and qualitative research have attempted to explain how exactly class makes a difference in education. For example, it has been suggested that schools transmit the dominant values of society (Parsons 1959, Karabel and Halsey 1977) and that these values are those of the dominant, ruling group whose needs, in terms of education for a viable work force, will be those that are catered for in the education system (Westergaard and Resler, 1975). The concept of 'cultural capital' has been put forward by Bordieu (1973) whereby the children of the dominant, middle class arrive at school already attuned to the ideals prescribed by an essentially middle class education system. They, therefore, 'fit-in' easily with the norms and values operated in schools and are at an advantage vis-á-vis their working class peers who have not had the benefit of this background. Bernstein (1970) has viewed the effect of class from the standpoint of language, arguing that both the middle classes and schools utilise an 'elaborated' code whereas the working classes use a more 'restricted' code in communication. As a result, the working class child is at a disadvantage in the classroom in not fully understanding and being able to interact within the format of the 'elaborated' code.

Attention has also been focussed on the attitudes of teachers towards pupils of different class origins (Sharp and Green 1975, Reid 1980); on the curriculum (Keddie, 1971) and upon pupils themselves. The latter category includes the work of Hargreaves (1967), Lacey (1970) and Ball (1981), who examined the effects of streaming and banding and how working class pupils could become discouraged by the process of being placed in low streams and so develop anti-school sub-cultures. Finally, the research of Willis (1977) and Corrigan (1979) has been important in portraying the perceptions of working class pupils and the reality of their lives in order to illustrate how these factors fundamentally shape their attitudes towards school.

Class factors at Leafield School

In this study, one major point of interest was what it actually meant to the pupils to be working class, and how they saw themselves (now and in the future) and how they 'handled' school as a result. The questionnaire with the whole 5th year included questions about what they had liked and disliked about school as well as what they wanted for themselves after leaving (see Appendix 1). This was designed to discover any unfulfilled needs among the pupils and also to see what, if anything, they had particularly enjoyed or found material to their needs at school. In addition to this, aspects of class and class consciousness were also explored with the twenty in-depth informants, and it is their statements that are turned to first by way of setting the scene.

Pupils' perceptions of their class position

Of the 20 in-depth informants (10 white and 10 West Indian-origin), 18 came from working class family backgrounds. Just two pupils had both parents in professional/white collar employment, whilst the remainder had mothers who were mainly in nursing, catering, cleaning, factory work, clerical work or housewives, and fathers who were bricklayers, decorators, electricians, porters, drivers and factory workers.

Table 5.1 lists parental occupations for all 20 informants and a cross-check against school records revealed that these 20 formed a representative cross-section of parental occupations for the entire 5th year. The school record cards, although not completely up to date, indicated some 90 per cent of fathers in either skilled or unskilled manual employment (or unemployment) with a slightly lower figure of 80 per cent for mothers (which included many listed simply as 'housewife'). Mothers' occupations revealed a higher incidence of clerical and secretarial work typical of women's work (Deem,1978, Oakley,1981).

Table 5.1
Fathers' and mothers' occupations for in-depth informants

FATHERS	No.	MOTHERS	No.
Teacher	1	Stores manageress	1
Agricultural engineer	1	Receptionist	2
Bricklayer	2	Laboratory assistant	1
Electrician	1	Cashier	1
Painter and decorator	2	Clerk	1
Printer (redundant)	1	Nursing [b]	3
Welder	1	Nursing assistant	2
Factory worker	1	Catering assistant	1
Mechanic	1	Factory worker	1
Driver	2	Housewife	3
Hospital porter	1	Not known (lives separately)	1
Manual workers (details N/K, father living separately)	6	Deceased	1
		Unemployed (1 ex-catering assistant) (1 ex-cleaner)	2
TOTAL	20	TOTAL	20

[a] moved to self-employment, making garage doors
[b] level of qualification not known

Source: In-depth informants and school record cards, Leafield School (1984)

Whilst it can be debated whether a pupil with a qualified electrician for a father and a receptionist for a mother is or is not of working class origin (see Acker 1980, Heath and Britten 1984), it should be borne in mind that these 'ordinary kids' from 'ordinary families' had their own definitions of where they stood in the economic and social hierarchy. Their definitions were not based on the occupational status of their parents in the manner of say, Goldthorpe's scale (Goldthorpe, 1983) neither did they utilise any Marxian notion of selling their labour to the owners of production. Instead, pupils relied on a firm conception of themselves as 'working class' based upon commonsense truths about the reality of their lives:

> Vanda (black less-achiever): 'I reckon I'm working class and have a poor chance of moving upwards'.

Similarly, other pupils who also saw themselves as working class had this to say:

> Philip (white less-achiever): 'Well, there's the working class and those on top of them get it easy .... It's probably fair if you've worked for it, but some get it handed on, or win it. Good luck to them! But the dole should be more.'

> Duncan (white less-achiever): 'I don't like snobs, stuck up people, especially them in the posh houses of Foxlease - too near Hillrise [his council estate] which is a dump and completely working class.'

Despite leaving school at Easter with no formal qualifications, Duncan was well-able to articulate his notion of class differences and his sense of injustice that such differences existed. He went on to say:

> Duncan: 'I don't think it's fair to be so unequal but it will keep happening. I think it's stupid to do the Pools and for one person to get rich. I don't think a bricklayer should get less than a clerk. A bricklayer uses his brain too, and with no office computer to help!'

Duncan's father was a bricklayer and he was experiencing the irregularities of contract work whereby there were often weeks of unemployment between jobs. Duncan was speaking in support of him having seen the limitations this placed on the financial rewards his father obtained for his labour.

Pupils frequently blamed 'the Government' for the inequalities which they saw around them, especially unemployment:

> Duncan: 'It's bad at the moment, I haven't got anything behind me or to look forward to. She's [Mrs Thatcher] not doing a good job really.'
>
> Eric (black less-achiever): 'The country's diabolical, terrible at present. She hasn't done a lot for the working class .... unemployment always strikes me as possible ....'
>
> Delia (black less-achiever): 'I'm not really interested in politics but I will vote Labour because they don't take one person's side. They take everyone's side, they help people. Not like the Conservatives, they want what's right for them.'

Delia's views indicated a definite concept of 'them' and 'us'. 'Them' were the affluent sector of society who were well off and tried to organise society to their own advantage. 'Us' were large groups of people in society who needed help to get jobs and avoid poverty. This divide was articulated in a different way by another pupil:

> Bedford (black less-achiever): 'This country's run for the rich, not really for the poor. I can remember when Labour was in, my mum was better off. One thing sticks in her mind. It was £25 for food then but it won't last a week now. Never heard of unemployment then but do now. A Labour government could do little, gone beyond it now.'

Views such as these were complemented by those of other pupils who could see how the Conservative government benefitted some people in society but not all:

> Peter (white less-achiever): 'Margaret Thatcher is the pits but Tories are OK for you on the money side.'

Peter indicated that those who had accumulated some wealth could gain from Conservative policies but he did not place his own family in this fortunate category. Indeed, he saw his mother, who was separated, as struggling financially and was keen to obtain a skilled apprenticeship in order to secure a permanent, well-paid job so he could help her:

> Peter: 'Mum's recently got a full-time cashier's job and she's part-time in

The Yew Tree some nights of the week. Her car's pretty old now and the rent's £22 per week. It's criminal!'

The most striking feature of pupils' definitions of where they stood in social or class terms was their overall acceptance that nothing could be done to change their lives for the better. Bedford has already been quoted as saying that he feared a Labour government would not be able to curtail rising unemployment and other pupils agreed with him:

Eddie (black less-achiever): 'I used to like Labour but not now. Ain't worth voting if you ask me. Neither of them can do anything about unemployment.'

This fatalist acceptance was present in the thinking of most working class informants. Where a preference was stated, pupils saw the Labour Party as trying to do most to help people like themselves and their parents, but half did not intend to use their vote upon coming of age. Some felt it was pointless to vote, others were simply not interested in politics and knew little of what the various political parties stood for.

Of the eighteen informants from working class homes, seven intended to vote when they became eligible and five did not. Six others were unsure. No one intended to vote Conservative. Their concerns were mostly about jobs although the most despondent ones, like Eddie, thought the employment situation was 'hopeless' and did not intend to vote:

Sheilah (black achiever): 'I won't vote when I'm 18. Possibly later. Britain's not very good at present. I remember the Young Socialists coming to the school, I sympathised. YTS is cheap labour. You should do a full-time job and should be paid.'

Sheilah was one of the two high achieving black informants from working class homes. She lived with her mother who was currently an unemployed catering assistant, and her comment above indicated that she had thought out her political convictions to some extent. Two others had also reflected on political solutions with widely differing results:

Peter: 'I tried the Young Socialists, they were a drag. Like Russia, too many rules. You couldn't get in or out. I wouldn't sell their newspaper but I did organise Discos. I got roped in too much. What they say sounds alright, but you can't put it into practice. They talk of revolution, but I said it was my time to get out.'

Peter then, also considered left-wing solutions to the class position he found himself in but decided they were untenable. In complete contrast, Duncan considered the opposite solution:

> Duncan: 'I've got this friend, he's a kind of Nazi, a racist. I don't think that's quite right .... but I've got sympathy with the National Front over numbers.'

Duncan had previously said that he had not got anything behind him (meaning qualifications) and that he had nothing to look forward to (see p. 109). He was worried about unemployment and felt that his father did not earn a fair wage as a bricklayer. He felt threatened by immigration. He had also 'been nicked for aiding and abetting', an experience concerning the taking of a motor bike which had left him with a low opinion of the Police. He claimed to have been beaten up by officers in a police car, and as such did not have a lot of confidence in them.

With no qualifications, a keen dislike of Asians (see p. 98) and a Police record, Duncan felt his chances of finding a job were poor. His only suggestion to ease this problem was a startling one:

> Duncan: 'I don't like the treatment of old people. The retired get too much from firms and the government. They should make way for young people .... possibly put them in a field and bomb them.'

He was completely serious in making this suggestion.

Duncan was not alone in perceiving unemployment as a threat. All but one of the fourteen less-achievers (i.e. those not taking any O-levels) from working class backgrounds acknowledged its existence and that it could happen to them. The majority, however, just accepted its existence and were not at all sure that anything could be done to alleviate the problem. They simply hoped that it would not happen to them and were prepared to be flexible in order to obtain work (see Chapters 6 and 7).

These comments from working class boys and girls, white and black, serve to illustrate their perceptions of their own position in society. They did not feel particularly important, nor that they were 'going places'. Indeed they saw themselves as largely needing 'help' to find a job and to create a life of their own. They saw other people as being in the 'posh' or 'comfortable' sector in society whilst acknowledging themselves to be working class.

They were not particularly angry or assertive in their demands for change and harboured few, if any, hopes about the unemployment situation.

Working class, less-achieving pupils

It has been indicated that eighteen working class Leafield in-depth informants had a clear idea of where they stood in society (i.e. firmly in the working class) and that they had a working definition of how that differentiated them from other, more favoured individuals in society. Fourteen of these were also less-achievers inasmuch as they were not sitting any O-levels, just CSEs, and this, in conjunction with their general acceptance of a reduced lot in life, led to a lack of any real hope for a fulfilling and rewarding future. This fuelled disinterest, inertia and lowered expectations, virtually guaranteeing that they would continue to fail at school and would ultimately find it difficult, if not impossible, to find interesting, well-paid work.

Simply being from a working class home led to a particular view of the world which informed the perceptions pupils held about education. Brown (1987) in his study of 'ordinary kids' argues in favour of a common working class understanding being present in pupils' attitudes to school:

> Despite important differences in the attitudes of ordinary boys and girls to school subjects and jobs, these differences are mediated and cross-cut in important ways by common class cultural understandings which lead both male and female ordinary kids to share the same orientation to school and the same understandings of what it is to be an ordinary working class pupil in school (Brown, 1987, p. 67).

At Leafield this common understanding operated to the effect that working class less-achievers displayed little, if any, enthusiasm for school. This was not borne out of a failure to succeed but rather it was something they felt about school in an overall sense. Similarly, Corrigan (1979) found that his working class boys had never seriously taken on board school values of academic achievement at any point in their school career.

At Leafield, life and futures were seen very much in terms of what pupils saw around them in their own families and among their friends. Pupils drew on the experiences of these people in assessing what might also happen to them. As Day (1987) states in relation to her 12 representative school leavers from Piertown:

They were confident from their peers and family they knew what the adult world of work was like (Day, 1987, p. 150).

The only way to succeed in life that Leafield pupils could see was 'to get a good job'. In their terms, 'good' meant well paid and secure, with interest value being a secondary feature, or bonus. A detailed discussion of job aspirations follows in the next chapter, but for the present the important thing is that as pupils consistently saw this as their main goal, they wanted their education to be relevant to that goal. It was this desire for relevance that led to the major criticism of school voiced earlier by working class pupils, namely that school was 'boring'.

The irrelevance of schooling

Much research has indicated how 'ordinary' working class pupils see school as irrelevant to their future lives. Brown (1987) found that pupils saw school as being a useful preparation for office work (and hence middle class destinations) but not matching up to working class needs. Similarly, both Davies (1979) and Day (1987) researching girls, and Raby (1979) and Corrigan (1979) researching boys, found disenchantment with the whole school process.

Queries about the relevance of lesson content cropped up frequently during periods of observation at Leafield:

'What's this got to do with us?'

muttered one boy involved in a history project on the local community as it was last century. He later described it as:

'totally boring' and 'a waste of time.'

The extent to which pupils could convey their absolute boredom during lessons has already been discussed in Chapter 2. Probing this boredom led to expressions of the perceived irrelevance of subjects and their content to the lives of pupils and their deep desire for change in the curriculum to relate their schooling more directly to the outside world, especially the world of work.

Phillips (1984), in a longitudinal study conducted in a Welsh comprehensive school found that pupils preferred subjects which they considered useful for future employment. Griffin (1985) found that girls only valued information of practical use in getting jobs. Leafield pupils expressed similar sentiments:

> Shirley (white less-achiever): 'The [subject] choices weren't flexible enough. We needed more practical things, to do with real life.'

Other pupils (predominantly girls) could be more specific about what those 'practical things' should be:

> Vanda (black less-achiever): 'More lessons on world wide knowledge and things like how the council works and political parties.'

> Delia (black less-achiever): 'I would have liked World Affairs ... famine, war in Iran, things like that.'

> Peter (white less-achiever): 'I'm into politics and law, so I'd 'av liked that.'

Whilst boys could agree that broader knowledge of the world today would be interesting, a lot of their concerns were linked directly to the need to prepare themselves for jobs:

> Duncan (white less-achiever): 'In my spare time [two afternoons per week due to being barred from some lessons] I just had to report to Mrs Young [head of 5th year] and do boring copying and paper work for her. They could have given me extra work in the lessons I liked, I would have done that, or arranged work experience.'

Pupils simply could not see the point of some of the things they had to learn at school. For example, Philip could not see the usefulness of languages:

> Philip (white less-achiever): 'Don't see the point of French. Most places they learn English don't they?'

Looking at life from Philip's standpoint he was absolutely correct. He was very unlikely to need French in his future jobs and not at all likely (due to disinterest) to take the type of continental holidays that would bring him into contact with the local people or seek work in France. He would far rather have spent his time trying out different types of work or concentrating on subjects that offered practical, saleable skills in the job market. Observed in some of his French lessons, Philip seemed desperately uncomfortable, occupying himself with constant knee-trembling as he struggled to maintain his dignity in the face of virtually no knowledge of French whatsoever. He could not pronounce French words correctly, or complete the simple sentence 'Je m'appelle Philip'. His inability was matched by total disinterest:

> Philip: 'I hated French. Only in it because I got kicked out of catering. I liked that but she said I didn't bring my stuff enough, but I only forgot twice.'

Philip appreciated catering because of its utility in later life, it therefore had meaning for him. Similarly, he appreciated the letter writing practice he did in English. Again, this was perceived as a useful skill in securing work:

> Philip: 'Catering was OK, it was useful and I like writing letters [for jobs] in English. Most other things were a waste of time.'

Philip had essentially opted out of school and its values. School had lost its relevance and in turn, teachers lost the battle to maintain his interest. His sights were clearly fixed on the outside world of work and the only practical thing the school could then offer to maintain his attendance was to create as much work experience as possible and to organise early entry into a YTS placement.

Philip's dissatisfaction with the content of schooling was shared by others. Questionnaire responses indicated that school was appreciated for having taught pupils to read, write and add up money, but for very little else. As Natalie put it in relation to one of her Maths lessons which she found crushingly boring:

> Natalie (white less-achiever): 'It's so boring. What we got to keep doing these angles for?'

As Raby and Walford (1981) state, school was 'generally regarded as an inevitable phase of life which had to be endured' (p. 22).

Neither were attempts by staff to make lessons more relevant very well received. Three boys were observed during a community studies lesson covering local Leafield history. They had the following to say about it:

> 1st boy: 'That photo of Mr Lea. He invented Leafield didn't he?'

2nd boy: 'What did he want to go and do that for?'

3rd boy: 'Some kind of nutter I reckon.' (laughter)

Davies (1979) reports a similar cynicism among girls in her study, stating:

> To them they are doing the same thing they did last week, last month, last year .... attempts to 'make relevant' the curriculum .... are treated with equal weariness, are viewed as equally insulting (Davies, 1979, p. 63).

The knowledge offered in lessons was not the knowledge that pupils wanted. The curriculum contained things that teachers perceived as relevant knowledge and there was a cultural and experiential gap between the givers and receivers of that knowledge. Keddie (1971) has argued that teachers define what is valid knowledge and there were similar indications at Leafield. The example above is a case in point, so too is the following one when spontaneous pupil knowledge was not accessed in the classroom even when it related directly to the topic in hand. A clear example of an opportunity missed was observed during a Religious Knowledge lesson on 'Suffering' when a lively, though disjointed, discussion developed. The text book stated that animal suffering was 'natural' but various pupils disagreed:

'Yeah, what about fox hunting.'

'And experiments.'

'Whale's blubber in margarine, that's not natural.'

'Experiments on animals don't always tell you about humans, take Thalidomide.'

The class soon fragmented into various discussions of related issues, one group talking about factory farming and another listening to a girl who said the Animal Liberation Front were awful for putting poison in Mars Bars. Another girl got onto the topic of Aids as a type of suffering, suggesting that this was 'God's punishment' for the wrong doing of homosexuals.

In short, within the space of a few minutes the class had come to life and demonstrated a great deal of personal knowledge on contemporary issues and a desire to discuss these, but the teacher did not use this knowledge to develop the theme of the lesson or encourage debate. Instead, he steered the lesson back to the set text and the class continued to undertake a cursory reading of the main points in the chapter. The lesson resumed a 'sterile' approach detached from modern day issues.

Bergqvist and Saljo (1987) also report teachers' failure to access pupil knowledge and incorporate it in lessons. This renders pupil knowledge irrelevant or illegitimate and thus fails to make the link between pupils' current level of understanding and what is being taught. A rift then develops between pupils' common knowledge and the formal knowledge on offer in the classroom.

The rift between the curriculum and these pupils' interests can be attributed to a cultural gap between educators and working class consumers. This rift is not so much a deficit on the part of working class pupils as a difference between their social world and that of their mostly middle-class, educational superiors. Bourdieu (1973) explains this in terms of a model whereby working class pupils lack the cultural capital that is gained in middle class homes which share the same dominant culture as the school. Bernstein (1975) also acknowledges that principles of power and social control are reflected in the knowledge transmitted in schools. If this is the case, then it is little wonder that Leafield's working class pupils rejected the knowledge that was on offer, and set their sights beyond the school gates instead.

The fact that school did not produce the goods as far as learning about the 'real world' was concerned exacerbated the desire of the vast majority of working class pupils to get out of school as soon as possible. Many non-exam takers left as soon as they were old enough to do so without waiting for the end of term, and even those with exams to take were longing to be released:

> Natalie (white less-achiever): 'I want to leave school. Do some growing up before going to college.'

Natalie felt that 'growing up' was something that happened outside school when you had time to discover the real world. School was a narrow entity that existed separately and 'kept you away' from everyday life.

Working class pupils felt the divide between school and 'real life' very deeply and they eagerly shared their grievances with the researcher in this respect. However, this did not mean that on a daily basis they were passively accepting the status quo. Challenges in the classroom were frequent and some extended beyond expressions of boredom and the creation of diversions. Pupils could be, and were, the instigators of constructive criticism and requests for alternative knowledge. From observations such challenges, often expressed as simple pleas for change, were not taken up by teachers on the pupils' behalf. Teachers would sympathise with pupils, and sometimes agree with them, but indicated that there was nothing they could do to change the situation:

> White, male pupil (in a non-exam Science lesson): 'I wish we could take an exam in this Sir, have something to show for it.'
>
> Teacher: 'Yes, you've had a bit of a raw deal this year, perhaps I can set you an end of term test.'

In one instance, two girls in a Biology lesson raised the issue of contraception and sex education with the teacher. 'I'll talk to you later about it' was the teacher's reply. However, no further mention of this issue was made by her either during, or at the end of, the lesson.

The above examples demonstrate a willingness among pupils to engage in positive criticism of educational content and to suggest alternatives they would find more interesting, but complaints were also levelled at educational process. During another Biology lesson the class were asked to view a video and take notes ready to answer questions afterwards:

> White, female pupil: 'But we've never been taught how to take notes. What are we supposed to do?' (she clearly seemed lost at the suggestion)
>
> Teacher: 'Yes I know, it would have been better if this had been done in the 4th year, but this is at least a late start and better than not at all.'

No further assistance was offered and this pupil and her friends copied the set questions off the overhead projector but made no attempt to take notes or list relevant points as the video proceeded. The pupils had expressed a need for assistance but none was forthcoming. This issue of note-taking arose again during another video for a different subject involving a different set of pupils, but again no practical guidance about how to proceed was offered. In a similar context, Natalie also complained about her CSE Biology:

> Natalie (white less-achiever): 'We never do experiments in Biology. Just one last year.'

Natalie became very bored when copying work from the chalk board or working from set question sheets. She wanted active as opposed to passive learning, and in its absence she lost interest in the subject.

The futility of exams

> Brown (1987) states: If what is taught in schools is viewed as irrelevant .... then the same can be said for qualifications (p. 74).

This statement was also borne out at Leafield. Of the 18 working class informants, 12 were due to sit between three and eight CSEs whilst 2 (the white boys, Philip and Duncan) were not put in for any exams at all owing to their poor performance. (These two boys went onto a programme of extended work experience.) These 14 boys and girls were not at all sure that CSEs would be useful afterwards in obtaining work. Their criticisms of CSEs fell into two broad categories:

(a) that one or two CSE passes were quite useless on their own and would not help in getting a job, and

(b) that securing a job depended more on personal contacts or personality than CSE results.

The subsequent experiences of the CSE school leavers did bear out that personal contacts were important in finding work and this issue receives attention in Chapter 7. However, for the present it is important to consider that pupils already viewed CSEs negatively before they had entered the job-seeking phase and that this influenced their motivation towards achieving in the exams that lay ahead of them. As Raby (1979) states:

> Most of the youngsters did not perceive that academic success or failure would affect their career aspirations, because most of them aspired to jobs which did not, or were perceived not, to require formal qualifications .... (Raby, 1979, pp. 255-6).

Day (1987) also reports that her Piertown informants rejected the usefulness of exams (O-levels) in doing a job, although pupils conceded they could be a passport to getting a job. At Leafield, working class less-achievers were sceptical about the utility of CSEs on both counts:

Eddie (who passed one CSE out of two taken and failed to sit a third): 'School is rubbish, I don't know why, it just is. Loads of people get jobs without exams, it helps a bit - but not that much.'

Sonia (who passed five out of seven CSEs): 'First year after leaving school they [CSEs] don't help you, nobody asks you .... it's your attitude to things and how you look.'

Similarly, pupils who admitted to being disappointed at their results could cite their actual job-seeking experiences to demonstrate that their lack of CSEs had not really mattered. This was treated with relief by some who had been apprehensive about securing work and as proof that exams (and by extension, school) were a waste of time:

Shirley (who passed one out of two CSEs and failed to sit a third): 'I knew of a job before my exams so I didn't really try.'

Tessa (who obtained low grades in the six CSEs she took): 'My exam results were terrible .... I was petrified for my Dad to see them. He was disappointed and thought a job would be difficult [to find]. Maths was low but I only got one wrong on the Marks and Spencer test and I got the highest score ever at Boots.'

This widespread lack of faith in CSEs was supplemented by the fact that many pupils had been shocked to discover how few CSEs they were being entered for. The decisions were taken by staff at Christmas and were not popular. Both the validity and timing of these decisions were questioned by pupils. Among informants, many less-achievers felt they should have been given the 'benefit of the doubt' and allowed to sit subjects. Pupils reported disappointment or anger from their parents about their low number of exam entries but there was also evidence of pupils' and parents' tacit acceptance of the school's decision:

Bedford (black less-achiever): 'I'm taking three CSEs, got told off for that. Mum expected more.'

Duncan (white less-achiever): 'I hoped I'd be put in for five CSEs but in the end, just before Christmas, I was told I could only do one CSE in Religious Knowledge and what good will one CSE do you?'

This low estimation by teachers of what he could take and pass came as a shock to Duncan and his parents, but no-one queried the school's decision. Duncan admitted that things had gone down hill in the last year through getting into trouble with the Police and confrontations at school. In the end he left at Easter to join a YTS workshop.

The news about how few CSEs they were being entered for led to widespread disenchantment with school. Pupils taking no CSEs began to drift away from school and into jobs or YTS at the earliest opportunity. Others lost the motivation to even sit the exams and a spate of pupils left at Easter, especially if they had jobs lined up.

Views of school polarised rapidly after the exam decisions were announced. Those with substantial numbers of CSEs to sit began to prepare in earnest whilst the remainder consolidated their opinions that exams were a 'waste of time'. Teachers were well aware of the drop off in school attendance that followed the announcement of the exam entries and, indeed, it was policy to delay these decisions until Christmas to avoid widespread absenteeism throughout the 5th form year. Pupils though, criticised the decisions for coming so late. Many were truly shocked to learn how few exams they were sitting and felt it left them no time to catch up or improve their work to reverse the situation. It was as if they had never really taken in the fact they were being continually assessed and could be precluded from a chance to sit an exam. Taking their school work seriously had been deferred for too long and in consequence, the Christmas decisions were a moment of truth.

To some extent these lesser or non-achieving pupils had been strung along for some time by their teachers. Encouragement led to confidence among pupils that they were doing alright, and lack of strictness (i.e. lack of 'pushing' and 'stretching') led to complacency. Teachers were treading a fine line here, not wanting to demoralise the weaker students with criticism (e.g. over poor work or non-existent homework) and wishing to give encouragement up to the last moment so giving all pupils the chance to prove their worth. Their working class pupils seem not to have responded well to this approach. This leads on to another issue, that of working class pupils' criticisms of their teachers.

Perceived teacher failings

One criticism that came across loud and clear among working class informants was that they felt their teachers were not sufficiently interested in them. This interest was gauged by the fact that pupils did not feel sufficiently encouraged by their teachers. In short, they wanted to be 'pushed' and 'stretched' and felt that in not doing so, their teachers had let them down. In both Stanworth's study (1981) and Delamont's (1980) girls spoke of being insufficiently 'pushed' but at Leafield both male and female less-achievers felt this way:

> Eric (who failed to sit his three CSEs): 'I could have got more out of school, didn't try hard enough .... would have done more if pushed by teachers. It makes you feel they're interested in you and wanted you to do well.'

> Bedford (who took and passed three CSEs with low grades): 'I know I was marked off as a dosser. I felt prevented because they thought I mucked about.'

Implicit in the complaints of some pupils was a resentment aimed at the 'posh' pupils, whom they saw as being favoured by teachers and having an easier time at school:

> Sonia (who passed five CSEs): 'Some don't bother about us and go back onto the brainy people. Lower grade groups, they don't even help you. They think you're dumb and that's it.'

Many studies have similarly shown that working class pupils are quick to spot the fact that they are located in low streams and that such pupils gain the impression that teachers are not interested in them (e.g. Hargreaves 1967, Lacey 1970, Ball 1981). These studies also demonstrate the link between perceived position in the academic meritocracy and actual achievement, arguing that such pupils then 'opt out' of school and fail by virtue of the 'self-fulfilling prophecy' (see Becker 1963, Rosenthal and Jacobsen 1968). There were also indications of resentment amongst Leafield pupils concerning the low streams they were placed in and this was blamed for dragging down their performance:

> Tessa (who obtained six low grade CSEs): 'I'm certain that if I'd been in a quiet class with cleverer ones I would have tried harder, not to look ignorant. Miss Wilson tried to push me, but not really a good talk.'

> Peter (who sat and passed two CSEs and failed to sit a third): '[I was] in General Science with knobheads and thickies. Two brainy people in that

class, me and Tracy. I was upset it wasn't a CSE course as I was getting good marks.'

At Leafield, working class, non-O-level takers certainly did not feel very important and could see a difference between themselves and the 'posh' pupils. The term 'posh' was used to describe those who were taking O-levels such that being 'brainy' was synonymous with being 'posh' in the eyes of working class less-achievers. Thus, a distinction in terms of academic ability was taken to be a distinction in terms of class by such pupils. This was not necessarily the case as will be discussed later in this chapter, but suffice it to say that that is how the hierarchy was viewed by the majority of informants.

Both Hargreaves (1967) and Griffin (1985) report similar views where streaming created a divide between achievers and less-achievers whereby achieving pupils were viewed as 'posh'. In the case of Hargreaves' (1967) study this divide came between CSE-takers and non-exam students but at Leafield it fell between O-level takers and CSE-takers.

The distinction between the 'brainy/posh' pupils and less-achievers at Leafield was made even more pronounced by the different classroom interactions experienced by pupils according to ability. Both higher and lower achievers acknowledged that low ability group lessons and unstreamed lessons were peppered with noise and disruption:

Sheilah (taking both O-levels and CSEs): 'Noisy pupils were a problem. Spoiled your concentration.'

Natalie (taking CSEs only): 'Them in the other group, the posh ones, they do alright.'

By 'other group', Natalie was referring to the main O-level takers, who split off into a separate form called the Exam Group after the Christmas exam decisions were taken. From observations of this group, their lessons were certainly a more straightforward academic exercise. There was little mucking about and no serious disruptive activity. Non-exam classes, and some CSE classes were always 'at risk' of disruption by pupils who were not involved in the work and wanted to create diversions. Typical activities such as bag lobbing, stupid remarks, flicking small items across the room and scraping chairs have already been described in Chapter 2 and were employed to full effect by the disinterested.

Some indications of a split between working class CSE-takers and non-exam takers was discernible over the issue of discipline in the classroom.

Some 10 per cent of questionnaire informants wanted stricter teachers and more classroom discipline. These were pupils who could be categorised as 'ordinary kids' (see Brown, 1987) who were taking some exams:

> Tessa (who passed six CSEs): ' I think they should have harder teachers. Higher levels, posh, never used to have any trouble but our group in the middle had tearaways and that, and we just used to mess about and never used to do nothing.'

These pupils, therefore, blamed teachers for their lack of discipline, and by extension, for their own lack of achievement. Non-exam takers saw things somewhat differently. They felt that teachers picked on them unjustifiably, and that they were not liked by those teachers:

> Delia (due to sit three CSEs but missed all three due to being off sick): 'Mr Morris talks to you as if you was skiving ... Mr Lukes said I was a skiver and it's really shameful in front of a class to be called a skiver. I wasn't doing nothing.'

> Shirley (failed to sit one of her three CSEs): 'Some teachers made sure you knew it if they didn't like you.'

> Philip (who took an early YTS): 'They just treat you like little kids.'

All informants hated the idea of being treated like a child, but it was the working class, less-achieving pupils who noticed and resented this treatment from teachers the most, primarily because theirs were the very lessons where disruption would take place and teachers would have to exercise some degree of enforced control. But did teachers really dislike their working class pupils or hold negative views of them? Both Hargreaves (1967) and Sharp and Green (1975) have indicated teachers do treat pupils differently according to how they are perceived and that their perceptions of pupils owe something to class factors.

Teachers at Leafield professed to care equally for all their charges and to judge pupils on their own merits. These 'merits', however, proved to include non-academic factors, as evidenced by the following descriptions of pupils provided by their form teachers:

> Shirley's form teacher: 'Rather stroppy and difficult, from a big family. Her mum gets in a violent temper and so can Shirley. There is a nice

side to her ... but she skives a bit. She's an underachiever, hasn't worked hard. Her mum works in Sainsbury's. She goes around with Lisa's crowd, getting into fights.'

Elements of Shirley's home life were, therefore, invoked to explain her temperament and level of involvement with school work. She was also judged by the friends she chose. Implicit linkage was also made between the mother's occupation (erroneously for she was currently a doctor's receptionist) and Shirley's underachievement. Similarly, Philip's form teacher had this to say about him:

> Philip's form teacher: 'Oh, a naughty boy, a baddie. His brothers were a nuisance at the school and he lives up to this. A bit aggressive, a bit noisy. Difficult in the classroom. He's not academic, banned from the workshops because he's such a twit there.'

In this case, clearly Philip's teacher had a very negative attitude towards him. His behaviour was described as 'naughty', 'aggressive' and 'difficult' and he was labelled 'a baddie' and 'a twit'; all judgemental statements, supported by the fact that his brothers had also been a 'nuisance'.

Hargreaves, Hestor and Mellor (1975) describe precisely this process of forming negative pupil typifications based on evidence garnered about older siblings and developing into a reputation that is utilised for subsequent members of the family. Clearly, Philip fell foul of this process. Notes on Philip's personal file revealed that in P.E. he was considered to be:

> 'talented and keen' (especially at football),

but the remaining comments were:

> Maths: 'Not achieving his potential'.
>
> Woodwork: 'Wasting ability'.
>
> English: 'Lacks concentration'

plus a general comment of 'not interested'.

Philip was also seen as 'noisy' and 'difficult' and as 'not academic'. Here too, he was fitting the teacher's typification of the boisterous and unruly pupil lacking in intelligence, a view commonly expressed by teachers in discussing working class, low achieving pupils (Hargreaves,1977). He was, however, 'talented and keen' in football, an skill considered to be in keeping with working class origins by middle class teachers who presume to judge.

Chapter 4 has already indicated how black pupils were the subject of stereotypical typifications by their teachers, and these two white working class, less-achieving pupils were similarly categorised according to perceived characteristics which, by themselves, need not have had any bearing upon academic performance. As a result, implicit understandings about class differences were developed and maintained by teachers and these should be borne in mind when considering that most working class informants felt that teachers did not really try to push them and were, in fact, not really interested in them.

Working class pupils saw school as selling them short. They were not at all sure that teachers acted in their best interests and school did not seem to tally with their needs and the reality of their future lives. When, in addition, schooling only seemed to offer non-relevant topics these pupils wanted to extricate themselves from the education process as soon as possible and try their hand in the job market instead.

However, for a small section of informants this mis-match did not exist. These were the pupils with middle class backgrounds or middle class aspirations, and the fact that school held far more meaning for them serves to support the view that a class divide informed attitudes to school.

Middle class and working class achieving pupils

A distinct difference in attitudes to school was discernible between the majority of working class informants already discussed and a minority of other pupils which consisted of two specific 'types'. These were (a) a small group of pupils of middle class origins and (b) a further small group of achieving pupils of working class origins. In all, 6 out of 20 informants fell into this category and the main difference between them and the bulk of working class informants was a polarisation in attitudes towards school and its worth for the future. This polarisation was also evident in questionnaire returns from the whole year group.

Before examining the views of these pupils it is necessary to define what is meant by both 'middle class pupil' and 'working class achieving pupil' in this context. In this study a pupil was taken to be of middle class origins if the main bread-winner of the family was in white collar professional or technical employment. Thus, in principle, a pupil with a bricklaying father and part-time secretarial mother would not be classified as middle class, whereas a pupil with a teaching father and factory working mother would. There have been criticisms of class schema which fail to give adequate weighting to wives' employment (see Heath and Britten 1984, Garnsey 1978), so in this study the possibility of any influence from mothers with middle class jobs was considered. In the event, however, some pro-school (achieving) and some anti-school (less-achieving) pupils had mothers in middle class, office work such that no correlation could be found between mothers' occupations and pupils' levels of achievement. Neither was there any correlation between mothers' occupations and pupils' attitiudes towards school.

The term 'working class achiever' refers to pupils from working class homes who were taking O-levels as opposed to CSEs. The divide was placed here because the pupils themselves categorised each other according to the ability groups they were in. This was also the line that differentiated pupils regarding a polarisation of attitudes towards school such that 'achieving' pupils had positive reactions to school and 'less achieving' pupils had negative reactions similar to those found by Hargreaves (1967).

The relevance of schooling

That school was seen as worthwhile by middle class and achieving, working class pupils was clear from their positive attitudes towards their preferred subjects and favourite teachers. In their questionnaire returns, school subjects were described as 'interesting' and teachers as 'helpful'. Most importantly, the role of schooling was not questioned.

It is difficult to convey the positive attitudes these pupils adopted towards their school work. Evidence for it was found not so much in what they said as in what they did. Classroom observations revealed passive conformity in lessons, quiet attention to the teacher, and concentration on work set in class with work completed to the deadline set. Conformity and acceptance of the norms and values of schooling meant that the education process ran smoothly and became something of a 'non-issue'. These pupils had few grievances and found it difficult to articulate opinions about school other than saying it was 'good' or 'interesting'. Their acceptance of school and its norms and values is perhaps best illustrated by the fact that the majority of O-level takers approached during their 5th form year made it plain that they were 'too busy' to spend time discussing school with a researcher. 'After the exams' was a frequent response, for these pupils were well-tuned to the deadlines of revision and exams that lay ahead and were wanting as few disruptions as possible. Their goal was very clearly getting through the exams and they approached them seriously.

In contrast, less-achieving pupils were not too busy to say how they felt about school. On the contrary, a whole host of pupils were keen to express their views; they were only too pleased to be able to air their grievances in the hope that something might 'get done' to change things.

When some of these achievers did sit down and talk about school at the start of the 6th form, their seriousness of purpose and absolute acceptance of the validity of the examination process was borne out in their statements:

> Lynn (working class achiever): 'I always liked school, including 5th form. Fun there, teachers were nice and lessons interesting. Being interested was definitely linked to how you got on.'

> Pauline (middle class achiever): 'I enjoy school. Always have done.'

These comments, and others like them, demonstrated an overall willingness to work and an acceptance of school subjects as worthwhile. Their criticisms concerned barriers which prevented that work from taking place or which made the process of learning less efficient or less pleasurable. Education, per se, was not questioned:

> Pauline (said when in 6th form): 'There were times when we were all a bit wound up and felt it was a bit disorganised, teachers not informed, lack of efficiency and that. We had no proper Chemistry teacher and this didn't help.'

This was in stark contrast to the less-achieving pupils who did not accept the usefulness or interest value of many lessons and found the process of schooling completely irrelevant to their future lives and very boring.

For achievers, however, school subjects certainly had relevance. Paul, for example, was of middle class origins. His father was an Agricultural Engineer and his mother (separated) was a Stores Manager in industry. Paul did not experience the mis-match of interests at school that his working class less-achieving peers did. He was involved in various after-school activities and had parents who could afford the additional expenses that clubs and trips entailed. His exam subjects were directly in line with his career interests (see next section). In short, school was offering an academic route towards a career and this was wholly in line with his needs. The school, therefore, seemed better able to meet the demands of a middle class pupil like Paul than one from the working class even though it professed to be a 'community' school and served a predominantly working class area (OPCS, 1982b).

The utility of exams

A second major difference between the middle class and achieving, working class pupils and their less-achieving working class peers lay in their approach to exams. Again, those involved in taking O-levels had little to say on the topic being too busy preparing for them, evidence in itself of the importance examination passes held in their eyes. One boy, studying for seven O-levels and four CSEs summed up what the exams meant to him:

> Paul (middle class achiever): 'O-levels I find are a way of getting you ready, giving you loads of information and facts. When you get to A-levels you start using the facts.'

For Paul, O-levels conveyed necessary information and learning that would be needed to progress to more applied studies. His acceptance of them as necessary meant that he did not question their content, and their usefulness was seen, not in terms of practical utility for daily life, but in terms of the access they promised to further education. They were a passport to further and higher education and, in his case, to university entrance, in order to be an Agricultural Engineer like his father.

All informants who were taking O-levels had their sights set on further education. They did not necessarily intend to follow a highly academic route involving A-levels but they wished to progress to the 6th form to take vocational or subject-specific courses to help them find an interesting job:

> Sarah (working class achiever): 'I want to do a year in the 6th form. An RSA Secretarial course then off to work.'

Taking and passing O-levels clearly had utility for these pupils. Their exams were part of a process towards employment goals and as such they had relevance. This is in contrast to the working class pupils mentioned earlier for whom CSEs held little relevance in finding work (see pp. 119-20). As Raby (1979) states, school seemed relevant to top stream pupils but not to the remainder.

Perceived teacher merits

Another polarisation of attitudes concerned the way teachers were viewed differently by achievers and less-achievers. Working class less-achievers, as discussed earlier felt they should have been pushed more, and that teachers lacked interest in them preferring the 'posh', brainy pupils (see p. 122).

Questionnaire responses indicated that achievers, in the main, felt they had gained greatly from their teachers. They had their favourites and the reasons cited for liking particular members of staff revolved around the perceived interest that that person took in the pupil and how well they got their subject across. Likes were therefore based upon factors that assisted the pupils in succeeding in their work, be it through personal encouragement or a flair for making the subject stimulating:

> Sarah (working class achiever): 'I had a lot of help leading up to the exams .... English, poor at it, but Mr Rogers got me through it.'

> Sheilah (working class achiever): 'It was OK last year [in 5th form] and some teachers I really liked .... a good relationship with teachers really helps your work and they take more interest.'

Naturally enough, achievers could find some teachers (or their subjects) boring, others helpful, and there was considerable overlap amongst achieving and less-achieving pupils on this topic. However, the general feeling amongst achievers was that teachers (good or bad) did their best for you. As a result the contract to work hard and learn was not threatened. Working class less-achievers were not at all sure that teachers had their best interests at heart, and some also indicated that teachers lacked classroom control which allowed disruption and noise to interfere with their performance. Achieving pupils agreed over teacher classroom control and the noise factor, but in the main they were largely buffered from the worst effects of this via streaming:

> Pauline (middle class achiever): 'Maths was very streamed right from the start, and English. A lot of others were mixed so a fair bit of noise. A lot has to do with the teacher. The vague ones were annoying and those who can't get discipline.'

> Sarah (working class achiever): 'I didn't find trouble-makers a problem. I could cope with them for fifteen minutes at Registration.'

As a result they were able to proceed with their work in line with their own objectives and did not perceive noise and lack of discipline as being associated with teachers' disinterest in them as the working class, less-achievers did.

Teachers, for their part, spoke quite positively about their achieving pupils whether of middle or working class origins. Examples of form teachers' comments about achieving pupils are as follow:

> Form teacher about Paul (white, middle class achiever): 'His attendance is fine, excellent. Lives with his father. Good lad, helpful, fairly responsible. Very intelligent doing between eight and ten O-levels with 6th form ahead. Possibly a university entrant if he has the right attitude and works .... Dislikes violence and violent people. Fairly relaxed but can be tense occasionally, possibly due to home and school pressures to complete his work. The father is very supportive, wants his son to do well so the boy's trying to live up to that. There's an older brother in the 6th form now .... they'll both succeed if motivated.'

> Form teacher about Sarah (white, working class achiever): 'Definitely one of our brighter pupils .... A good worker, conscientious. Lives with her mother. Has had some trouble recently with some girls in the non-exam group. Got hit over taking someone else's boyfriend, but she's getting over that now.'

As with working class less-achievers, teachers brought home background, siblings and other non-academic criteria into their verbal assessments. In talking about Paul and Sarah teachers spoke enthusiastically and with a degree of pride. Here, their tone was far more positive; for example, being in a single parent household was not connected to problems as it was for less-achievers and personal qualities such as disliking violence were given credit. Such pupils fitted teachers' notions of the 'ideal pupil' (Becker, 1952). A combination of their ability plus their 'helpful', 'responsible' and 'conscientious' ways meant that they were rewarding and a delight to teach. Such pupils, therefore, satisfied teachers' interests at hand whilst teachers satisfied those of pupils. The relationship between school and achieving pupils therefore seemed to be a 'symbiotic' one for the pupils also felt that schooling offered subjects and examinations which provided an entree into their chosen career areas and gained satisfaction from being able to demonstrate ability in their chosen subject areas. Both parties had similar expectations of school and there was little real discord between them.

The special case of working class achievers

Four pupils out of the twenty informants appear to spoil the perfect 'fit' of working class pupils being turned off school and middle class pupils being committed and successful. These were the four 'achieving' pupils from working class families whose attitudes to school and careers have been incorporated within the last section. These pupils were all girls, two white and two black. Their home backgrounds are charted in Table 5.2.

Table 5.2
Parental occupations and career aspirations of Leafield 5th form working class achievers

Achieving Pupil	Father's Occupation	Mother's Occupation	Career Aspirations
Sarah (white)	Council Manual Worker (living apart)	Hairdresser's Receptionist	Work in Travel Agency
Lynn (white)	Bricklayer	Nursing Asst. (nights)	Teacher (primary)
Colette (West Indian)	Welder	Nursing	Business Studies BSc
Sheilah (West Indian)	Ex-printer, now in USA (living apart)	H/Wife, Ex-catering Asst.	Skilled Office Work

Source: In-depth informants and school record cards, Leafield School (1984)

All four girls had two things in common, which in tandem, had placed them outside the experiences of the other working class pupils. Firstly, they had all found school work interesting and secondly they all had some degree of parental support.

The fact that they found school interesting enabled them to develop a good working relationship with their teachers in a way that was not possible for their peers who found school subjects boring. Form teachers spoke positively of all these girls, taking pride in their achievements irrespective of ethnic origins. For example:

> Form teacher about Sheilah (black achiever): 'She's a well rounded, mature, intelligent girl. Gifted in O-level subjects and sport. Pleasant personality.'

> Form teacher about Sarah (white achiever): 'Definitely one of our brightest pupils. A joy to teach.'

These harmonious pupil/teacher relationships encouraged performance and assisted these pupils in becoming achievers.

The effect of parental support

There is, however, the additional dimension of parental support and encouragement. The Central Advisory council for Education (1967) in its major report on Primary Schools states:

> .... the most vital factor in a child's home is the attitude to school, and all that goes on there, of his [sic] mother and father. The interested parent had the interested child (Central Advisory council for Education, 1967, p. 461).

Reid (1986) suggests caution in viewing the evidence for parental influence but indicates that:

> if achievement were related to certain parental values, then a potentially powerful explanation could have been identified (Reid, 1986, p. 216).

At Leafield parental support, taken in isolation did not appear to be sufficient to motivate working class informants to do well at school, but parental support plus a pupil's interest in school subjects served jointly to enhance achievement. The absence of one or other of these served to depress achievement.

It has already been described how disinterested pupils found school boring and irrelevant to the 'real' world outside school and in consequence could not relate well to teachers or become motivated in their school work. This has been analysed as a class-based phenomenon because the school curriculum did not match up to the needs of working class pupils and what they perceived as necessary to help them find 'decent jobs'. This disinterest in school could not be countered by parental support operating in isolation. Hence the working class parent who wanted their child to 'get on' and stay on in the 6th form could not instil in that child a positive image of school. Indeed, every one of 20 informants reported their parents to be in favour of them staying on to obtain additional qualifications. No pupil was being expected or pressurised to go out to work to earn money. The less-achieving pupils, however, had already 'voted with their feet' and decided that further schooling was a waste of time. Pupils had, therefore, taken on a working class perspective and were more inclined to follow in their parents' footsteps than heed their advice to 'break the mould'.

Although parental support for the 'idea' of education without any insight or past experience may not be very helpful for pupils, parents cannot be blamed for the underachievement of their children when they have tried to express their support for them gaining qualifications and 6th form studies. To cite specific examples of parental support, Bedford remembered his mother always wanting him to be 'a heart doctor' and he knew she was disappointed that he did not continue at school after the age of sixteen. Eddie's father wanted him to go to college, Shirley's parents wanted her to carry on in the 6th form but said 'It's up to you'. Similarly, Tessa was horrified at her poor CSE results because she knew her father would be angry and disappointed. Parental support for education came from both mothers and fathers, including fathers separated from their families who nevertheless kept in touch and tried to encourage their children. It also came from both white and black parents. This support though seemed powerless to alter the opinions of school that working class disinterested less-achievers held.

However, parental support did act as encouragement for the pupils who already liked school. The extent to which this encouragement affected their performance and willingness to stay on in the 6th form can be judged by Colette's experience.

Colette was of West Indian origin and her father was a welder, her mother a nursing assistant. She recounted how during her moments of depression over poor O-level grades her mother had humoured her into persevering:

> Colette (black, working class achiever): 'She would say to me things like "Let me see, we haven't got any doctors or lawyers in the family so you've got to be something like that".'

Sarah and Lynn, the two white working class achievers had also received support for gaining qualifications and as this combined nicely with their own interests, both intrinsic and extrinsic motivation were present.

Similarly, Sheilah, the other West Indian-origin working class achiever, spoke of the encouragement and advice she had received at home regarding staying on to undertake a B-Tec National:

> Sheilah (black, working class achiever): 'I talked with my mum and older sister and mum's pleased I'm staying on to do it because my sister did the B.Tec earlier and she was alright.'

These working class pupils then, received the kind of parental support and advice normally associated with pupils of middle class origins. Their parents aspired to white collar or professional employment for their daughters and this plus their children's interest in school work and their ability enabled them to progress academically through the school and examination system. Parental support for middle class occupations was therefore indicated as an important element in working class informants' achievement although it did not seem to have an effect in isolation. Other working class parents would have loved their sons and daughters to remain at school and do well but their children lacked motivation for they could not see the usefulness of school or exams. These pupils were the less-achieving informants who 'voted with their feet' to extricate themselves from the school process as soon as possible.

Does class make a difference?

In this chapter it has been suggested that working class informants had a very clear understanding of what it meant to be working class and that the majority of them then viewed school as being largely irrelevant to their future lives. They did not see the utility of exams (or more specifically CSEs) and the subjects on offer held no meaning for them. Neither did they see teachers as being particularly interested in them. Middle class informants did not see any separation between their best interests for the future and what school offered and could see the relevance of both subject content and exams for their future training and careers. These pupils viewed teachers as encouraging them and showing interest in their performance.

This was explained in terms of a clash of cultures along class lines whereby the school operated on essentially academic and meritocratic principles in line with the dominant middle class values that abound in education, values that were not shared by the majority of working class pupils. It was also indicated that teachers labelled pupils according to factors linked to their home and therefore class backgrounds, and not just an academic criteria alone, serving to exacerbate a class divide.

Finally, an explanation was offered for the achievement (in middle class terms) of a minority of working class informants on the basis that both they and their parents were acting uncharacteristically for their actual class position in that these pupils were interested in their school subjects, and were positively encouraged by their parents. That these pupils were a minority, and that 16 out of 20 informants maintained strong allegiance to either their working or middle class origins, with attendant anti- or pro-school attitudes indicates that class has an important bearing on how schooling is received.

The 'success' of the working class achievers and the main difference between them and their less-achieving peers appeared to lie not just in their interest in academic subjects per se, but in the fact that their utility was recognised in providing access to middle class occupations. This indicates a link not only between class and attitudes to school, but also between class and aspirations, an issue which is taken up in the next chapter.

6 Choosing for the future

Introduction

As pupils approached the end of their compulsory education they had to make some important choices about staying on at school, seeking further education, trying to find work or accepting YTS placements. An important feature of this study was to research this decision-making process in order to establish the extent to which gender, race and class affected both choices and outcomes. In consequence, the focus now shifts onto the 5th formers' career choices, the influences involved in making those choices and a critique of the careers advice available at the school.

In this respect, the 5th formers in this study did not drift towards leaving school. Indeed, they talked about it at home, with their friends and thought about it a lot. From the replies on the 5th form questionnaire it was evident that the majority of pupils had availed themselves of the careers talks on offer as some 75 per cent reported attending these. In addition, nearly 80 per cent indicated that they had talked to relatives (parents, siblings and others) about selecting and seeking employment. The effect of this was quite pronounced in that pupils frequently opted for a path already taken by another member of their family or one suggested by them. This held true for both boys and girls, achievers and less-achievers, blacks and whites, details of which are explored below.

Perhaps the most important thing to establish at the outset is that the vast majority of Leafield pupils of both genders and all racial origins, did not make career choices, but job choices. The school's intake was predominantly working class (OPCS 1982b) and some 90 per cent of 5th formers at the time of this study had parents with working class occupations, according to school record cards. As such, the majority of pupils did not think in terms of a 'career' and 'job satisfaction'. It is in this light that Leafield's 5th form choices must be viewed, for as Corrigan (1979) states:

> they don't see their world in terms of choice and career, when the job comes it comes in a harsh and real form .... you have to go and it's boring (Corrigan, 1979).

All pupils were asked by questionnaire the following two questions:

Q. What would you most like to do when you leave?

Q. What else are you prepared to do if necessary? (see Appendix 1)

These two questions were posed to elicit both pupils' deeply-held desires and their realism, and to compare these replies with the actual experiences of the 20 in-depth informants. The resultant data indicated a strong influence on choices of both class and gender, but not of race. These are now considered separately.

The class dimension in job choices

There is a wealth of research to support the notion that class position is a major determinant in pupils' job choices. Corrigan (1979) discovered that boys in his study stuck closely to their manufacturing origins in thinking about future work, stating:

> At no stage in either the interviews or the questionnaire do they reach out from their class backgrounds and use a comparison that comes from outside (Corrigan, 1979).

Finn (1984) also concluded that the dominant influence on decisions and expectations for the future came from class and cultural backgrounds. Other researchers focussing on girls have indicated the importance of parental occupations in formulating choices (Delamont 1980, Furlong 1986), which by extension, implicate class origins in forming pupils' aspirations.

At Leafield, class origins and parental occupations played a major part in determining pupils' job choices. Only 7 pupils (3 girls and 4 boys) aspired to professional employment or university in questionnaire returns and of these, two were known to be of middle class origins for the pupils concerned were among the in-depth informants.

At face value this could seem surprising as some 21 girls and 18 boys were sitting sufficient O-levels to warrant 6th form entry (subject to satisfactory grades) and had already split off from their usual form groups at Christmas to become an 'Exam Group'. However, this lack of aspiration becomes understandable in terms of class position when the parental occupations and home backgrounds of informants are taken into account to shed light on this phenomenon.

Achievers

Of the 20 informants, 6 were from the Exam Group mentioned above and defined as 'achievers' in Chapter 5. Their occupational aspirations and parental occupations are detailed in Table 6.1.

Table 6.1
Exam group informants by ethnicity, to show parental occupations and career aspirations

Pupil	Ethnicity	Father's Occupation	Mother's Occupation	Career Aspirations
Paul	White	Agricultural Engineer	Stores Manager	Agricultural Engineer
Pauline	White	Science Teacher	Hosp. Lab. Tech.	Occupational Therapist
Sarah	White	Manual Worker	Hairdresser's Receptionist	Work in Travel Agency
Lynn	White	Bricklayer	Nursing Asst. (nights)	Primary School Teacher
Colette	West Indian	Welder	Nursing Asst.	Business Studies B.Sc.
Sheilah	West Indian	ex-Printer	Housewife ex-Catering Asst.	Skilled Office Work

Source: *Leafield informants and school records (1985)*

It was noticeable that many of these achievers had job aspirations in line with the actual occupations (or past occupations) of a parent or sibling, and not in line with their own level of achievement and ability to continue with Higher Education. Thus, despite ability, there were indications of a 'pull' towards class origins such that middle class pupils chose careers closely aligned to the career of a parent and working class pupils chose occupations below the level associated with their academic achievements. This created a tendency to under-aspire in working class pupils, whilst middle class pupils chose careers in line with their ability.

Four of these informants aspired to a profession and two of them had professional parents. All six were well placed academically to progress towards middle class occupations. Their experiences are interesting in shedding light on how class position and family influences can affect aspirations and career choices.

Paul's father was an agricultural engineer and his mother was an stores manager. Paul had his sights set on taking three A-levels and he listed his eventual aim as a career in agricultural or electronic engineering. Paul's career choice was strongly influenced by his parents, especially his father with whom he lived:

> Paul (white, middle class achiever): 'My parents helped in my decision, pushed me a bit. I've got a brother and sister older who did A-levels.'

Paul's form teacher confirmed that the boy's father was supportive of the school and 'pushed' the boy to the extent that he was perhaps 'under a bit of pressure from the father.'

Paul recounted his earlier childhood experiences of growing up in a farming environment and how he saw this as satisfying work. He recalled travelling around with his father and took pride in the links his family had with the farming community. He had kept up some of his father's old contacts in the country and was a member of the Young Farmers' Club. He also lived in a country village outside Bridgehurst, and was the only informant to do so.

Not only did Paul select an occupation that was already 'in the family' but he showed a strong leaning towards entering that career in the same way as his father. In the 6th form he began to think about an HND instead of a university degree because he could see it was more practically based:

> Paul: 'You see, I enjoyed Control Technology [in 5th form] .... projects and working with people. More action-type, more machinery work.'

This was directly in line with his father's experience who started off as a foreman in agricultural engineering. Paul was displaying a similar interest in the practical rather than the academic side of the industry.

Pauline was the only other informant to have professional parents. Her father was a science teacher at a local college, having previously been in laboratory work. Her mother was a laboratory technician in a local hospital. Pauline herself wanted to be an occupational therapist.

Here again, the scientific and professional interests of her parents were conducive to Pauline's own interest in science. Pauline took and passed eight O-levels with an average pass grade of 'B' and went on into the 6th form to take two Science A-levels and English Literature. She was a quiet, modest and serious pupil:

> Pauline (white, middle class achiever, about her new A-level studies): 'They're interesting but Biology is harder than I thought it would be. Chemistry is hard but I like it - although I doubt if I'll pass.'

Her results at O-level were the best grades in the school that year and her fears for her ability would appear unfounded.

Pauline had given some thought to her future career and had taken some active steps before settling for occupational therapy:

> Pauline (black, working class achiever): 'I first thought of nursing then I heard of this through a cousin doing a week's work experience in occupational therapy. Also, I went to the careers talk on occupational therapy. So I did some work experience in that too and decided it was OK.'

Pauline intended to go on to a polytechnic or special training college for occupational therapy. She said that her parents had never pushed her as regards career choices but clearly, with both parents in scientific work and a medical orientation, it is not surprising that she should feel comfortable and confident about a career that combined science with a caring profession. Pauline also chose a 'practical' occupation rather than an 'academic' one despite her excellent O-level achievements. In this too, she was following in the footsteps of both her parents and a cousin and was influenced by them in choosing a middle class occupation.

The noticeable feature of the remaining achievers was that their parents were in typically working class jobs and that pupils themselves held modest career aspirations below the limits of what could be open to them based on their examination successes. Thus, whilst it was still true that there was a parental influence on career choices, this influence was now exerted in such a way as to curtail not enhance career aspirations. This created the beginnings of class perpetuation between generations for both middle and working class pupils, even in the face of proven academic ability.

Sarah, for example, sat eight O-levels and passed six, plus four grade 1 CSEs and was considered by the Head of 5th form to be 'one of our brightest pupils'. Sarah, however, tended to underestimate her achievement and had heeded the advice of her mother and experience of her older sister in selecting a career:

> Sarah (white, working class achiever taking an RSA secretarial course in 6th form): 'I never felt very academically inclined. It was very hard work to get Cs [at O-level], so my mother thought don't flog it to do A-levels, go for a secretarial course, so I did. My older sister had already done the same course at Leafield and did OK afterwards.'

Sarah's mother was a receptionist in a hairdressers and her father, who did not live with them, used to be a manual worker with the local council although Sarah was not certain about his current job. Although she was within range of A-level achievement, she found studying hard going and was happy to take an easier route towards employment as encouraged by her mother. Here again, family influences were involved and, like Pauline, she chose a 'tried and tested' route that a member of her family had already negotiated successfully, in this case depressing the level of her aspirations, albeit that her preference for working in a travel agency was a form of white collar employment.

Another example can be found in Sheilah who was again pronounced to be 'very academic' by her form teacher. She sat seven O-levels and five CSEs passing five at O-level. Like Sarah, Sheilah also had her sights set more on getting a practical qualification that would lead to employment and she made choices below the level of the options open to her based on her examination results. In her case she chose to do a one-year B.Tec. National in order to go straight into office work afterwards. She hoped that this job would include some computer or accountancy training to make her more specialised and was happy to continue some part-time (perhaps day release) studies once she had started work. Here too, both maternal advice and sibling experience prevailed to influence her:

> Sheilah (black, working class achiever who began a B.Tec. course in

office skills): 'B.Tec. takes one year and I can convert it to a Higher Diploma with one extra year. Then straight into a job, preferably computing office work ... My mum's pleased I'm staying on, my sister did the B.Tec. earlier.'

Both Griffin (1985) and Furlong (1986) researched girls' aspirations in comprehensive schools and found evidence of low expectations. Furlong also found girls' female relatives had a powerful impact on their choices:

> The single most important influence on the occupational aspirations of young women is that of their mother and female friends and relations (Furlong, 1986, p. 375).

To supplement Furlong's contention, for Leafield working class achievers the influence of those female relations served to limit occupational choices and confine them to what Glass (1954) and Heath (1981) refer to as short-range mobility. Thus, class origins impeded such pupils in striking out towards occupational goals compatible with their proven academic ability.

So far, it has been suggested that familial influences both enhanced and depressed the aspirations of achieving working class pupils. Enhanced them because working class parents openly supported and encouraged their children to stay at school and aim for qualifications but also depressed them by suggesting employment choices below the level of their children's ability. However, the two working class pupils who did make professional career choices revealed an ambivalence towards those careers which indicated that even they were wishing to enter those occupations for reasons other than middle class aspiration.

Lynn for example, was one of these two informants to 'break the mould' in the absence of familial occupational links. Lynn's father was a bricklayer and her mother was a nursing assistant for disabled people. In a breaktime discussion about future career choices she had this to say about her family and her decision to be a primary school teacher:

> Lynn (white, working class less-achiever) (said fondly and without rancour): 'Both my parents are thick .... My mum's nice but ever so thick. I just want to do a job with children and think the holidays would be good as well as it being an interesting job .... Teaching was my own idea, it came from my own interests. I must have a job I enjoy as it won't seem like working.'

Lynn could not say why she had proved to be academically able but she had always liked school. Her parents were supportive and she had a good relationship with them; she knew she wanted a 'more interesting' job than her mother's.

In this instance, it is worth noting that Lynn's preference for teaching was because she wanted 'a job with children' and that teaching seemed to offer the 'easiest' and most interesting option. Her articulated sympathies lay not with teaching per se, or the imparting of knowledge in an academic sense but with children. In this, she was very similar to many lower ability working class pupils but her O-level successes enabled her to consider more professional employment with children that would lead to a career. She had doubts about her ability to succeed but was, nevertheless, undertaking three A-levels and one O/A level:

> Lynn: 'Not sure I can do it, but it's nice to try.'

Colette, the other black achieving pupil, similarly did not set her sights too low. She and her parents had been told many times that she was 'university material'. As a result, she had originally anticipated passing her O-levels, entering the 6th form to take three A-levels and then going on to college or university to take a degree in Business Studies.

The problem for Colette was that on her own admission, she had become 'too complacent'. She thought she could be active in sports, music and drama and still pass her exams without spending a lot of time on her work:

> Colette (black, working class achiever): 'The trouble was I was really fed up with school. I always worked hard and then I asked "What's it all for?" I got to the stage I said "I can't take any more".'

Colette felt that all the time her less-achieving friends had been enjoying themselves she had been working studiously, then near exam time they had been able to knuckle down to work whilst she had reached her 'cut off point'. The end result was that she failed four out of seven O-levels and obtained 'D' and 'E' grades in the other three:

> Colette: 'My mother said "How could you do this to me?" but later she said not to worry .... I can tell you I was so depressed at that time.'

In consequence, Colette's plans had to be revised and she spent here first 6th form year re-taking her O-levels, this time successfully. After that she embarked upon her A-level programme, one year behind her peers.

The interesting thing about Colette was that she had become 'really fed up with school' and began to resent all the effort she was putting into school work compared with some of her non-O-level friends. She was in danger of 'slipping' and becoming one of the less-achievers and only strong parental encouragement (see p. 134) kept her going. Colette then, can be viewed as 'sticking it out' rather than enthusiastically being involved in academic attainment. As she herself said:

> Colette: 'I don't know whether it's motivation, or laziness about going out to work.'

Lynn and Colette were the only two working class informants who had opted for academic or professional careers, and as demonstrated above, neither were particularly committed to what they had chosen in a 'career' sense, although for different reasons. Lynn's motivation was that she primarily wanted to work with children and Colette showed signs of continuing with her original plan because it was preferable to going straight out to work. The jobs that lay ahead of them, after qualifying, were not valued for their intrinsic worth as by Paul and Pauline, rather they offered a pragmatic solution for the future.

In this, Lynn and Colette were acting similarly to Sarah and Sheilah who had made different but nevertheless pragmatic decisions in choosing short term skill-orientated training in readiness for the world of work.

Pragmatism has been noted as a particular feature of working class girls' occupational choices by Griffin (1985) and by Raby and Walford (1981) and as a feature among all working class pupils, both boys and girls. Indications at Leafield were that working class achievers were also thinking along such lines.

Less-achievers

As has already been stated, only 7 out of 193 pupils who returned questionnaires aspired to professional middle class employment or to university. The remainder selected jobs from a narrow range of skilled and unskilled manual employment with boys opting primarily for skilled trades or garage/mechanic work (26 per cent) and girls primarily selecting 'caring' jobs (15per cent) or office/secretarial work (13 per cent) (see Table 6.3). As these choices were also gender specific they are discussed in more detail in the next section which examines gender and aspirations but for now it is important to consider the class relevance of pupils' preferences. Raby and Walford (1981) found that job choices among their urban comprehensive school pupils bore a direct relation to the practicalities of the local labour market and many other researchers (e.g. Corrigan 1979, Baqi 1984, Griffin 1985) reveal a realism in pupils' choices that reflects what is feasible and attainable in the job market. Delamont (1980) indicates that parents' own jobs are considered in making these choices and as King (1987) states:

> children do not encounter the occupational structure directly, but construct subjective definitions of work through their family and school experiences (King, 1987, p. 297).

Certainly, at Leafield, there was nothing to indicate that pupils in any way stepped out of their class origins in selecting jobs. Furthermore, 16 per cent of all pupils said they were prepared to consider 'anything' if their first choice was not possible, indicating an acceptance of whatever was available in the job market. This can best be seen by examining the job preferences of the 14 working class less-achieving informants. Table 6.2 shows both preferred and second job choices in relation to parental occupations.

From this table it can be seen that pupils chose largely from the range of occupations they saw their parents and siblings participating in, such that any mobility that might be aspired to was only from unskilled/unqualified manual work to skilled or qualified manual work (e.g. Peter, whose father was an ex-welder making garage doors, wanted to obtain an apprenticeship). These less-achieving pupils acted in accordance with Willis' (1977) lads in taking their aspirations from what they saw around them, thus being instrumental in their own working class entrapment. Neither their first nor second choices lay outside the domain of working class jobs, pointing again to the beginnings of inter-generational class perpetuation; indeed some had deliberately selected the job of their same-sex parent:

> Philip (white, working class less-achiever): 'I'd really like to work down Parkers on their coaches [he had done some work experience there] but otherwise I'd like to be a painter and decorator like my dad.'

Philip, who found school totally irrelevant and boring (see p.p 114-5) could indeed 'come alive' when talking about the world of work. One breaktime by the bicycle sheds he proudly talked about his father, a painter and decorator:

> Philip: 'He can do wonderful ceilings and that, plaster them real smooth. He does a lot for that .... [named local period property]'

Philip was animated and enthusiastic in what he said, quite unlike the silent and stumbling boy observed painfully enduring a French lesson. He saw his father's world as the 'real' world and was keen to leave school behind him. Whereas his form teacher described Philip as a 'baddie', a 'nuisance' and a 'twit', he was more than efficient in delivering a building quotation from his father for a prospective client, getting back to them in twenty four hours.

Table 6.2
Parental occupations and job aspirations of less-achieving working class informants, by ethnicity

Pupil	Ethnic origin*	Father's occupation	Mother's occupation	Job preferred	Alternative job choice
Peter	W	Door maker (living apart)	Cashier	Fire service	Anything
Philip	W	Painter and Decorator	Clerk	Coachbuilder	Painter and Decorator
Duncan	W	Bricklayer	Nursing Assistant	Building work	Army
Bedford	WI	Labourer (living apart)	Nurse	Electrician	-
Eric	WI	Hospital porter	Housewife	Electrical Engineering	Garage
Eddie	WI	Electrician	Not known (living apart)	Anything	YTS
Winston	WI	Not known (living apart)	Nursing assistant	College	-
Shirley	W	Delivery driver	Doctor's receptionist	Catering	Factory
Natalie	W	Driver	Housewife	Work with animals/F.E.	YTS
Tessa	W	Factory mechanic	Factory machinist	Work with children	Office work
Delia	WI	Not known (living apart)	Unemployed cleaner	Hairdresser	-
Sonia	WI	Not known (living apart)	Deceased	Anything	F.E.
Vanda	WI	Manual work	Housewife	Shop work	-
Diane	WI	Not known (living apart)	Catering	Nurse	Catering

* W = White   WI = West Indian-origin

Source: Leafield informants, questionnaires and school records (1984/5)

Duncan similarly wanted to work on a building site and his father was a bricklayer. This, despite the fact that he had referred with some bitterness earlier to his father suffering spells of unemployment between jobs and receiving low wages (see p. 108).

Furthermore, three pupils were prepared to consider any job at all and flexibility is perhaps best demonstrated by Shirley who completed her questionnaire by post, having already left school (unofficially) before Easter. She wrote on her form:

> Shirley (white, working class less-achiever) 'I would have liked to have catered somewhere but fortunately I ran straight into a job in a factory .... I will stick to the job I have.'

Shirley then, quickly accepted the first job offer she was made and was prepared to 'stick to it' without searching for something better. Indeed, she even left school early in order to take it. Her instrumental approach to work epitomised the work ethic of most less-achieving informants whereby anything was swept aside in order to secure a job. This issue receives further attention in Chapter 7 which focusses on employment destinations.

Finally, the parental advice that was forthcoming for achievers in helping them decide future careers and appropriate 6th form courses, was also forthcoming for less-achievers in deciding their futures. In relation to this, no parents of informants had insisted they leave school to get work (see p. 134) and some openly preferred their children to stay on in the 6th form:

> Vanda (black, working class less-achiever): 'My mum, she supported me in my decision to go into a shop but both mum and dad wanted me to go into 6th form.'

> Shirley (white, working class less-achiever): '[They were] all for me going to college but said "It's your choice, so do what you want to do".'

These parents then, might have liked their sons and daughters to continue at school but they did not press them to do so. Neither did they articulate specific job targets or goals that would be best served by staying on at school thus enabling pupils to see the rationale for doing so. None of the parents of these pupils had themselves stayed on at school beyond the minimum school leaving age and their children, in following in their footsteps were 'doing as they did' rather than 'doing as they said'. Thus there was a realism on the part of pupils in sticking to tried and tested routes rather than delve into the unknown. This too served as a mechanism for intergenerational class perpetuation and was further compounded by the job contacts parents could often make for their children via friends or their own workplaces. This factor is discussed in more detail in Chapter 7 when examining employment destinations.

Gender and job choices

Another notable feature among Leafield 5th formers was the gender differentiation in employment aspirations, as reported in the questionnaires.

The girls

With stunning clarity, both girls and boys chose stereotypical occupations that would polarise them into two separate spheres of the workforce. Table 6.3 indicates the first and second choice occupations that they chose.

The largest category of employment cited by girls as their main choice was 'looking after children' with 10 per cent of girls mentioning this. The next most popular choices were shop work (9 per cent), office work (7 per cent) and secretarial work (6 per cent) such that these four categories combined to account for 32 per cent of all girls' choices. A further 14 per cent wanted what has been collectively described as 'glamour' jobs in reception, hairdressing, beauty work, fashion design or art. Engineering was completely unrepresented in the girls' choices and just one girl wanted to work with computers. Nobody wanted outdoor manual work and the two girls who wanted professional careers chose occupational therapy and accountancy, both of which can be associated with either the 'caring' role or office work, thus lying within the realm of what is considered 'suitable' women's work (Sharpe, 1976). As such, gender-specificity in job choice transcended occupational class divides.

One interesting feature of girls choices was that 5 per cent nominated YTS as their main choice whereas no boys opted for YTS in the first instance. In addition girls were far more willing to opt for 6th form or further education (8 per cent against 2 per cent for boys), although these differences disappeared when alternative choices were taken into account. Girls, therefore, displayed a tendency towards greater readiness to stay in education, or embark on some type of vocational training than boys, whose sights were more set on paid work. Furlong (1986) suggests that this willingness to continue studying is a way of girls avoiding unemployment

Table 6.3
First and second choice occupations of 5th formers, by gender, as cited on 5th form questionnaire

Destination	Girls (%) 1st choice	Girls (%) 2nd choice	Boys (%) 1st choice	Boys (%) 2nd choice
Anything	14	16	10	17
6th form or F.E.	8	10	2	10
H.E./University	1	0	0	0
YTS	5	10	0	14
Uniformed Forces	1	0	6.5	5.5
Unskilled (outdoors)	0	0	6.5	1
Unskilled (Rail/P. Office)	0	1	5.5	0
Unskilled (Garage)	0	0	9	2
Unskilled (Factory)	1	0	1	1
Unskilled (Domestic/Catering)	1	1	1	0
Skilled (trades)	1	0	17	10
Skilled (factory)	0	0	3	1
Skilled (catering)	3	1	3	2
Shop Work/Sales	9	14	5.5	3
Reception	2	1	0	0
Fashion and Art	8	4	3	2
Hairdressing/Beauty	4	1	1	0
Child care	10	2	1	1
Animal care	2	0	1	2
Nursing Assistant	0	1	1	1
Nurse	3	0	0	0
Office/bank work	7	9	1	3
Secretarial	6	4	0	0
Computer work	1	0	4.5	1
Engineering	0	0	3	2
Technician/Technical	1	1	2	0
Professional	2	3	5.5	2
Not stated	10	21	6.5	18
Total number = 193	**Total number = 100**		**Total number = 93**	

Source: Questionnaire, Leafield 5th formers (1985).

but this did not seem to be the case at Leafield. Girls were faced with only 4 per cent unemployment as school leavers locally and female informants actively chose further studies at either A-level or for vocational purposes (e.g. Sarah, Pauline, Sheilah and Natalie). In this they differed from the boys who were more likely to start in 6th form but drop out as soon as any paid job arose (see p. 158).

Much attention has been focussed on the tendency of girls to opt for traditionally female roles, and occupations seen as 'feminine', and school processes have been implicated in the formation of girls' attitudes by Delamont (1980). Researchers have identified a wealth of factors influencing decisions among them being home influences (e.g. King, 1987), the desire for marriage (e.g. Dex, 1982), pressure from boys to exclude girls from non-traditional spheres (e.g. Culley, 1988), teachers' attitudes (e.g. Stanworth, 1981) and the quality of careers advice (e.g. Griffin, 1985). Each of these issues will be addressed in turn in relation to Leafield girls using data from informants and school observations.

Furlong (1986) suggests that mothers and other female relatives are instrumental in girls' aspirations because:

> persons of the same sex within the family are most likely to be experienced as significant others (Furlong, 1986, p. 375).

At Leafield, girls certainly referred most to female relatives in talking about family discussions on jobs as evidenced by Sheilah and Sarah (pp. 142-3) who listened carefully to their mothers and sisters in deciding what training to undertake and what jobs to aim for. The fact that the mothers of all these girls operated in entirely 'female' spheres (see Tables 6.1 and 6.2) must, by Furlong's reasoning, have an effect upon expectations.

A powerful message from Leafield girls was their keen interest in 'working with children'. In this they were being unrealistic in terms of jobs on offer in the labour market. Some 80 girls packed the careers talk on 'Working With Children' (the average attendance at careers talks was about 40), and 10 per cent (the largest single category) wanted such work according to the questionnaires, yet local opportunities in this field were severely limited. The local College of Further Education course for Nursery Nursing was over-subscribed each year and in any event, the ability levels of the girls most interested in such work fell short of the entry requirements for the course. As the local Careers Officer told me 'They wouldn't be able to pass the entrance test anyhow'. Tessa's experience seemed to confirm this:

> Tessa (white, working class less-achiever): 'I tried to get into college before my results so as to work with children. Went for a test for being a nanny at the College of F.E. There was this stupid Maths test on shapes and how would they fit. Was told they'd be in touch but never did; 200 apply each year and 23 are chosen, so I just gave up.'

As the girls would need to be qualified to work in any professionally organised creche or nursery school, the only other option remaining open to them was the informal sphere of child-minding and babysitting, neither of which provided regular, paid employment. However, girls who specified such work were being realistic on two accounts. Firstly, they readily saw that such jobs were in short supply and were perfectly prepared to consider other work instead. Indeed, 16 per cent of girls said they would do 'anything' as an alternative to their main choice. Secondly, they elected to incorporate their interest in children into their private lives instead:

> Shirley (who leapt at a machinist's vacancy before school had ended): 'I loved kids on my work experience, but hopefully I'll have my own.'

These girls were also being realistic in another sense, inasmuch as they saw marriage and raising children as an automatic part of their future lives. Most girls saw marriage and having children as likely, but a long way off:

> Shirley (white, working class less-achiever): 'I haven't really thought about the future .... Don't really want to get married for a long time yet, and kids, but not for a long time .... Not interested in boyfriends at the moment, I'd rather go out with my mates.'

Girls therefore anticipated later family ties, but as Griffin (1985) states:

> Marriage and motherhood seemed distant if inevitable events (p. 188).

Admittedly, when pressed, these girls of 15 and 16 years of age would see their 20s as being 'the longer term' and the majority wanted to stay at home while their children were young, but there was no evidence that girls saw employment as a temporary phase whilst waiting to find a partner and start a family, and some wanted to delay marriage in order to develop a career first:

> Tessa (white, working class less-achiever): 'I'm only interested in being settled in two years time .... I do want children, about two years after getting married .... stay at home with them 'til they're ready for school.'

> Delia (black, working class less-achiever): 'I don't want to get married, not yet anyway .... I would like kids, yeah! Would prefer to keep working, I've got my mum [to look after the children].'

> Natalie (white, working class less-achiever): 'I would delay marriage 'til after my career takes off.'

The 'longer term' outlook varied in its length from pupil to pupil and Tessa's longer term was only two years hence. Achieving and middle class pupils were more inclined to delay the idea of marriage slightly in order to develop a career. They were also more concerned about the impact of children on their lives, but still saw themselves having children at some stage:

> Sarah (white, working class achiever): 'I'm definitely not interested in marriage until my late 20s .... having kids causes delays .... I want to be free of those constraints.'

> Pauline (white, middle class achiever): 'Can't really see myself getting married young .... don't know about children .... I would want to share looking after them with my partner.'

It is suggested, therefore, that in listing 'working with children' as a main job preference, the girls who made that choice were making something of a 'statement of intent' about their future lives. They saw raising their own children as an integral part of their whole 'career' future and specified such work as a long term goal whilst simultaneously considering any job for the time being. In this they were reacting to the labour market in a similar way to the boys who spoke of wanting to qualify in skilled trades as their ultimate objective but were nevertheless prepared to take 'lesser' employment (see Table 6.3). Girls were, therefore, being highly pragmatic taking their working lives as a whole, and as Griffin (1985) states, perhaps:

> Our ideas on the 'transition from school to work' need to expand to include young people's relative positions in the sexual and marriage markets (Griffin, 1985, p. 188).

A further interesting feature of girls' choices at Leafield was the distinct lack of interest in 'male' occupations. No-one listed science, technology or engineering among their choices, and only one girl opted for work with computers. Culley (1988) argues that the siting of computer equipment in Maths blocks (associated with the male domain) and the off-putting influences of boys in 'hogging' equipment are factors to be considered in turning girls away from the field and a scenario of this type prevailed at Leafield (see pp. 60-1). Measor (1984) similarly indicates that pressures to conform to female stereotypes, emanating from both teachers and male peers, serve to negate girls' interest in science. The experiences of Natalie, whose dream was to become a vet, are worth exploring in this context. Her teachers had ensured that she took all the right science subjects to achieve her goal, but a number of things about what was taught, how and in what atmosphere conspired to inhibit her performance and turn her off science:

> Natalie (white, working class less-achiever): 'I never found school subjects interesting, even Biology - just about plants [said with disinterest]. I loved Chemistry, quite interested in Physics, but I would have preferred it if more girls were involved, it puts me off. They [boys] put me off by messing about.'

It should be borne in mind that Natalie was one of the two girls who so unwillingly demonstrated their successful experiment to a class full of boys in a Physics lesson (see p. 59). She had also said that sometimes the girls worked outside in the corridor to get some peace and quiet (see p. 65). However, she was critical of the teacher as well as the male pupils:

> Natalie: 'School doesn't encourage girls in science. Mr Perry tends to talk to the boys and ignore the girls' questions. You know, it's mostly girls going for this vet's course [Animal Technology]. I find that really interesting. You see, boys have done the school subjects needed but go into Engineering more and A-levels, not animals. Yet I needed them and felt put off.'

That Natalie felt 'put off' and excluded in science is quite clear, although it is not clear that teachers actually did undermine her in the way she perceived. Two of her male science teachers were very supportive and knew of her interest, including Mr Perry. Neither of them were seen to discriminate against girls during classroom observations. In any event, the important issue is that Natalie felt like an outsider in science classes where she was outnumbered by the boys, and where she felt the teacher gave boys greater attention. As a result Natalie did not do well in her science subjects. She took CSEs not O-levels and was forced to modify her 'dream'. The effect of this on her career aspirations was that she finally opted to go to the local College of Further Education with greatly modified ambitions:

Natalie: 'I want to do a year at College followed by Zoology at some level or possibly then go straight into a job with animals. I'd like to start at the bottom and work my way up but I don't think I'm brainy enough.'

Another important factor for Leafield girls was the quality of careers advice provided by the school. To begin with there was a marked lack of careers talks on topics that related to girls' interests. Whilst to have such things may well have the effect of promoting, and hence perpetuating, a gender divide in occupations (an argument put forward by Cockburn (1987) in relation to vocational training and YTS), to omit girls' interests is to provide them with distinct messages about the unimportance of their needs and their secondary role to boys in a world dominated by male-oriented occupations. Such was the situation at Leafield where, in the first term of the 5th year the weekly programme of career talks included ten topics on skilled trades, the Armed Forces and technology and just two that could be regarded as relevant to girls' job preferences. These were 'Working with Children' and 'Department Store Work'. As previously stated, there was a heavy attendance at the former, but after the 'gloom and doom' messages about the few places available in Nursery Nursing girls were left with just one other talk that term, essentially on shop work. In addition, the school poster advertising the schedule of talks for the term emphasised the male weighting in careers talks by displaying a bold, 4-inch high logo of a man's head wearing an industrial safety helmet.

Careers advice and school work experience placements did not always match up to girls' expectations. One girl in the 5th form who was taking woodwork (and was good at her work) explained that she was interested in Joinery during her talk with the careers teacher. She complained bitterly afterwards when her work experience placement turned out to be in a children's day nursery. Similarly, Natalie was totally disgusted with the advice she received:

Natalie (whose dream was to become a vet): 'I told Mr Rogers I wanted to do Chemistry, Biology and Physics to build up to A-levels for University and he said it was too late, they were all booked up and there was nothing they could offer .... he said, "Work in a Pet Shop, at least it's working with animals". So did the YTS-day people.'

In this respect it was interesting that Mr Rogers had indicated his belief that girls harboured aspirations that were too low. He put this down to their working class origins, yet faced with these two girls above who were keen to break out of the mould, one in terms of gender stereotypes and the other in terms of class barriers, he himself acted stereotypically in underestimating their ability and did not take them seriously. There were similar incidents with the boys (see p. 160), and on one occasion, an infuriated teacher disclosed that Mr Rogers had failed to redress the situation when a visiting speaker from a local factory had turned to the girls present and said:

> 'I'm talking to the boys now. There'll be a secretarial speaker coming later to talk to you girls'.

Griffin (1985) also reports the incidence of limited and sexist careers advice to girls and the Fawcett Society (1984) reports girls as remembering very little about the advice received, indicative of its poor impact. They write:

> Most girls claimed that the information they had been given was of very limited value, apart from the help in writing letters of application and completing applications forms (Fawcett Society, 1984, p. 12).

The boys

Such then were the factors surrounding the issue of girls' aspirations and job preferences, but boys' selections were marked by the same features. To begin with, boys were similarly governed by traditionally male spheres of employment in their ideal job choices, and they chose predominantly from the range of skilled, working class occupations that they saw around them through friends, older brothers and their fathers (see Table 6.3). By far the most popular choices were skilled manual trades and these were desired by 17 per cent of the boys, with a further 9 per cent preferring car mechanic or garage work. This was entirely consistent with job opportunities on the nearby industrial estate which incorporated a large car manufacturing plant, confirming the findings of Raby and Walford (1981) that job choices related to practicalities of the local labour market. The boys very definitely valued skilled trades as opposed to unskilled assembly work. Aspiring boys wanted apprenticeships because they valued having a trade and saw it as a form of security against both poor wages and unemployment. Only one boy listed unskilled work as his first choice.

The third most popular choice with the boys (6 per cent) was the Armed Forces or uniformed services. Corrigan (1979) also cites this as a favourite with his northern town teenage boys and refers to local high levels of unemployment as being a major influencing factor; but for the local availability of skilled and unskilled 'masculine' jobs such opportunities in the Forces may also have been far more popular with these southern town boys.

When considering alternatives to their main choices, boys demonstrated a highly flexible approach with 17 per cent saying they would consider 'anything' and 14 per cent prepared to take YTS. In this respect it is interesting that no boys voluntarily selected YTS as their first choice of destination. It was something they considered as an alternative if regular work could not be found. A further 10 per cent were prepared to stay on in the 6th form or go to college but 10 per cent stuck to their original choice of a skilled trade. For some, acknowledgement of future family responsibilities created a 'push' towards finding such secure and well-paid work:

> Peter (white, working class less-achiever who wanted a skilled trade): 'I would like at least one child definitely, sometime. But I've got to sort meself out first.'

The prospect of parenthood therefore increased boys' desire to 'get a good job' but for girls, the caring and mothering role, so powerfully incorporated in their future expectations, served to decrease aspirations.

Boys' preferences bore little relation to girls' preferences in most occupations. Boys were massively more interested in both skilled and unskilled manual work and the Armed Forces whilst girls preferred the caring jobs (i.e. with children and animals), office work, and 'glamour' jobs in hairdressing, fashion and reception work. There was overlap in catering with equal numbers (3 per cent) of boys and girls wanting this and also some overlap in shop work.

That this should be the case is not surprising. Like girls, the boys looked to their same-sex parent for inspiration. Some boys spoke proudly of their fathers' jobs as skilled craftsmen and wanted to follow in their footsteps:

> 5th form white boy (after a careers talk): 'My dad was a mechanic and I grew up with motorbikes. Now he's a stonemason, he's worked five years on one job. I want to be a mechanic but my brother's into stonemasonry.'

Some wished to 'improve' upon the job status of their father but they did so by still remaining within the traditional scope for their gender. In total 17 per cent of boys aspired to skilled trades and a further 6 per cent aspired to other skilled work. King (1987) states that some working class parents do aspire for their children and that for boys this takes the form of encouraging them towards apprenticeships. Among the seven working class less-achieving males, three (Peter, Bedford and Eric) specifically wanted apprenticeships and were encouraged both at school and at home to take such a course:

> Bedford (black, working class less-achiever): 'I want to be a qualified Electrician and Mr Rogers suggests City and Guilds so I'll stay on for that.'

Such was the pull towards apprenticeships that Peter knew exactly what to do when an offer arose:

> Peter (white, working class less-achiever): 'I started at the College of F.E. on a B.Tec. course but heard immediately of a job at Petts [local printers]. A full apprenticeship in printing so I jumped at it.'

Boys were also subject to the same stereotypical set of values that served to restrict girls' choices. Ten careers talks in the first term of the 5th year had a masculine 'flavour' to them, with three on motor trades, two on building trades and two on engineering: two others related to the Armed Forces. Figure 6.4 sets out the full list for the term:

Royal Air Force
Car plant work
Navy and Marines
Building Trades (general)
Engineering (general)
Building Trades (electrical)
Motor Trades (general)
Engineering
Work with Children
Motor Trades (apprenticeships and YTS)
High Technology + Computing
Builders Merchant/Do-it-Yourself Store Work
Department Store Work

Figure 6.4 Titles of career talks at Leafield school, autumn term, 1984

The popularity of these talks was such that 36 boys and one girl attended Motor Trades and this was the usual pattern when traditionally male-orientated industries were being covered. However, as if this weighting in favour of skilled trades was not sufficient, Mr Rogers went further in banning three boys from attending the 'Working With Children' session. Upon discovering their names on the booking sheet he announced:

'Oh no, I'm not having that. If they show up I'll chuck 'em straight out.'

His immediate reaction was that they must be 'skiving off lessons' to put their names down for such a topic and indeed, he may well have been right for he knew the boys concerned quite well. However, he also steered another boy away from what is considered 'female' employment. This boy responded to a work experience placement for an office typist but he was turned down by Mr Rogers because, he said, the employer wanted a girl.

Mr Rogers was also one of the teachers in the Head's 'old righties' category who felt too much was made of racism and sexism (see pp. 47-8) and he was not averse to sexist humour (see pp. 49-50). This, plus his reaction to both girls and boys who showed non-traditional employment interests, suggested that he, as well as most pupils, harboured fixed, gendered ideas about occupations.

Race and job choices

The major finding regarding race and job choices was that no real difference could be detected between black and white pupils in what they wanted for the future. All 14 non-white 5th formers (i.e. of Asian, West Indian or Eastern origin) returned questionnaires and Table 6.5 therefore includes the responses of the entire cohort of Leafield's black 5th formers for the year.

The results in Table 6.5 are indistinguishable from selections made by white pupils and differences in black pupils' choices were similar to white pupils' in that the same gender divide operated to separate 'mens' and 'womens' work. In other studies (e.g. Warr, Banks and Ullah, 1985), black pupils have been said to have lower commitment to the labour market leading to suggestions that this contributes to higher rates of black unemployment. Eggleston et al. (1986), however, found no evidence for this in a large-scale survey of black and white school leavers. They suggest that where black pupils do hold aspirations higher than whites these are perfectly realistic in view of their levels of achievement. This was also the case at Leafield. The numbers involved were very small, but out of fourteen black pupils just two boys aspired to professions and two girls to the 6th form and university. In all four cases, their hopes were in line with their ability. In relation to the boys, one Eastern-origin boy wished to be a Dentist and an Asian-origin boy wanted to go into business. In both cases their academic record and family connections meant that their ambitions were feasible. Here, it should be noted, that neither of these two boys was West Indian in origin and that it was West Indian-origin girls, not boys who intended to enter the 6th form and university. Again, their career plans were well-tuned to their academic success and were by no means unreasonable. Fuller (1980) found that West Indian girls were more likely to try to use education as a way of securing better paid and higher status jobs than their male counterparts. Evidence at Leafield is small but does not contradict her findings.

Table 6.5
First and second choice occupations of Leafield non-white 5th formers, by gender, as cited on 5th form questionnaire

Destination	Girls (Nos)		Boys (Nos)	
	1st Choice	2nd Choice	1st Choice	2nd Choice
Anything	1	1	1	0
6th form/F.E.	1	1	0	1
H.E./University	1	0	0	0
YTS	0	1	0	1
Unskilled (garage)	0	0	0	1
Skilled (trade)	0	0	1	0
Skilled (catering)	0	1	0	1
Shop Work/Sales	1	0	0	0
Hairdressing/Beauty	1	0	0	0
Nurse	1	0	0	0
Engineering	0	0	1	0
Professional	0	0	2	0
Unstated	0	2	3	4
TOTAL NO. OF PUPILS	6	6	8	8

Source: Questionnaire, Leafield 5th formers (1985)

One thing that black girls did not do was to state an inclination towards working with children, something that was common in white girls' choices, but in all other respects their goals could not be distinguished from those of white pupils. Black girls had very similar views about marriage:

> Sheilah (black, working class achiever): 'I haven't got a steady boyfriend at the moment and don't really want one. I would like to get married and have children in my late 20s. I would take a break to look after my kids but would prefer a husband who shared everything...'

> Vanda (black, working class less-achiever): 'Marriage? Much later on, in my 20s or 30s. Then two children and stay with them all the time 'til they're grown up.'

They also received similar help and encouragement from their parents in deciding about their futures. For example, Sheilah and Colette reported strong support and advice about careers from their mothers (see pp. 135, 144) whilst Winston and Bedford had received advice from their mothers, both of whom suggested they consider the College of Further Education.

With reference to these two West Indian-origin boys, it should be noted that both had supportive mothers, and their fathers, although not living at home, maintained contact with both boys and took an interest in them. Bedford, in particular, was close to his mother and had this to say about her:

> Bedford (black, working class less-achiever: 'I'm close to my mum. I talk to her a lot .... she made me want to be a heart doctor, not stuck in a factory.'

Despite this support, Bedford did not have high education motivation or achievement. Neither he, nor Winston had enjoyed school and Winston had very definitely 'gone his own way', being absent from school and not concentrating on his work. It is doubtful that Winston would have taken the initiative himself to continue his education and only parental 'nudging' and support succeeded in keeping him there. However, the important point is that black pupils did enjoy parental support for both educational and occupational goals.

In terms of the careers advice at school black pupils again fared similarly to whites, receiving the same limited and stereotypical talks and advice as their white peers. Their uptake of these talks and their views of their work experience were in line with those of all other pupils and it is to the pupils' critique of careers advice that this study now turns by way of a final comment on how pupils were assisted in formulating choices for the future.

The careers service at Leafield

Careers advice

Mr Rogers, the careers teacher, was allowed two hours per week on his timetable for careers work and there was a financial supplement to his basic salary in acknowledgement of his extra duties. However, the two hour allocation was totally inadequate for the task in hand. Forty visiting speakers per year had to be arranged, involving a great many telephone calls; good relations had to be forged with local employers and colleges; there was a host of administrative duties; up to date careers literature had to be assembled and displayed involving liaison with the local authority's Careers Service, and all 5th formers were interviewed to see what they were interested in pursuing after age 16 years. There was also the need to be available to pupils with individual enquiries.

Work experience

In addition Mr Rogers was responsible for finding work experience placements for most members of the 5th form, amounting to some 200 placements. The work experience scheme operated to provide pupils with a good insight into at least one occupation before leaving school. The standard arrangement was for pupils to have a complete week in a place of work linked, wherever possible, to their field of interest. However, as the girl who wanted to be a joiner and the boy who wanted clerical experience discovered, work experience did not always match up to this ideal. Some of the more disruptive or non-achieving pupils were given longer term work experience placements and these could mean one or two days per week at work instead of attending school, and in some cases no school attendance at all.

At the other end of the achievement scales, some top O-level takers did not go on a work experience scheme because they were busy revising their subjects and had little time to spare. At Leafield, teachers accepted that preparation for exams was more important and work experience was either deferred until after the exams or deemed unnecessary for pupils intending to pursue A-levels in the 6th form. Occasionally, a pupil who was undecided about whether to stay on at school or not was given the opportunity to undertake a YTS in time to re-enter the 6th form if they chose to.

Criticisms of careers advice at Leafield

Many pupils felt satisfied with the extent of careers advice and other services at the school, and on the questionnaires over 75 per cent stated that they found the advice 'very helpful' or 'good'. This was a higher proportion than discovered by Brown (1987) whose study of comprehensive school pupils revealed just 50 per cent being satisfied with what was on offer. However, at Leafield 8 per cent felt the service was poor and many more than this offered suggestions for how things could be improved.

The improvements suggested bore a striking similarity to those voiced in other studies. For example, Keil and Newton (1980) whose research found 60 per cent of pupils to be satisfied with their careers advice, nevertheless found that pupils (both male and female) wanted more visits, more work experience and more of anything connected to careers advice in general. Leafield pupils displayed the same tendency with girls demonstrating more interest in personal, one-to-one work experience or counselling than the boys. Table 6.6 lists their suggestions as given on the questionnaire.

Table 6.6
Pupils' suggestions for improving careers provision in school, by gender, as cited on 5th form questionnaire

Suggestion	% Girls	% Boys
More careers talks	26	24
More work experience	20	12
More individual career interviews	23	15

(Total number of Questionnaires = 193)

Source: Questionnaire, Leafield 5th formers, 1985.

From this it can be seen that at least one quarter of 5th formers wanted additional career guidance. Informants also voiced similar opinions:

Philip (white, working clas less-achiever): 'More useful would be more work experience, a week is no good.'

Sheilah (black, working class achiever): 'Different places to visit and

> interviewing practice would be helpful.'

> Tessa (white, working class less-achiever: 'Careers advice on how to conduct yourself at interviews would be good. I didn't expect a panel interview.' (Speaking about her recent interview at Marks and Spencer.)

Pupils clearly wanted more help in making the transition into work and as in other spheres their requests were essentially practical. They wanted the opportunity to learn about more types of employment and they wanted to practice different kinds of work. They also wanted assistance in making introductions to employers (e.g. through learning how to write letters and present themselves). In part, their resistance to lessons cited earlier as boredom and disinterest, was due to the perceived lack of relevance these subjects held for the real world. Here also, in careers advice pupils were wanting to get closer to reality to help them with their choices. They also criticised work experience schemes for being too short and wanted the last year of school to be far more related to trying out different types of work and finding a job.

Pupil critiques of careers advice and work experience

Inevitably, some pupils felt thoroughly let down by the advice they had been given at school. This then gave them a negative view of the whole service:

> Paul (white, middle class achiever in the 6th form on an A-level course): 'I didn't think much of it. Two weeks ago I was told about the B.Tec./HND route to University. Wish I'd known because HND is a different, more relevant way in [to jobs]. I enjoyed Control Technology, projects .... more action type things .... Thought B.Tec. was an office skills course, didn't see its potential to go on.'

> Sheilah (black, working class achiever): 'It wasn't really all that helpful. The leaflets catalogue was not really helpful. Work experience - not really learning, just do the work for a week .... A man interviewed me and told me about staying on or going on YTS.'

> Peter (white, working class less achiever): 'Well, it's not really good enough. Just talks and a quick word with someone doing careers, they don't follow it up.'

Leafield informants therefore appeared to be as disenchanted with their careers advice as the Asian pupils studied by Brah (1984) who states:

> The majority indicated that careers advice in school was by and large limited to one or two meetings during the fifth year with the careers teacher and an occasional careers convention (Brah, 1984, p. 25).

Baqi (1987) in her study of YTS trainees also found that careers advice was described as being 'insignificant'. It would not be true to say that the majority of Leafield pupils felt this way, but a significant minority (25 per cent) did, and criticisms came from both achievers and less-achievers, girls and boys, blacks and whites.

Through the work experience route, pupils gained an insight into at least one occupation whilst still at school. Pupils took stock of the work they had sampled and considered whether or not it would suit them upon leaving. They were highly perceptive in their comments:

> Peter (who was put on extended work experience): 'I got put on a Butcher job. Didn't get a chance to serve until three months gone. Got the dirty jobs cleaning out the fridge, packing and mincing pet meat. Also the tea-boy.'

He had also had another experience which disgusted him:

> Peter: 'My work experience in Townsend's boatyard was £1 per hour, below the minimum wage level.'

Two girls had similarly negative experiences which served to change their minds over what type of work they wanted and when to leave school. Tessa, for example opted for shop work after her placement:

> Tessa (white, working class less-achiever): 'I didn't like my office work experience, it changed my mind about it. Just a skivvy.'

Similarly, Sheilah, who was undecided about whether to enter the 6th form or not, was provided with an early YTS placement to help her make her choice. She opted for the 6th form after sampling unskilled office work:

> Sheilah (black, working class, less-achiever): 'I did a Solicitor's YTS for one month but didn't like it. The job wasn't very interesting, doing general dogsbody work .... It's all right for them just talking to their clients but it's the people down below who do all the running around'.

Shilling (1988) argues that vocational experiences do not necessarily facilitate the transition from school to work and do not always create a favourable attitude towards work. He suggests that pupils can and do 'see through' the exploitation that is involved in wage labour. Certainly Tessa and Sheilah decided against office work on such grounds, and experiences such as theirs could account for the fact that 9 per cent of girls ranked office work as their second choice rather than their first (see Table 6.3). It was not clear that Tessa's alternative of shop work would provide her with anything better, but this is explored in more detail in Chapter 7 in relation to her actual shop destination (see p. 176-7).

Apart from officially organised work experience, a quarter of informants also had part-time jobs and these consisted primarily of shop work, waiting, newspaper rounds and (for girls) babysitting. Finn (1984) states that such work provides pupils with useful contacts for later entry into full time employment and that at the same time:

> employers themselves value this labour market experience, as demonstrating a youngster's initiative and discipline (Finn, 1984, p. 41).

Leafield pupils certainly valued their little jobs, but more for the spending money they provided than the experience they could then use to 'sell' themselves to employers or for the contacts they could develop. Indeed, no part-time job of any Leafield informant led to subsequent full-time employment for most jobs were essentially very part-time in nature (e.g. split shift waiting at table):

> Peter (white, working class less-achiever): 'I'm a waiter down at Harwood [residential centre]. Brilliant money, £1.76 an hour.'

Both achievers and less-achievers took part-time jobs but achievers tackled things less likely to interfere with school work (e.g. Saturday shop work) and were more inclined to drop their jobs as exams drew near. For example:

> Sarah (white, working class achiever): 'I used to do Saturdays in a newsagents but I gave it up last term. Couldn't really do both.'

Less-achievers took on greater amounts of work often with awkward split hours before and after school (e.g. newspaper rounds and catering/waiting in nearby residential homes). Sometimes, the part-time job interfered with school work but pupils still felt that the financial rewards made working part-time worthwhile:

Tessa (white, working class less-achiever): 'My exam results were terrible .... also had a job at night, used to do waitressing 6.30pm to 8.30pm and this took up all evening. Only did homework at weekends.'

Such jobs plus their work experience organised by the school became a pool of useful knowledge upon which pupils could assess what they might like to do in the future. Some liked and some disliked the things they had tried, but either way the money was considered useful and the experience valuable. With a new employment phase of their lives opening up in front of them, full of unknown quantities and a bewildering array of industries and types of work, this experience of the work place plus careers advice (from both school and parents) provided crucial reference points from which to view and evaluate available options.

A smooth transition?

In many ways the transition from school to work was unproblematic for Leafield pupils. They were in receipt of advice on jobs and careers from both parents and the school which did not threaten the current order of things. In addition, unemployment was not a desperate problem locally. Advice was both class specific and gender specific but few pupils had complaints on either score. As a result, both boys and girls had a clear idea of the type of work they would entertain. Their choices were divided along traditional 'gender' lines of women's and men's work. They were also extremely realistic and pragmatic in relation to employment vacancies in the local area and in the case of girls, in relation to their whole future lives which were seen as involving marriage and motherhood. In this respect both genders showed signs of bearing in mind long-term family plans, for whilst girls spoke of delaying marriage in order to establish themselves in work before a break, boys spoke of wanting 'good' skilled jobs to provide them with long-term security and a decent wage in order to support a family.

Pupils were satisfied with the support they received from home in making this transition but were less satisfied with what was offered at school. They particularly wanted more direct work experience and practical careers advice aimed at how to secure a job, although pupils used the experiences they had had to good advantage for it informed their ultimate decisions.

Overall, the actions of both the school and the pupils served to perpetuate class and gender divisions in society. The school served to steer pupils towards the needs of the labour market in such a way that it:

reproduces and legitimates a pre-existing pattern in the process of training and stratifying the workforce (Bowles and Gintis, 1976, p. 265).

It also steered all pupils, irrespective of class origins, towards occupations traditionally associated with their own gender. Simultaneously, working class pupils in setting their horizons in line with, or slightly above, that of their same sex parents, were instrumental in their own gender and working class entrapment (Willis, 1977). Middle class pupils similarly ensured their own transition into the realms of the middle class by choosing occupations similar to those of parents.

Racial origins had no apparent effect on ambitions and aspirations at Leafield. No distinction could be made between black girls and white girls choices, or between those of black boys and white boys. Black pupils also received similar careers advice to white pupils both in school and at home. More girls than boys were interested in gaining white collar qualifications in the 6th form and it is argued that this was more connected to the acceptability of 'office work' for working class girls than to any deep desire for self-advancement. When black girls were intersted in white collar work, their choices were entirely reasonable in view of their proven academic ability.

Overall, of the three major variables gender, race and class, gender proved to be most powerful in steering attitudes towards work and job aspirations. Thus, whilst Roberts et al. (1983) found gender to be a more important divide than race in the aspirations of their Birmingham school leavers and King (1987) found gender to interlink with class in forming pupils' orientations towards work and/or marriage, at Leafield, gender transcended both race and class factors to become an all-pervasive influence on the aspirations of pupils. Put simply, knowing the career or job aspirations of a pupil, was far more likely to indicate their gender than either their class or their racial origins. Without exception, informants selected gender-specific occupations and girls incorporated a vision of subsequent marriage and motherhood as part of their career aspirations.

However, aspirations and expectations do not necessarily coincide with actual destinations. Chapter 7 of this study now focusses on this aspect of transition into the adult world to establish whose hopes were matched by reality and whose were not. In the process, gender, race and class factors will be examined to establish whether they operated to the same extent in actually securing work or whether they took on different weighting in the 'outside world'.

7 Expectations and destinations

Introduction

With a crucial phase in their lives beginning, this study now turns to the actual early destinations of Leafield informants. In so doing, the relevance of gender, race and class in the job-seeking, YTS or educational endeavours of pupils will be traced to establish their impact on the process.

Actual 5th formers' destinations

The actual destinations of Leafield 5th formers in 1985 are recorded in Careers Office data on destinations based on their own records and their own questionnaire with school leavers (see Table 7.1). Although their data do not offer any gender or ethnic breakdown they do indicate far higher proportions of pupils in education, YTS or unemployment than ever intended to enter those fields when compared with the first choice preferences of questionnaire informants for the same year. These preferences, listed in detail in Table 6.3 are condensed into column 4 of Table 7.1 for ease of comparison. Careers Office data refer to the known destinations of 236 Leafield 5th formers and this study's questionnaire to the responses of 193 pupils from that same academic year. Although the two sets of figures are not absolutely comparable they are a strong indicator of unfulfilled aspirations and of many pupils having to accept second best, or even more flexible alternatives to their chosen futures.

Table 7.1
Destinations of Leafield 5th formers (as at 31st October 1985) compared with pupils originally aspiring to those destinations from earlier questionnaire

Destination	Nos	%	% Aspiring to that destination beforehand
6th form (1 yr course)	40	15.00	Nil
6th form (2 yr course)	20	7.50	5.00
College of Further Education	4	1.50	Nil
Employment	55	20.50	72.00*
YTS	88	33.00	2.50
Unemployment	29	11.25	Nil
Unknown	30	11.25	-
TOTAL PUPILS	266	100%	79.50%

* This figure excludes 12% who were prepared to consider 'anything'.

Sources: Bridgehurst Careers Service, Statistics for 1984/85 year (cols. 1-3); 5th form questionnaire, Leafield School, 1985) (col. 4).

Brown (1987) found that 60 per cent of his pupils were not following their previously chosen routes eighteen months after leaving school and from the evidence of informants, the local Careers Office and questionnaire respondents, Leafield pupils appeared to be following a very similar pattern, for over 50 per cent aspired to employment but did not achieve this objective.

In addition, Table 7.2 shows that of the one-third of Leafield 5th formers who went onto YTS, 10 per cent became unemployed by the end of the year with a further 15 per cent remaining in YTS for a second year. Allowing for these additional pupils whose work ambitions would not be fulfilled, it can be estimated that at least 55 per cent of Leafield 5th formers did not achieve their ambitions in relation to jobs within 12 to 18 months of leaving school despite their highly realistic aspirations. This figure could be as high as 70 per cent if the destinations of some of the 'unknowns' and pupils willing to take 'anything' are taken into account.

Table 7.2
Destinations of 5th formers who entered YTS one year after commencing training (as at 31st October 1986)

Destination	No.	%
Job with Host Employer	34	40.5
Job Elsewhere	25	30.0
Further Education	1	1.0
Continuing YTS	13	15.5
Unemployed	8	9.5
Unknown	3	3.5
TOTAL PUPILS	84	100%

Source: *Bridgehurst Careers Service, Statistics for 1985/86 year.*

Attitudes to work

One important consideration in this respect is pupils' own attitudes to work. Here, it must be emphasised that the pupils at Leafield were not work-shy. Many of the less-achievers were just bursting to leave school and get out to work and for the most part, both achievers and less-achievers who stayed on in the 6th form had a specific job or career in sight and were not continuing their education in order to avoid going out to work. Indeed the reverse was sometimes the case, a pupil would sometimes start in the 6th form or College of Further Education because no suitable job had been found, but leave immediately upon finding work (see p. 181).

For the less-achievers in particular, leaving school and starting work represented entering the real world at last. It provided financial rewards and with these the promise of some degree of independence and increased respect from parents:

> Shirley (white, working class less-achiever): 'I was pleased to get out to get paid. Treated a lot more like an adult by my parents, especially dad.'

For those who entered the 6th form, this also represented an important progression into the adult world. All such informants said they were now granted a lot more freedom and were no longer treated 'like children':

> Sheilah (black, working class achiever): 'We're treated differently now,

not like kids .... they treat you like equals .... and attendance not so rigid, just let them know you won't be in.'

Paul (white, middle class achiever): 'It's harder .... you do it to get what you want. You're treated more like adults, it's up to you if you get your work done.'

There was no evidence at Leafield to suggest West Indian-origin pupils were less committed to work than their white counterparts as suggested by Warr et al (1985). Indeed their aspirations and motivation towards employment could not be distinguished in any way from those of their same sex white peers, a feature noted by Drew and Jones (1988) in relation to Sheffield and Bradford black school leavers. They were, however, apprehensive about what the outcome of their job hunting might be:

Eddie (black, working class less-achiever): 'You can only try can't you? You know, do your best to find something.'

Shirley (White, working class less-achiever): 'You won't catch me on the dole. I'd do anything rather than be signing on.'

Less-achieving pupils set themselves highly realistic ideals in terms of their occupational choices and were even more pragmatic in what they were prepared to do if necessary. Tables 6.2 and 6.3 in the preceding chapter reveal job preferences and alternative choices for in-depth informants and 5th years respectively. The range of jobs selected as 'preferred' demonstrate a willingness to accept limited scope in employment opportunities. As Raby (1979) states:

The jobs to which they aspired strongly reflected the jobs available in the local area in which the youngsters lived (Raby, 1979, p. 256).

Beyond this, pupils were prepared to take alternative work, YTS, or consider 'anything' rather than be unemployed or forced back into school. This pattern was borne out in the actual early destinations of informants who, if anything, displayed greater pragmatism in the event than the pre-Easter questionnaire suggested, indicating a wider acceptance of YTS in particular, as an alternative if first choices did not materialise. In addition, there was no evidence of pupils 'pricing themselves out of the market ' in seeking work. Pupils were more concerned to get any job than worry about the rate of pay, a finding similar to that of Main (1987).

Among the less-achievers no-one stayed on at school beyond the minimum school leaving age. They were all very keen to start work or move on to further education away from the school environment and two did so before the school term had officially ended.

Achieving pupils were equally realistic in their choices, bearing in mind their O-level successes. Indeed, if anything there was a tendency to under-aspire vis-á-vis achievement (as discussed on p. 141-3) regarding career choices and this aspect is developed later in this chapter concerning actual destinations (see p. 179).

First destinations of informants

An examination of informants' data reveals some interesting features of the employment they found. The first destinations of the fourteen less-achieving informants are shown in Table 7.3:

Table 7.3
Less-achievers: first destinations of informants upon leaving 5th form, by gender and ethnic origin

First Destination	White Boys	W.I.* Boys	White Girls	W.I.* Girls	Total
6th form/college	1	2	1	0	4
YTS	2	1	0	3	6
Temp. or P/T Empt.	0	0	1	0	1
Perm. F/T Empt.	0	1	1	1	3
Unemployment	0	0	0	0	0
TOTAL	3	4	3	4	14

* W.I. = West Indian-origin

Source: *Leafield informants (1985)*

Table 7.4 then shows the first destinations of the six achieving informants indicating that without exception, all six continued with their education.

Table 7.4
Achievers: first destinations of informants upon leaving 5th form, by gender and ethnic origin

First Destination	White Boy	W.I.* Boy	White Girl	W.I.* Girl	Total
6th form/college	1	0	3	2	6
YTS	0	0	0	0	0
Temp. or P/T Empt.	0	0	0	0	0
Perm. F/T Empt.	0	0	0	0	0
Unemployment	0	0	0	0	0
TOTAL	1	0	3	2	6

* W.I. = West Indian-origin

Source: Leafield informants (1985)

Permanent work

Table 7.3 shows that only 3 out of these 14 less-achieving school leavers were able to find a permanent job as their first destination after school. Furthermore these ppupils had introductions to their jobs from family or friends. Griffin (1985), Day (1987) and Brown (1987) all report the belief among pupils that 'who you know, not what you know' is more important in securing work. Jenkins (1982) and Finn (1984) go beyond this by demonstrating that family and other informal contacts were of prime importance in finding work, especially for Easter leavers (Finn, 1984).

At Leafield, informants have already been demonstrated as taking heed of parental advice in formulating job aspirations and making choices, but here it is apparent that parents or friends were instrumental in every case of a pupil actually obtaining permanent work. An inference to be made from this is that pupils found it difficult to obtain permanent jobs without such help.

> Shirley (white, working class less-achiever): 'I started my job in early March .... Another Leafield girl, Julie, got a job there and I went there, cycled 15 miles and saw the Production Manager. Got an application form and filled it in. Got the job and started the following Monday.'

Shirley ditched her opportunity to revise for three CSEs in order to take this job although she returned on the due dates to sit two of them, passing with low grades. For Shirley there was no question of lingering at school in the face of such an opportunity, one which she actively pursued under her own initiative. This was in line with advice from her parents who favoured securing any job rather than being too selective:

> Shirley: 'Their advice used to be to get a job and keep looking for something better. Helping me to sort it all out .... That backing made me feel good.'

Brown (1987) found some non-achieving pupils to be in favour of leaving at Easter in order to 'beat the rush' for jobs that inevitably followed the summer term exodus. Shirley too, it would seem, protected her own interests by leaving school early to accept a job.

Vanda's job hunting also involved a friend's recommendation which led to success:

> Vanda (black, working class less-achiever): 'I applied for two jobs then a friend said there was a job in Hatfield's [local greengrocers]. I went in and three days later I got it.'

Similarly, Eric had an introduction to a juke box company. In this case, his mother had worked for them in the past and she still had contacts there having previously been secretary to the Manager. She phoned him and made her son known to him:

> Eric (black, working class less-achiever): 'I knew the Manager through my mum and my aunt. It led to an interview and I was OK.'

Eric was particularly pleased because the job involved training in electrical wiring. His preference had been for an apprenticeship in electrical engineering when asked earlier by questionnaire and this job suited both his needs and his interests. It did not offer a formal apprenticeship but it was good enough and Eric took the pragmatic route of accepting something closely in line with, but not 'spot on', his earlier employment choice.

The only other person to secure a job was Tessa, and this was a part-time job with a major department store. Tessa's parents had also tried to help her find work in the following way:

> Tessa (white, working class less-achiever): 'My parents were very helpful. Used to ask around at work regards what I wanted. Dad insisted I went out each day to look for work. Had ten applications at least and two interviews.'

Tessa's part-time work came as a result of this intensive job hunting and was taken in preference to a full-time YTS shop assistant placement with another large store:

> Tessa: 'I had both but dad chased the [department store] medical so I knew which one to take.'

Thus Tessa would have accepted a YTS counter assistant placement if nothing else had been on the horizon but faced with a choice between a part-time job shelf-filling and a full-time YTS she much preferred the part-time, permanent job:

> Tessa: 'It's part-time 7.00am to 9.00am but I do extra shelf-filling and till work [as a relief if permanent staff fail to turn up for work]. I earned £92 as my record but the lowest weeks are £30 for minimum.'

One important feature of this job for Tessa was that it had 'prospects'. Tessa felt that if she worked well and displaying willingness, she might be offered a permanent, full-time job as a shop assistant and this would give her access to promotion under the company's training scheme:

> Tessa: '[I] could be a supervisor inside a year like the boy next door. I don't moan at moves. I like Foods and don't like the rest of the tills but says nothing.'

Kirby and Roberts (1984) found that part-time work with prospects was seen as preferable to either staying on at school or accepting YTS. Tessa felt the same way, she never considered the former and did not like the idea of the latter.

In this context, Tessa was one of the 10 per cent of girls who had earlier specified their ideal job to be 'working with children'. Her alternative, acceptable choice was 'office work'. She had previously followed up both of these choices before settling on the idea of shop work. She had failed to be selected onto a local Nursery Nurse course at the College of Further Education and had disliked her office work experience placement, declaring she was 'just a skivvy' (see pp. 151-2, 165). In the light of this experience, Tessa felt that part-time shop work with prospects, where she might be rewarded for her willingness to be flexible and stand in for absent staff, was infinitely preferable to the monotonous routine of office work. She was prepared to stick with something that enabled her to demonstrate her own worth in the hope that this would lead to advancement onto the full-time, permanent payroll. It was a well thought out strategy informed by the success of a neighbour whom she hoped she could emulate, and in part, both her parents and the experience of a male peer were instrumental in the job choice she made.

Brown (1987), found that only 18 per cent of his school leavers obtained permanent jobs and that a further 72 per cent went either into the 6th form or YTS. Whilst Leafield numbers are small, it can be seen that just 22 per cent of school-leaving informants (3 out of 14) obtained full-time employment. The jobs found were in line with stated job choices cited before leaving in all cases except Shirley's. She, however, did not complete her questionnaire until after starting her job in March and indicated that she was prepared to 'stick to that' rather than look elsewhere (see p. 148).

These jobs were also found either as a result of a direct parental contact, information from a friend or family member 'pushing' after interview. Dex (1982) and Jenkins (1982) have indicated the importance of parental contacts of this kind but have emphasised that white pupils benefitted more from such contacts than blacks. At Leafield, however, Shirley and Tessa were white whilst Vanda and Eric were black, thus the informal network appeared to work equally well for all four pupils irrespective of race.

Nevertheless, it has to be said that 11 less-achievers did not enter paid work. Of these only two had intended to continue their education at the College of Further Education and the remainder had specified jobs, not education or YTS, as their preference. This means that out of a small group of 14 less-achieving school leavers in a southern town with below national average unemployment there were nine who could not meet their objective of getting a job. This despite their modest and realistic appraisal of jobs and what they would like to do. The routes of these pupils were subsequently through further education or YTS as a means of training in readiness for later full employment and the pathways taken by these pupils are traced in the following two sections.

Staying on or going to college

One option that was open to all informants was either staying on in the 6th form or going to the College of Further Education. It has already been stated that no parents were pushing their children out into the job market and none would have raised objections to their child continuing with any form of education. Most would have preferred it if their son or daughter had chosen to stay on at school (see p. 134).

Pupils were also encouraged by their teachers to stay on in the 6th form if they so wished. Pupils knew that various vocational courses were open to them and that 6th form was not just a place for the 'posh' and the 'brainy ones'. A combination of a course plus substantial work experience was also possible, and there was always the option to enter the 6th form in order to re-sit failed exams or take O-levels where CSE grades had proved promising. In addition, virtually every pupil acknowledged that 'you're treated more like an adult' in the 6th form which was something very dear to their hearts and a source of grievance in the lower part of the school. Yet this knowledge was not sufficient to lead less-achievers into 6th form studies:

> Eric (black, working class less-achiever): 'I could have got a lot more out of school, didn't try hard enough and I've got a slight regret already. But for my job I would have regretted it and wanted to stay on .... wouldn't feel like a school kid in 6th form.'

> Peter (white, working class less-achiever): '6th form is like a totally different world .... so much more relaxed, smaller. They've got more time for you.'

Despite this, neither Eric nor Peter considered staying on at school. Eric got a job with a local company:

> 'Wiring up juke boxes .... apprenticeship included.'

Peter started a B.Tec. course at the College of Further Education because he:

> 'wanted to get out of school badly.'

One reason for this was that pupils still saw school as largely irrelevant to the outside world. It was better to leave and try one's hand in the job market or obtain vocational training than stay on, wasting time at school. In

Natalie's view it was necessary to leave school in order to start learning about the outside world, and it was the beginning of 'real' adult life:

> Natalie (white, working class less-achiever): 'I want to get out into the real world. Do some growing up before going to college .... I want time to go around town, I've got an ambition to visit the local museum [of science]. I've never been to one.'

An additional reason for less-achievers not staying on at school could be that in the 5th form they had been involved in taking CSEs not O-levels. Failed O-levels were worth re-sitting for they were an entree into A-levels and a useful 'selling point' in the job market. There was, therefore, plenty of relevance in 6th form re-takes for passing meant the freedom to continue with career plans. CSEs did not have this same buying power vis-á-vis further education and pupils were, in any case, sceptical about their utility in securing work (see p. 120). They saw no real point in staying on to re-sit CSEs, it being better to try one's hand at employment which was, after all, the ultimate goal.

Achievers

Achieving pupils then, had no conflict of interests in deciding to enter the 6th form, and indeed, from Table 7.4 it can be seen that all six achievers did so. An average of 50 pupils entered the first year of the 6th form each year, the usual uptake being 20 per cent of the 5th form. Two thirds of these took one year courses primarily of a vocational nature such as B.Tec. National, RSA and Pitman's examinations or City and Guilds. A few re-took failed O-levels or CSEs. Among these were Colette, who was the only informant who needed to re-sit failed and low-grade O-levels. She did so rather than give up her plan to read Business Studies at university level.

For the remaining five achievers 6th form was a part of a natural progression into their chosen careers. Pauline and Paul, the two middle class achievers, began the A-level programmes intended to lead them towards occupational therapy and agricultural engineering respectively. Lynn, a working class achiever, was also taking A-levels in preparation for training as a teacher. The remaining two working class achievers, Sarah and Sheilah, chose less academic routes with the intention of moving out into the world of work after one year in the 6th form. Both girls began courses directly in line with their aspirations stated in 5th form. Sarah began an RSA secretarial course and armed with this qualification her intention was to work in a travel agency. Sheilah began a B.Tec. course in Business Studies and still wanted to leave school after a year and work in an office in accordance with her earlier plan. She hoped that some computer or accountancy training would be incorporated in that job and still preferred this idea to staying on longer at school or college. In this respect, it should be borne in mind that both Sheilah and Sarah had received limiting 'sensible' advice on careers at home from their mothers and sisters (see pp. 135, 142). Both girls had been encouraged not to aim too high and to obtain a qualification that would equip them for easier access into the job market. Both girls stuck to this course of action despite good O-level achievements. Sarah passed six O-levels (mostly 'C's and 'D's) plus four grade 1 CSEs, and Sheilah passed four O-levels (also mostly 'C's and 'D's) plus one grade 1 CSE. However, neither girl wavered from her original choice to use 6th form as a quick way towards a practical 'saleable' skill in the labour market.

Less-achievers

According to Table 7.1, four less-achieving informants also entered either 6th form or went into further education via college. These four were Peter and Natalie (two white pupils), plus Bedford and Winston (two West Indian-origin boys). This was true as far as initial destinations were concerned, but for some their time in further education was very limited indeed and it would be untrue to depict these pupils as becoming seriously engaged in studies beyond the minimum school leaving age.

Bedford for example, cited 6th form as his preferred destination after 5th form. This decision was taken in the light of poor CSE passes and the fact that he resisted YTS as 'cheap labour'. By the summer of 1985, he had obtained three CSEs with low grades and had been told that he did not work hard enough by his teachers:

> Bedford (black, working class less-achiever): 'Got told off for that. Mum expected more.'

However, he had been a bit unlucky. He lost a lot of time in his final 5th form year through hurting his arm (which was in plaster for a number of weeks) and this disrupted his work experience with a firm of electrical contractors, and also meant he had difficulty in writing for the best part of one whole term. Bedford wanted to be a qualified electrician and agreed to the careers teacher's suggestion of staying on to sit City and Guilds to help him into the trade for he saw this as being preferable to YTS. However, the call of paid work was too great and within a few weeks of term starting he left to accept a job on a building site. Some months later he had had a succession of such manual jobs and was to be seen digging a hole in the road in town:

> Bedford (chest deep in a hole he was digging): 'Oh yeah, that's right, I didn't stay long. Had lots of different jobs since then, like this one.'

Bedford was the only one of these four to enter the 6th form. The others preferred to move to the College of Further Education.

In Peter's case college was an alternative to school which he hated, YTS which he was ambivalent towards and unemployment which he found unacceptable. Like Bedford he began a B.Tec. course because he valued having a skill and had left school with just two CSE passes. Peter had shifted from his earlier questionnaire decision to be a Fireman and now wanted to have a trade. As with Bedford, he was not prepared to consider YTS but B.Tec. studies were an alternative route towards relevant skill training. He too, left his course as soon as a job materialised. Peter was delighted with what he had found. He spoke with great pride and enthusiasm about his new trainee's position with a firm of printers. It represented both a wage and training in something he perceived as worthwhile. For him there was no question of staying on at college in the face of a job of this calibre. He had been ready and willing to join the world of work for at least the last year of schooling and had undertaken both work experience and part-time jobs. He was well satisfied with the position he had secured:

> Peter (white, working class, less-achiever): 'I like it a lot. There's a 3-month trial period then a 3-year apprenticeship. Binding, printing, litho, typesetting, art work .... really good after lots of part-time work. £54 a week take home pay!'

Winston was the third boy to enter a College of Further Education having passed two CSEs with low grades. Winston was organised by his mother into moving to another part of the country to live with his father and into attending the college serving that area. He too started a B.Tec. course. It is not known whether he stayed the course as contact with him was lost at this point, but certainly he was there, and enjoying it, according to his mother as the first term drew to a close.

The only other person to undertake a course at the local college was Natalie, and she represented the only one of the four less-achieving informants to be there through her own efforts and dogged career motivation in the face of obstructions.

Natalie held a dream of becoming a vet, and wanted to work with animals in some professional way. She had felt insulted when the careers teacher at Leafield had seriously suggested working in a pet shop on the grounds that 'at least it's working with animals' (see p. 155).

As with Paul and Pauline, the achieving pupils who had a specific career in sight, Natalie also had been strongly influenced by her family, albeit in a different way. She had grown up on a farm and had gained a passion for animals:

> Natalie (white, working class, less-achiever): 'One teacher once said I was brainy enough to be a vet and told my parents but they've never shown any interest. My father grew up on a farm and took it for granted.'

Natalie had not had encouragement from home but had developed an interest in her father's husbandry work from talking to him and remembering things from her early childhood. She also had a fond recollection of going around with her grandfather who had run a farm and with whom she had been raised as a youngster. Such was her desire to work with animals that she could say this about the future:

> Natalie: 'I don't think I'd ever get married, my life would be complete if I got a zoo job.'

However, her ambitions had to be modified by her level of achievement for she knew that her grades were not good enough to continue with A-levels. She had been offered just one O-level in Chemistry but refused this 'because it meant staying on after Easter.' In the event she took seven CSEs including three science subjects and passed five of them, with mostly '4' grades.

Despite her 'poor' advice from the careers teacher, she had been placed on one week's work experience with a local animal rescue sanctuary which she loved. Then, a fortuitous event enabled her to pursue what she wanted. She attended the local YTS Open Day held at the local college where yet another person suggested pet shop work for her, but Natalie explained what else had happened to her that day:

> Natalie: 'I found out that same day by accident about their Animal Technology training course. I was talking to this man and I just

happened to have asked the Head of Department and he showed me round and everything. Saw the animals and that. He was very encouraging, the most ever.'

Albeit that luck had caused her to speak to precisely the right person on the YTS Open Day, to her credit, Natalie had attended that day with the intention of pursuing her interests if possible. Later, she was accepted for Animal Technology which was a full-time 3-year course at the college. Later, two months after starting the course she had this to say:

Natalie: 'It's quite difficult, Biology is O-level-like and the technical subjects .... I'm working better at the F.E. than at school, got 80 per cent recently in a Physics test on energy.'

Natalie was delighted with her success in getting on this course which she had achieved in the face of very 'negative' advice from careers advisers and no particular interest in her ambition from home. The course work was harder than she imagined but she showed every sign of wanting to stick the course. Indeed, in view of her job aspirations, she had every reason to do so.

The utility of continuing education

Overall, Natalie was the only one of four less-achievers to be in further education of her own volition. Winston was somewhat 'press-ganged' into college by his mother and the other two boys who had primarily wanted work, abandoned their studies as soon as a job arose. There was every sign that continuing education was, therefore, used primarily as a stop-gap by less-achievers who wished to avoid both YTS and unemployment. Dex (1982) arrived at similar conclusions in her longitudinal study of black and white school leavers for the Department of Employment.

For achievers, however, the picture was quite different. The studies and examinations that could be undertaken in 6th form represented a logical progression towards career objectives whether these involved A-level study leading to higher education, or a 1-year vocational course in preparation for skilled work. Again Dex (1982) has shown that girls have a greater tendency towards staying on at school than their male counterparts and this has been linked to girls' greater desire to obtain qualifications leading towards better paid, clean, white collar employment. Both Dex (1982) and Eggleston et al. (1986) found that black girls in particular used 6th form to retake exams, whilst Fuller (1980) and Dex (1982) argue that black girls use education to further their ambitions far more than black boys, who tend to reject school more.

At Leafield there were some indications that girls in general were more likely to utilise 6th form studies than boys but not necessarily for highly academic routes. Nine girls and no boys used the 6th form to re-take CSEs in 1984 but boys and girls were roughly equally represented in 6th form as a whole and took A-levels in almost equal numbers (12 girls and 14 boys) in 1985. Among the informants, there was a tendency for girls to use the 6th form in pursuance of white collar or professional employment. Here, both white and West Indian-origin girls were involved in these ambitions such that there was nothing to choose between them. Two white and one West Indian-origin girl were aiming for professional careers or university and one white plus one West Indian-origin girl wanted qualified office work after a 1-year 6th form course. The white girls represented three out of ten white informants and the black girls two out of ten, thus both white and black girls used the 6th form for these ends in similar proportions.

White and black male informants leant more towards the labour market as evidenced by the two boys (one white and one black) who deserted their studies in favour of paid work. Overall, just five girls (three white, two black) and one boy (white) stayed in the 6th form, on their intended courses for the whole of the academic year and their studies were for particular white collar or academic qualifications. No West Indian-origin boys opted for such a course of action, thus as both Riley (1985b) and Eggleston et at. (1986) state, boys more than girls opted to leave school and try either work or vocational training, and this seemed particularly true for West Indian-origin boys at Leafield.

The uptake of YTS

The idea of going onto the Youth Training Scheme had a mixed reception at Leafield School. The careers teacher, Mr Rogers, was very much in favour of it and had a reputation among pupils for singing its virtues:

> Natalie (white, working class, less-achiever): 'Mr Rogers does plug YTS .... but not necessarily at a high level.'

Natalie was referring to her own careers interview when Mr Rogers had suggested she work in a pet shop in view of her interest in animals. She was disgusted because her aim was to work with animals in some qualified way.

Mr Rogers himself made no secret of favouring YTS for school leavers. He was observed explaining to one pupil who was not keen on applying for a placement:

> Mr Rogers: 'What have you got to lose? If you get a job you can leave and if not, well, you're getting trained.'

Negative Attitudes Towards YTS

The feeling that you got the 'bum jobs' on YTS, or were 'used' led job-seeking pupils to prefer almost any kind of permanent work to a 'scheme'. This general feeling can be summed up using the questionnaire data. No boys and only three girls from a total of 193 pupils cited YTS as their preferred choice upon leaving school. However, the pragmatism mentioned earlier regarding job choices was again displayed over YTS. An average of 12 per cent of questionnaire pupils (10 per cent of girls and 14 per cent of boys) were prepared to go on a scheme if nothing better was available.

Mr Rogers suspected that family influences were largely responsible for pupils' negative reaction to YTS. He felt that in listening to the youngsters' objections:

> Mr Rogers: 'You can hear the parents talking, that's very clear'.

Evidence from informants would appear to substantiate his opinion, for pupils referred to both family and friends in citing their reasons for rejecting YTS:

> Bedford (black, working class, less-achiever): 'I dislike YTS - cheap labour. All my family thinks so, but others at school don't agree and think I'm a swot for not going on it.'

> Shirley (white, working class less-achiever): 'The girl next door did YTS in a hairdressers. All year they said how good she was .... saying she'd be kept on. In the end, he didn't, said he couldn't afford it.'

In Shirley's case, she secured a permanent job before the official school leaving date so never needed to reconsider its utility, but pupils also formed independent opinions of YTS based on their personal experiences:

> Sheilah (black, working class achiever): 'I did a solicitor's YTS ... doing

general dogsbody work.'

In Sheilah's case her early YTS experience was sufficient to make her change her mind and enter 6th form to gain some extra qualifications in the hope that then she would be able to secure a full-time job (see p. 165). Kirby and Roberts (1984) also found that YTS and school work experience was viewed as 'cheap labour'. Brown's (1987) informants felt the same way but acknowledged that YTS could provide useful training.

At Leafield, some informants were ambivalent towards YTS. They resented the pay, and comments about 'cheap labour' were frequent, but on the other hand most pupils recognised that it was better than doing nothing. Doubters were influenced by what their parents said, just as the anti-YTS pupils had been and their ultimate decision could go either way according to what was said at home.

Peter, who was prepared to consider YTS and took home lots of leaflets, was discouraged by his mother. He lived alone with her, and money was a bit tight. She steered his thinking in a way that Griffin (1985) reports happening to her female respondents:

> Peter (white, working class less-achiever): 'I originally wanted YTS as a mechanic but the Careers Office said don't go in for the main things that everyone else does. I liked computer studies but you got far behind if you didn't have one at home. Got booted out of that eventually for messing about and put on a Butchery job work experience .... got lots of leaflets from the career talks and mum said YTS means going out to get a flat.'

Peter took a further education route towards City and Guilds training, which he dropped immediately upon securing an apprenticeship in printing (see p. 181). However, it is worth noting that his interest in YTS was only in the 'mechanic' area, an area in which, as Mr Rogers explained, the old-style apprenticeships had now ben replaced by linked YTS schemes. Peter's interest in YTS was, therefore, instrumental in that it might provide him with training for a skilled, manual trade, a popular choice with many boys. This he subsequently found for himself in printing.

This instrumental approach towards training and employment displayed by Peter and others who had found jobs with 'prospects' for themselves (e.g. Tessa) was also evident in the thinking of those who did accept YTS placements. In all cases, YTS was used because it was viewed as a potential entree into permanent employment with the same employer or as useful experience in readiness for snapping up a permanent job as soon as one arose. However, in practice, the experience was frequently more disjointed than anticipated.

YTS placements and subsequent employment histories

From Table 7.3 it might be thought that YTS was a popular option for school leavers because 6 out of 14 less-achieving informants went straight onto a scheme upon leaving school. However, it is insufficient to look at these figures without considering:

(a) the pupil's own attitudes to YTS and why they accepted their placements, and

(b) their early work histories upon joining their schemes.

In view of this the intentions and experiences of YTS trainees appear below.

Philip and Duncan were two white boys who hoped that something substantial would come of their YTS placements, indeed they had received some promises. Philip left school at Easter with no CSEs and had been on two days work experience per week with a firm of coach builders since Christmas to help combat his poor attendance and his disaffection with school. This became his full-time YTS placement after Easter when he became 16 years of age and he hoped it would lead to a permanent job:

> Philip (white, working class, less-achiever): ' .... because I've been told so by the boss.'

Philip did not hold out a lot of hope about finding a job by himself and this had led him into an acceptance of a YTS placement, saying that jobs 'weren't very good'. When asked what he meant by this he said that there were not enough jobs to go round and those that were available were not always suitable. Philip was not an easy person to talk to. His ability to express himself was limited and his comments were frequently monosyllabic and non-explanatory. Pressed on the question of why jobs were no good he offered in a simple but accurate sentence:

> Philip: 'Perhaps because jobs and people don't match up.'

Philip was concerned that unskilled jobs were in short supply and that he did not have the qualifications to apply for the skilled jobs that were available. He wanted to work his way into painting and decorating like his father, and eventually to be self-employed in the absence of being successful in coachbuilding.

Philip's hopes that his YTS placements might lead to a permanent job did not come to fruition. Indeed, he did not give them time to do so. At a follow up interview in November 1985, he had left his YTS to take a job as a delivery driver's mate with a soft drinks company. He could not give his reasons for this choice other than to say his new job was 'better'. He had made the change four months earlier in favour of this job which was full-time but casual, not permanent. Indeed, the company was closing its local depot in three months time.

Duncan similarly used YTS because it held a promise of something better. He started a workshop scheme after Easter in his year of leaving (as he was taking no CSEs), on the promise of a bricklaying placement later on if one arose, the latter being his preferred type of work. However, Duncan also felt the lure of a 'proper job'. He left the workshop to take a painting and decorating job although he soon became disillusioned with it:

> Duncan (white, working class less-achiever): 'I left after a month because the pay was so bad. £36 for a 45 hour week!'

After a month's unemployment he was 'bored' and the Careers Office found him a second YTS placement doing carpentry in a community workshop.

> Duncan: 'There's a good atmosphere there, it's a good laugh .... but I'll probably start looking for a permanent job after Christmas.'

These two YTS takers were white, but the remaining four were of West Indian origin. There was a proportionately higher uptake of YTS among black informants than white and Baqi (1987) suggests that black pupils in particular use YTS rather than be unemployed. At Leafield there was evidence to suggest that less-achieving black girls had greater difficulty in securing paid work straight from school than either their black male, or white male and female counterparts. Thus other pupils avoided having to consider YTS as an option because job seeking proved fruitful. Black girls by this token, were more likely to be forced to accept YTS or nothing.

Eddie, who failed two CSEs and passed one was placed in a community printing workshop. Regarding his job preferences, he had stated on his questionnaire that he would take 'anything'. He was proud of his opportunity to train in printing over a consolidated period of time:

> Eddie (black, working class less-achiever): 'It may go on for two years including printing work.'

His ambition was to 'go up in printing' and his expectations were modest:

> Eddie: 'I want a decent job, normal hours. I would expect prejudice because I've heard of it from family and friends.'

Eddie was another difficult boy to talk to. He approached school and life with general disinterest, as well as conversations with the researcher. Earlier, he had this to say about school:

> Eddie: 'School was rubbish. I don't know why, it just was .... school's alright for reading and writing, nothing else.'

He and his brother lived with their father.

> Eddie: 'Mum's not around - we don't speak of her.'

He thought his father has a job as an electrician with an agency but he was not sure if he was qualified. His father had wanted Eddie to stay on at school or go to college but Eddie was not interested. He accepted YTS 'because there's nothing else.'

The other three West Indian-origin YTS-takers were girls. Of these, Delia missed all three of her CSE exams through being ill, although teachers suspected her of simple absenteeism:

> Delia (black, working class less-achiever): 'I left at 15 because I was ill and they sent a letter about I couldn't do my exams .... I had a chest infection. They knew because of notes.'

Delia wanted to be a hairdresser and a suitable YTS placement was found for her.

> Delia: 'I did get YTS in a hairdressers but had to stop because my blood was low. The doctor said it was too much standing.'

Despite these suggestions that perhaps hairdressing was not an appropriate occupation for her, Delia still wanted to train as a hairdresser. Of all the informants she was the most unrealistic in her outlook in view of her health and had been unemployed for some months at the time of the follow up interview.

> Delia: 'The things I wanted they said I couldn't do, like hairdressing and work in a shop because of my health record. I wanted to be a nurse but they said it was too hard.'

As a result, Delia was sat around at home most days of the week with her mother who was on social security benefit. She was in danger of forming a similar occupational pattern to that of her mother who had had various part-time jobs over the years:

> Delia: 'My mother was a cleaner for Habervilles [a private hospital] but now she's unemployed cos of high blood pressure. Doctor said stop work, even a cleaning job.'

Her vision of the future was more of an escape route than a progressive plan of action:

> Delia: 'Money for a start. I don't want to get married, not yet anyway. Possibly emigrate to another country, to my mum or dad's country, Jamaica or Barbados. Saw Barbados at 14. More family over there, everybody's friendly with everyone. It's OK around here, don't get any racial remarks or anything, but her next door is a bit moany.'

Sonia, who was also unemployed at the time of the November follow up, had similar hankerings to 'return' to the West Indies. She lived in care because her mother was dead, her father was in custody and she had not got on well with an aunt with whom she had previously lived. She had passed five out of seven CSEs and started off on a YTS placement with a large chain of newsagents having specified a preference for shop work. Here she had hit racial prejudice:

> Sonia (black, working class less-achiever): 'A part-time woman used to talk about blacks causing trouble .... and she was saying I talked a lot to my friends when I was working.'

Sonia reported this to the Careers Office and she was offered a move to another branch. It is interesting to note that the Careers Office did not challenge the employer on the event that took place, and their 'solution' was to move Sonia elsewhere. Lee and Wrench (1987) have argued that YTS perpetuates existing racist bias in the labour market and that managing agents are powerless to stop employers' racism. Austen (1987) takes a similar view. In Sonia's case, the Careers Office did not confront overt prejudice on the part of employees with the employer, choosing to remove Sonia rather than tackle the racism she encountered. At this point Sonia declined the transfer, preferring instead to seek permanent work. At the time of the follow up she had had three recent interviews with two more coming up shortly, one in a frozen food store and one in a hairdressers.

Sonia was a quick tempered girl and this had got her into trouble both in and outside school. Swearing at teachers in school had given her a bad reputation and she had been taken to court for fighting with a girl who called her 'A dumb nigger' at a leisure centre. She was given a conditional discharge. Her life did not go smoothly. Sonia's ambition was to get herself settled into a well-paid job and then do some travelling:

> Sonia: 'I don't want no kids. If I had a hairdressing job I'd stay with it. Get a flat and do it up real posh. All before I'm 18. I want to do it before I'm 18 cos I get chucked out of here then [her warden-assisted bed-sit in town.] I was born in America. My dad was from Trinidad and my mum from St Vincent. I was 10 years old when I came from there. I'm trying to save to go back to the West Indies for a holiday.'

She was the only female informant to be very anti-children, although two achieving girls were ambivalent on this issue. Her ambition to get a regular job and have a smart flat was all the more poignant because she had not had a home to really call her own for some years.

The final pupil to be involved with YTS was Diane and little is known of her progress because contact with her was lost after 5th form. During her last few months in the 5th form, Diane had gained a reputation with her teacher as 'a silly girl' despite being 'quite able'. She was often absent and anti-school in her attitude. Diane wanted to be a nurse and she had been down for eight CSEs but only turned up to take six of these and was unclassified in three of them. The remaining three she passed with '4' and '5' grades. There was no real scope for Diane to pursue her nursing interests with such grades and she drifted away from school and was always 'busy' or 'going off to an interview' when the researcher called to see her. The Careers Office had tried to place her on a YTS but Diane also proved herself to be as elusive with them. From the little she said, Diane was not favourably inclined towards YTS and preferred to try interviews for permanent jobs, but the type of work she aimed for and her success rate are unknown. However, she was unemployed and seeking work during follow up in the November of the year of leaving.

The major pattern in the uptake of YTS was that pupils simply used schemes as a stop-gap until permanent jobs turned up. Even Philip, whose employer intimated that he might be taken on full-time did not turn down the 'here and now' offer of paid work when it arose. Only Eddie (West Indian-origin) stuck to his community workshop scheme and this was consistent with his negative view that both prejudice and unemployment risks were present in the working world.

For the white boys, the pattern was to leave YTS for a full-time job even if that job was precarious in nature or poorly paid. In view of the unsatisfactory nature of the jobs the boys secured they soon left or were made redundant, pivoting them back into another YTS or into another equally precarious job (see p. 181). For the black girls the situation was much the same. Disillusioned with her YTS experience Sonia decided to go for lots of interviews for jobs rather than accept a transfer placement. Delia did the same after her YTS proved unsuitable on health grounds, although she did not seek out interviews as actively as Sonia. Diane also spent her time looking for jobs and attending interviews. The main difference between these black girls and their white male counterparts was that the girls suffered long spells (a few months) of unemployment upon abandoning YTS whereas the boys managed to move into a succession of jobs, albeit that they left these shortly afterwards because they were unsatisfactory in some way. This leads to the question of racial prejudice amongst employers, something which can be hard to prove but which Leafield black pupils had some evidence for.

Racial prejudice in recruitment

The evidence that Leafield informants met with racial prejudice from local employers was by no means conclusive but black informants had experiences they could draw upon in forming the opinion that they would meet discrimination on the grounds of racial origins when seeking work. In this respect, informants could recall more 'concrete' examples of prejudice from their job-seeking phase than they could from daily school life. As racist remarks were passed at school (see p. 95-6), this selective recall can perhaps be taken as a measure that outcomes in the job market were more important to black pupils than outcomes in the school setting. Whilst comments about school were passed off light-heartedly, discrimination encountered in seeking employment was taken far more seriously. Here, black informants pooled their other life experiences with actual job-seeking experiences to create a whole picture of the world of work which left them feeling doubtful about their equal chances of finding a job:

> Eddie (black, working class less-achiever who settled for a YTS workshop placement): 'I would expect prejudice because I've heard of it from the family and my friends.'

> Sheilah (black, working class achiever): 'I think my chances of a job will be the same as anyone else's but there was a YTS form which asked for your colour, I wasn't sure about that.'

> Bedford (black, working class less-achiever): 'I think I'll have to do more to get a job. My mother was a teacher in Jamaica but she tried and couldn't get a job over here .... Black people cleaned up the country [after World War II] and then weren't wanted.'

Out of ten black informants, two felt they had encountered racism directly from employers. Sonia's experience on her YTS placement has already been discussed (see pp. 190-1), but Vanda believed she had faced something similar before finding herself a shop assistant's job with a greengrocer:

> Vanda (black, working class less-achiever): 'Half of it is colour in getting a job. I was on my second interview, I went in and there was this [white] boy, a right dimwit, and I heard it a few days later that he got it.'

Black youth suffers higher unemployment in Britain than white youth and both direct and indirect discrimination have been identified amongst British employers in, for example, Nottingham and Birmingham, in studies by Hubbuck and Carter (1980) and Jenkins (1982). It is unlikely that Bridgehurst should differ greatly from other cities in this respect and two black pupils out of a small cohort of ten were able to recall adverse experiences. Roberts et al. (1983) in a study of West Midlands black and white school leavers, found a relationship between race, gender and qualification level such that whilst all black pupils had to look longer and try harder in order to find work, it was the black, unqualified girls who fared least well in the employment stakes. At Leafield, it seemed also to be black, less-achieving girls that were disadvantaged in seeking work for both black boys and black achieving girls met with employment success. To be black, female and poorly qualified created something of a triple disadvantage to the extent that three out of four Leafield girls in this category were unemployed at the time of the post-school follow up.

Overview of informants' destinations

A final question to ask about informants is whether or not occupational aspirations were matched by reality, and if so, for whom.

For achieving pupils, all of whom entered the 6th form the answer is chiefly in the affirmative. Limited follow up on achievers two years after leaving the 5th form revealed that five out of six had been able to achieve their career goals without modification. Sarah (white) did secure work with a travel agent after completing her RSA secretarial course and Sheilah (black) obtained office work to her liking following her B.Tec. course. Lynn (white) and Pauline (white) obtained A-evel grades that allowed them to pursue teacher training and occupational therapy training respectively in line with their earlier ambitions. Colette (black), who was one year behind her peers in the 6th form due to a year spent retaking O-levels was all set to pass her A-levels upon last contact with her (May, 1988) and was awaiting the result of polytechnic applications to read for a B.Sc. in Business Studies. Only Paul (white) had failed his A- levels and not been heard of since that time.

For the less-achievers the answer has to be a qualified negative. Eric (black), Shirley (white) and Vanda (black) secured permanent full-time jobs straight from school through parental contacts or word of mouth from friends. A fourth pupil, Tessa (white), entered part-time work in the hope that it would lead to something full-time as it had for a neighbour. These pupils who found themselves a job or apprenticeship upon leaving school tended to stick with these, at least in the short term, and were generally pleased with their jobs.

Four further pupils, Peter (white), Winston (black), Bedford (black) and Natalie (white) opted for further education. Both Peter and Bedford left very soon after term began when jobs were obtained with Peter being thrilled about securing an apprenticeship. Thus there were indications that further education was used as a stop gap by less-achievers until paid work was found.

The pattern among YTS-takers was very similar. Placements were used primarily as something to do until a job turned up, but pupils who abandoned either education or YTS tended to find jobs of an unsatisfactory or erratic nature and there was more movement between jobs than for pupils who had secured work as a first destination after leaving school. As Corrigan (1979) states:

> They change jobs very quickly; have periods of temporary unemployment; get another job; can't stand it and leave (Corrigan, 1979, p. 92).

Both Duncan and Philip (white boys) were displaying this tendency in November, six months after leaving school, and subsequent follow up a year later revealed an extended pattern of intermittent work. By this time both boys had moved on to a succession of building site and factory jobs with Philip settling (at least for a few months) with a firm of timber merchants. In addition, even more less-achieving pupils were caught in the same spiral. Bedford smiled when reminded about being seen digging a hole in the road:

> Bedford (black, working class less-achiever): 'Oh yeah, I've had a few jobs since then. I'm down at Tindales now [local factory].'

Also Peter, who had been so pleased with his apprenticeship in printing had lost his job many months before for absenteeism and not knuckling down to the work. He proceeded to a variety of casual jobs on building sites and in factories.

It is not known whether Winston remained in his Welsh College of Further Education as contact with both him and his family was lost, but his female counterpart, Natalie did not stay her course. Despite all her efforts to get onto an Animal Technology course she was to be found on a supermarket check-out a year later:

> Natalie (white, working class less-achiever): 'You've got to be stupid to stick this job .... but I'm getting engaged and I'm saving up for my bottom drawer .... My boyfriend wants me to go back to college later when he's earning enough money. I'd like to go back.'

Marriage plans overrode her employment aspirations despite her earlier declaration that she would never get married and life would be complete if she got a 'zoo job'. The impact that marriage plans can have on curbing female career aspirations has also been noted by Griffin (1985) and King (1987) in their researches with school leavers.

For some, however, commencing YTS was a road that ended only in unemployment. Delia, Sonia and Diane (all West Indian-origin girls) experienced difficulty in either sticking to YTS or getting a job as an alternative. They moved into a pattern of intermittent work and 'signing on' and suffered more frequent and longer spells of unemployment than the boys who started on YTS.

Class, race and gender dimensions in destinations

Informants with middle class job aspirations and academic achievement to match experienced little difficulty in obtaining exactly what they wanted irrespective of their actual class and racial origins, but girls were the only ones to succeed in this category. Three white and two black girls were successful in achieving their ambitions but there were no black male achievers in the 6th form. Also the white boy, Paul, of middle class origins failed his A-levels. There had been prior indication from his form teacher that his attitude to work was not quite up to standard (see p. 131) and that he became disenchanted with A-levels upon hearing about the more practically orientated B.Tec. and HND routes he could have pursued (see p. 164). These factors could have contributed to his failure.

It is well documented that middle class pupils such as Pauline and Paul, fare well in the search for jobs (e.g. Halsey, Heath and Ridge, 1980), but it is less well documented for aspiring white and black pupils from the working class. Riley (1985b) has argued that able black girls can successfully compete in the job market and the job attainment of working class, black achieving girls at Leafield serve to support her findings. White achieving girls in the same class position also fared well, but for both groups there was some evidence of under-aspiration, and in consequence lower job attainment, than their academic ability merited.

The situation was different for working class less-achievers. Here, all the pupils had working class origins and black boys fared as well as white boys in gaining employment and training but black girls did not fare as well as their white counterparts. The only pupils to be unemployed four to six months after leaving school were black girls although they had declined YTS placements offered to them.

The uptake of YTS was predominantly from white boys and black girls with no or few CSE qualifications. Among these, the boys found it easier to move on to other paid work than the girls, a feature also noted by Dex

(1982). Hence, although both groups rejected YTS after a while, this resulted in long term unemployment only for the black girls. There was some evidence of racial prejudice exercised towards two black girls as an indicator of barriers to their finding work.

Overall, nearly half the informants (nine less-achievers) were not doing what they had intended six months after leaving school. This figure rose to include one achieving pupil within the next eighteen months. In the main, they accepted this with the same kind of realism displayed in formulating their earlier job choices. They simply accepted what they saw as the best among available options. Thus, just as initial job choices were based on what was available and practicable locally, so alternatives, including YTS, were accepted as a matter of course, when faced with limited opportunities.

Mission accomplished?

In conclusion, it can be said that job expectations were not being met at Leafield for the majority of pupils. From the patterns of job attainment that existed among the twenty informants, a 'hierarchy of success' could be discerned as illustrated in Figure 7.5.

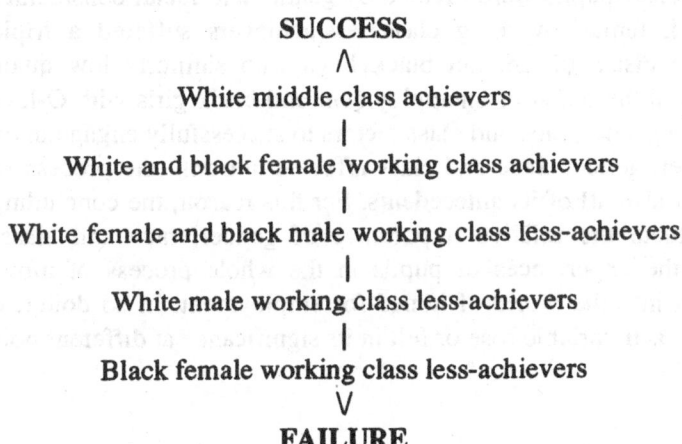

SUCCESS
∧
White middle class achievers
|
White and black female working class achievers
|
White female and black male working class less-achievers
|
White male working class less-achievers
|
Black female working class less-achievers
V
FAILURE

Figure 7.5 Diagram to show hierarchy of success in job attainment for Leafield informants according to gender, race and class factors

This 'hierarchy of success' indicates some subtle interconnections of race and gender in enhancing or detracting from life chances with gender playing a crucial role in association with level of achievement at both ends of the continuum of 'success' or 'failure'. Black girls in particular seemed to 'sink or swim' according to proven academic ability, this being the key to either their further education and choice of career or their unemployability. Black less-achieving working class boys held more of the 'middle ground', alongside white working class less-achieving girls, faring better than their white male counterparts. Crucially though, white boys with no CSEs gained access to more jobs than black girls with some CSEs, indicating greater difficulties for black girls in securing work.

Wright (1978), Roberts et al. (1983) and Riley (1985b) have researched some of these interconnections. Wright favours the power of class to override racial dimensions, whilst Roberts et al. and Riley favour the power of race in combination with gender and achievement as determining factors in labour market sucess. All are correct in their own way and for Leafield pupils different permutations of gender, race and class in conjunction with achievement served to create a 'hierarchy of success' built primarily along class lines but thereafter with a strong influence from first gender and then race in combination with academicqualification levels. The outcome of this was that middle class pupils stood a strong chance of job success but working class pupils were divided by gender and racial considerations such that black female working class less-achievers suffered a triple, if not quadruple disadvantage, but black boys with similarly low qualifications could avoid the worst of unemployment and black girls with O-levels could rise above gender, race and class factors to successfully engage in careers.

However, gender, race and class affected not only the process of finding work, but also all of its antecedents. For this reason, the concluding chapter will evaluate the relative importance of gender, race and class as they affected the experiences of pupils in the whole process of moving from education into the world of hoped-for employment. In so doing, it will be seen that each variable rose or fell in its significance at different points in the process.

8 Summary and conclusion

Introduction

This chapter seeks to review the evidence from this study in terms of the relative importance of gender, race and class in the school experiences, attitudes, aspirations and eventual destinations of Leafield pupils. These major forces on pupils' lives will be examined in turn to establish the areas of school life and transition to the adult world most affected by each. In addition, gender, race and class will be discussed in conjunction with each other for it is of key importance to examine collective as well as discrete effects of these three and to establish inter-relationships (if any) between particular factors. This is crucial in order to understand their impact at the level of the individual, for, as discussed in Chapter 1, individuals experience being male or female, and white or black and working class or middle class simultaneously within one identity.

The impact of gender

To what extent did gender affect pupils' lives at school and their eventual aspirations and destinations after the 5th form?

Evidence from participant observation indicated a major role for gender in shaping pupils' daily experiences and anticipated futures, a feature which was confirmed by subsequent questionnaire data and discussions with informants.

Experiencing School

Beginning with school experiences, it was apparent that gender firmly controlled interactions in the classroom (see Chapter 3). Firstly, pupils themselves operated a form of voluntary segregation in seating arrangements so that boys and girls sat almost exclusively with same-sex peers. Friendships were also based around pupils' own gender which ensured gender-specific clustering both in project or group work and at breaktimes when pupils walked or talked together with 'their mates'. Polarisation along gender lines was exaggerated by the girls' use of the toilets as a base during breaks (see also Griffin, 1985) and the boys use of the sports pitches and bicycle sheds.

Interactions between boys and girls were largely competitive, not co-operative. This applied again both within and outside the classroom. In class, there was much comparing of marks and indications of 'competing' between the sexes. Classroom 'mucking' was also frequently aimed at the opposite sex (e.g. via boys flicking items at girls or girls making remarks about boys).

Girls and boys also made highly gender-specific subject choices at Leafield, in some cases steered by curriculum limitations or teachers' actions (Delamont, 1980). In subtle ways this led to disadvantage among the girls, not the boys. For example, girls were loathe to enter metalwork or woodwork for they knew they would be virtually isolated among a group of males and recoiled from the teasing and barracking they would receive. Criticism was also likely from female peers who found such interests either strange, or deliberately orchestrated in order to be in boys' company. Boys entering the 'feminine' domain (e.g. needlework) were not faced with these challenges to either their interests or motives, and in another area, that of catering, courses were seen by boys and staff as useful in providing saleable skills in the job market, something not experienced by those girls who chose 'male' areas of the curriculum.

Similarly, girls lost out in typically 'masculine' areas of the curriculum such as computing and the sciences. Boys hogged both equipment and teacher attention in these lessons leaving girls on the periphery (see also Culley, 1988). Boys could also be loud and boisterous and some teachers took pains to 'protect' girls from this disruptive environment (e.g. by seating them outside the main classroom environment in corridors or in the library). By both types of event, girls became marginalised and not part of the mainstream learning experience.In a few lessons, teachers were seen to perpetuate the myth of the less confident girl pupil, and to ignore girls' interests. The boys were allowed to take up prime teacher time and attention thereby enhancing the hidden process which left girls on the margins (Measor, 1984).

Girls were also disadvantaged by virtue of sexual harassment that was meted out by the boys and not matched either in frequency or vigour by anything girls could perpetrate against boys. Sexual insults were a common feature of boys' arguments with, or about, girls. Girls were 'fair game' for horseplay (see also Cowie and Lees 1981, Wood 1987) including 'touching up', grabbing of bodies and gestures full of innuendo. Girls did not solicit such advances and, without exception, female informants aged 15 to 16 years of age were not interested in boys sexually but this did not stop the boys in seeing them as 'fair game'. Indeed, female disinterest can be seen as providing a 'challenge' to male dominance which boys had to negate by oppressive actions towards them.

Features of daily life at school such as those mentioned above affected pupils' perceptions of school. For boys, the arena was theirs, without let or hindrance, but girls were mindful that boys could, and indeed did, interfere with their educational progress in subtle ways. Girls' social groupings were also, in part, a response to the actions of boys. Girls displayed far greater solidarity with their female friends and placed greater emphasis on the importance of these friendships than did boys, frequently selecting 'female-only' refuges inside the school to be on their own, away from male interference (see also Griffin, 1985). This can be viewed as a strategy to combat the unwanted advances of boys and as a protection mechanism which in turn created separate spheres to an even greater degree and to a point which could even be described as antagonism between the sexes.

Future aspirations of girls and boys

Surmounting the above-mentioned considerations lay the fact that girls and boys at Leafield saw their futures quite differently. Girls both implicitly and explicitly incorporated subsequent marriage and childraising in their employment plans and aspirations for the future (see Chapters 3 and 6). They saw both of these events as being a long way off (i.e. some 5-10 years hence in their twenties), but acknowledged the effect that those aspects of live would have on their working lives. As a result, girls built in the prospect of marriage and motherhood into their job aspirations and expectations. Some, like Sarah, wanted to get their career underway and consolidated before marriage interfered, others like Delia and Vanda acknowledged that their paid work would have to stop, at least for a few years, whilst raising children. Either way, having a family was seen as having a profound effect upon their working lifes and girls' career and employment choices were significantly steered by the value placed on the 'caring' role of women in our society irrespective of their class background. Female job aspirations incorporated all those occupations deemed to be suitable 'women's work' (i.e. teaching, secretarial and office work; shop work; hair, fashion and beauty occupations; nursing and caring for children or animals). Such choices were heavily weighted by the type and quality of careers advice they had received at school which was essentially stereotypical in nature. Girls were primarily steered towards limited scope in shop and office work via career talks whilst boys were faced with a wide range of talks encompassing skilled manual trades and engineering. This advice was 'traditional' in being both gender and class-specific.

All the girl's choices involved providing services or care direct to other individuals thus fitting the acceptable stereotype of the nurturing and caring female figure. This was particularly clear in the case of the working class less-achieving girls who ideally wanted to work with children. Here it would seem that their lack of academic success had closed off certain career options for them, and their already limited scope in view of few qualifications was further compounded by the Parentcraft courses these girls attended. Skeggs (1988) found that girls' caring courses led them to see total mothering as the best way to rear children thus leading them away from the job market. Parentcraft therefore helped to restrict girls' horizons and Leafield girls, in stating an interest in working with children, were displaying realism as to where their futures lay both in terms of (a) weighing up their strengths and qualities (as indicated by school-based qualifications and curricula) which would govern their success in the job market, and (b) by adjusting their vision of the future to include a major role in looking after children, albeit in their own home and not as a paid occupation. Girls who made this choice were making a statement about what their whole futures would contain, a future in which paid work and family care would be integrated. A point made also by Griffin (1985) in calling for a fresh analysis of girls' aspirations.

For the boys no such meshing of potentially conflicting interests was necessary in formulating their occupational choices. Boys also selected work from their own 'male' domain favouring skilled trades and apprenticeships above any other type of work. This again was entirely consistent with their picture of the future. Boys saw a single, not a dual role ahead of them, one that hopefully involved work through to retirement age without interruption. For boys, the concept of marriage and having a family seemed equally as inevitable as among the girls but for them this had the opposite effect. For boys, having a family meant having financial responsibilities as the provider. A secure job, one that yielded a good wage, was therefore of paramount importance in this respect. Boys predominantly saw a skilled trade as offering these two desirable features of paid work. Firstly, having a skill meant being in demand and acted as a safeguard against unemployment; secondly, a skill was more saleable and commanded a higher wage in the job market than unskilled work. On both accounts, skilled work was seen as the 'answer' for life.

Early destinations

In terms of actually starting employment or remaining in education, male and female informants entered precisely the types of occupations or training generally associated with their gender. Those in work also acquired either their first or second choice destination as cited on their 5th form questionnaires. However, for the school leavers a pattern emerged whereby, within a few months of leaving, white male informants had fallen into a cycle of short-term unsatisfactory jobs and white girls were largely engaged in further education or settled into jobs. Race as well as gender appeared to be a factor in destinations such that whilst white boys were intermittent workers, black girls were the ones who were unemployed. This feature is discussed in more detail in Chapter 7.

Taking working class informants as a whole, more girls utilised further education than boys, a feature noted by other researchers (e.g. Fuller 1980, Dex 1982). Whilst this may well be to escape the worst effects of unemployment (as felt by less-achieving black girls), Leafield informants who stuck it through 6th form or college did so with specific career objectives in mind and not simply to fill in time. Here they were acting unlike their male counterparts who displayed a tendency to use further education only as a stop-gap until a job arose. Boys' greater emphasis on getting out of school and obtaining a 'decent' job as soon as possible reflected their implicit acceptance of an adult role as provider and supporter of a family and dependants. Girls escaped this imperative for their implicit assumptions incorporated breaks in employment and there was less single-minded emphasis on paid work. As a result girls found it easier to make the choice to stay on at school, for the pressure to join the workforce at the earliest possible opportunity was not as great. One irony in this, was that working class girls, in delaying entry into paid work, were actually improving their chances of obtaining work to their liking based on the returns that further qualifications would bring. Working class boys, it would seem, either did not favour or did not dare risk this option. Work was of paramount importance and success was spelt by securing it at the earliest opportunity.

The impact of race

Experiencing school

Aspects of race were far less overt at Leafield in terms of having an effect upon school experiences. Black pupils were not as vociferous in making complaints about the establishment, teachers or classmates as, for example, were white girls. Indeed, to establish how race affected school life it was necessary to 'reverse' the research process and rely mainly on observations of, and conversations with, white teachers and pupils rather than gather data on experiences directly from black pupils. Black pupils could not recount specific school incidents that had seemed racially inspired and tended to dismiss racist name-calling, treating it as a minor issue and with the contempt it deserved. It was therefore necessary to uncover the covert (and sometimes unintended) aspects of white racism at Leafield by other means, details of which are contained in Chapter 4.

Starting with the school curriculum, any multi-cultural inputs at Leafield operated on a particularly 'ad hoc' basis. Lesson content was governed primarily by the willingness of individual teachers to revise old teaching methods and introduce new material aids, and the Section 11 appointee was used mainly to ease the general teaching load and not solely to the benefit of ethnic minority education, a feature noted in other LEAs by Dorn and Hibbert (1987).

Racist humour

A great deal of white racism took the form of 'humour' and this was something practised by both staff and students. In both cases it would be more accurate to say male staff and male students. Again, white pupils, not black, were the ones who 'picked up' on this and were able to recount events. Teachers, in being familiar with pupils, indulged in jokes about ethnic minorities, their food, their customs and their names. White pupils viewed such banter as a positive attribute, one that demonstrated the teachers 'could have a laugh' (Beynon, 1984). Indeed, such humour was taken by white pupils to be 'proof' that their teachers were not racist, for in joking about the

Irish and Pakistanis, for example, teachers were seen as giving everybody the same treatment whether they were white or black.

White pupils similarly picked on racial differences to inform their 'mucking about'. Mimicking perceived racial differences (e.g. big lips and accents) and racist name-calling were forms of raising a laugh at a black person's expense. Such events that were observed always involved a white audience available on the scene to be amused, or at least, diverted momentarily from their other pursuits. Black pupils appeared not to allow such behaviour to interfere with their attitudes towards school, choosing to ignore it and guaging school more by their own levels of achievement.

In Chapter 4, it has been suggested that the absence of both a written multi-cultural and anti-racist policy served to encourage white racism, for no guidelines existed to help teachers who wished to combat classroom and breaktime incidents. However, even with such a policy, it would be possible to stick to the letter of the law without fully implementing its meaning, and pupils would still be largely at the 'mercy' of their teachers and peers in the relative privacy of the classroom. Indeed, Troyna and Ball (1985) argue that rising pupil/teacher ratios and falling teacher morale are not conducive to innovatory practices. As such, even with a written policy, things may not have changed at the 'chalk face' and the covert prejudices harboured by white pupils might not have been addressed.

White pupil racism

At Leafield the overt signs of racial jibing were slight but were just the tip of the iceberg providing only a glimpse of the bulk of racism which lay beneath the surface. White racism, as expressed openly by some informants, took the form of disliking different cultural practices (e.g. food and dress) and resenting the rights of 'immigrants' to jobs, houses and social security benefits. In this respect, no distinction was made between British-born individuals and those who had actually arrived from abroad. There was also an abhorrence of intermarriage and mixed race friendships in two male informants. One powerful message from these Leafield pupils was their intense hatred of Asians, or 'Pakis' as they were called. Here, all Asian people, irrespective of origins were termed 'Pakis' and it was this particular ethnic minority that was most resented for setting up shops, taking housing and accepting benefits. The cultural distinctiveness of Asian people was also resented owing to an implicit belief that people who live in Britain should try to be like 'us'. Here, West Indian-origin people fared slightly better, escaping the worst of white prejudice by virtue of speaking English as a mother-tongue, conforming to Western dress and enjoying (and also contributing to) popular music.

Here a link could be found between gender and white racism for white boys were more inclined to make perjorative statements than white girls. Conversely, white girls far more than white boys offered sympathy in their remarks when discussing the way black people were treated in school. Here it could be said that boys' greater dedication to finding and keeping employment for life led to their greater fear of 'foreigners' taking jobs, and the attendant risk of unemployment that could follow if too many people were seeking too few jobs. Girls, in incorporating the 'caring' role in both paid work and a projected home life, were more readily able to identify with the needs, welfare and problems of black people and therefore demonstrated a 'protective' and 'caring' stance in support of them. For both white boys and girls, these views were entirely consistent with what society expected of them and they expected of themselves.

Black pupils' aspirations

Moving on to black pupils' aspirations and job expectations, only black girls' lack of interest in working with children differentiated their job choices from those of their white counterparts. Black girls aspired to white collar office work, sales work, and hairdressing to the same extent as their white peers (see Chapter 6, Table 6.2) and in all cases, aspirations were realistic in view of their proven O-level or CSE ability. Black boys also made choices indistinguishable from those of their white counterparts. Black boys valued skilled trades just as white boys did and here again aspirations were practical and realistic when viewed against both personal academic achievement (CSE passes only) and available work in the local labour market (see also Eggleston et al., 1986). Black pupils were also just as keen to start work as their white peers and were equally industrious in seeking work, something also noted by Drew and Jones (1988).

One notable feature among the ten black informants (who represented the entire cohort of West Indian-origin pupils in the 5th year) was that there were no male achievers. No black boys had been put in for O-level examinations, but two of the six black girls had. These two girls found school interesting, unlike their black peers, and expressed the desire to continue with education in the 6th form in order to gain additional qualifications ready for the working world. Fuller (1980), Dex (1982) and Eggleston et al. (1986) have documented black girls' greater interest in utilising further education. As Wrench (1987) states:

This might be understood in terms of greater ambition and a determination to gain vocational training and educational qualifications by these young people, but might also reflect a knowledge of the greater difficulties they face in the labour market through racism (Wrench, 1987, p. 135).

At Leafield, the two black girls, Sheilah and Colette, who did stay on at school definitely did so in order to obtain qualifications required for the careers they had in mind (Sheilah wanted RSA secretarial skills in readiness for office work and Colette wanted A-levels to do a B.Sc. in Business Studies). Ironically, the pupils who left school at 16 years of age were the ones who anticipated racial discrimination in finding work (see Chapter 7 for examples of black pupils' concerns), but this did not lead them to reconsider their choice to leave school as soon as possible.

Early destinations

Race appeared to be an important factor in securing work but this interlinked with gender such that an overall statement regarding black pupils' employment destinations cannot be made without reference to gender. Beyond this, academic achievement was also an important factor such that:

(i) black achieving girls succeeded in obtaining the work or training they desired, and

(ii) black less-achieving boys succeeded in finding work or training in line with their objectives, but

(iii) black less-achieving girls were far more likely to rely on YTS or be unemployed after leaving school.

As previously stated, Sheilah and Colette, the two achieving black pupils succeeded in obtaining office work and A-levels respectively and entered into the work and higher education of their choice. This is in line with Riley's (1985b) contention that young black women who succeed academically are able to successfully challenge oppression and racism in the labour market. Two black less-achieving boys and one black less achieving girl were also able to secure employment but the two who did this most successfully had personal contacts to thank for it. Eric obtained his apprenticeship through the representations his mother made to her ex-boss, and Vanda found her grocery shop work through being told by a friend that a vacancy was coming up and approaching the proprietor directly. In Vanda's case the contact a friend could make was particularly helpful for she had already experienced a refusal from an employer where she suspected racial prejudice (see Chapter 7). Bedford also found work, or rather a succession of unskilled manual jobs, but these were without the benefit of contacts. The work he found was not as secure or satisfactory as that found by Eric and Vanda who were content with their jobs and remained in them at least until the time of the follow up interviews.

Parental and other informal contacts were therefore as crucial for black pupils in securing work as for their white counterparts. At Leafield, such informal networks seemed to operate as frequently for black informants as for white, contrary to the findings or other studies (e.g. Jenkins, 1982).

Parental contacts and informal networks were lacking for the four black pupils (one boy and three girls) whose first destination was YTS. Of these, only the black boy, Eddie, remained on his scheme and all three black girls were unemployed and actively seeking work at the follow up stage. There was some evidence that racial discrimination had taken its toll on two of these pupils, although they chose different solutions. Eddie, who had earlier expressed an expectation of prejudice amongst employers subsequently preferred the security of his two-year printing community workshop place to the vagaries of the job market and did not make attempts to break away from YTS in the way his less-achieving white counterparts did. Sonia, who also began YTS, came up against racism from a fellow employee who complained about her. After that she decided to abandon YTS and try for full time permanent work on her own, instead. The net result was that Sonia and two other less-achieving black girls, Delia and Diane, were the only three out of twenty informants to be unemployed at the time of the post-school follow up.

It can be argued that girls like Sonia, Delia and Diane do not represent the same calibre of prospective YTS trainees as white girls owing to the greater tendency of black girls to utilise further education thus reducing the quality of the YTS pool (Wrench, 1987), and that this affects their YTS success. However, this does not account for the unemployment of these three Leafield black girls. Delia had to leave her hairdressing placement for health reasons, Sonia left because of racial discord at her place of work and her rejection of a transfer, and Diane resisted YTS placement offers altogether.

What did distinguish these black girls, however, was their inability to obtain alternative employment upon giving up YTS and here they were singularly unsuccessful vis-á-vis their white peers. Their two white, male

YTS counterparts also gave up their YTS placements but did so because work was obtained elsewhere. This work, however poorly paid or unsatisfactory was nevertheless obtainable in a way that did not seem possible for black girls, indeed boys proceeded to obtain a succession of these jobs whereas black girls could not find any. Sonia and Diane in particular were very busy attending a host of interviews, perhaps indicating that there was resistance amongst employers towards engaging black girls that did not occur for either white or black boys. Indeed, the two black boys, Eddie and Bedford had not even needed to resort to YTS, for they found paid work instead and were able to keep themselves in work. In this respect, there was some indication that black boys were more successful than completely unqualified white boys because Duncan and Philip had left school with no qualifications at all and had started on YTS before being able to find 'proper' jobs. Black boys had avoided this step by securing a job.

Expressed another way, qualifications above the level of CSE were crucial to black girls in determining their job success, and lesser qualified black girls faced far more difficulty in finding work than either their white female or white male less-achieving peers, a feature also noted by Roberts et al. (1983). Black boys' experiences of the labour market were indistinguishable from those of their white male and female peers indicating a specific disadvantage in being female and black and poorly qualified.

The impact of class

Experiencing school

The subtleties of class origins pervaded many aspects of schooling and the transition into work, YTS or unemployment.

To begin with, class more than gender or race, affected pupils attitudes towards school. Thus, class origins informed opinions regarding the worth of schooling for both boys and girls, black or white. The main thrust of working class opinion was that school was both boring and a complete waste of time (see Chapter 5). Working class pupils saw no real relevance for their lives in the subjects they were forced to study and they could not see any application of the knowledge transmitted in school in their anticipated future working lives. By extension, exams, (and in particular CSE examinations) were seen as largely irrelevant in both seeking and acquiring work. There was widespread belief that employers were more concerned with physical appearance and personal qualities than pieces of paper, and that 'who you know, not what you know' was of major importance in securing a job. Evidence collected during the job seeking phase of informants would appear to show that pupils were correct in holding these views (see Chapter 7). Jenkins (1982), Finn (1984) and others have emphasised the importance of the informal network primarily for white pupils but at Leafield it was clear that the efficacy of such networks also held true for blacks and whites, males and females.

Middle class pupils at Leafield did not share the view that school was boring and irrelevant to their futures. Indeed, there was a complete polarisation of attitudes as recorded by Lacey (1970) many years ago. Middle class pupils found school interesting and the subjects they took had plenty of relevance, for they provided a vital link towards gaining the O-level and A-level qualifications required in order to train for the jobs and careers they aspired to. Polarisation at Leafield was also indicated by the less-achievers' terminology for achieving pupils whom they referred to as the 'brainy' and 'posh' ones.

This polarisation of attitudes towards school was obscured only by the pro-school attitudes of a few achieving working class pupils. Evidence from informants suggested that such pupils were unique in having both a genuine interest in school and highly positive parental support for education and its continuation in the 6th form. This support was forthcoming for a minority of pupils irrespective of gender although there was evidence that West Indian-origin mothers in particular, were keen for their sons and daughters to remain in education and seek further qualifications (see also Riley, 1985b).

With regard to the curriculum, there was evidence that some teachers made no attempt to access working class pupils' interests in the classroom (see Chapter 5). Pleas for alternative topics and teaching methods did not meet with a positive response. As such, middle class values in education predominated and pupils with middle class origins, or middle class occupational aspirations, were the ones most suited to the knowledge transmitted at school through familial 'cultural capital' (Bordieu, 1973). This enabled them to engage successfully with the values and knowledge on offer which would stand them in good stead for passing the examinations so crucial to their career aspirations.

Class and aspirations

Another important feature of class origins was the effect that this had on job aspirations. Almost without exception, working class informants selected working class occupations and middle class ones selected middle class occupations. Only middle class pupils made choices that could be termed 'careers'. For both classes, the impact of parental influences was marked, for all pupils were mindful of parental advice and parental job experiences in what they, themselves, aspired to. As in many other studies (e.g. Corrigan 1979, Raby 1979, Griffin 1985, Brown 1987), Leafield pupils selected occupations primarily from what they saw around them, both in terms of what parents and siblings did for a living and in terms of the scope available in the local labour market. The particular notice that pupils took of family advice in forming their aspirations and job choices, led, in the case of working class pupils to a perpetuation of their class position akin to the working class entrapment described by Willis (1977) in his study of how his 'lads' ended up on the factory floor.

This was compounded by the help parents and friends gave to school leavers via the contacts they could make with employers. The result of family contacts was intergenerational continuity whereby sons and daughters gained successful introductions to the work places or occupational spheres of a parent. The result of advice from working class friends also created situations whereby pupils came to be working either alongside or in the same industry as neighbours or friends, as happened to Shirley and Tessa, (see Chapter 7). Such advice and assistance was compounded by the traditional working class nature of careers advice at the school with talks centering on skilled trades for boys and shop, office and child-care work for girls.

The advice of working class parents was also instrumental in limiting the career aspirations of working class achievers. Thus, although support for education and qualifications was proffered, advice on occupations was cautious, such that vocational and short-term courses were more frequently suggested with the practical aim of assisting the young person into secure work. Far reaching, long-term and 'risky' goals were not advocated by working class parents and as informants invariably took parental advice into consideration, this led to a pattern of under-achievement in employment destinations among achieving, working class pupils vis-á-vis their academic ability.

Early destinations

Actual employment destinations for middle class informants closely followed their job aspirations but for working class informants the situation was different. Those who did secure work generally found themselves in either their preferred or second choice job based on earlier questionnaire returns. However, only 50 per cent were actually doing what they had aspired to 18 months after leaving and Careers Office statistics combined with Leafield School questionnaire data revealed that over half of all 5th formers were left with unfulfilled ambitions.

Working class informants relied far more on YTS or further education than they had originally envisaged doing (see also Dex, 1982), indicating that these two avenues were utilised as a 'stop-gap' until employment could be found. Indeed, working class boys in particular, soon 'ditched' their placements in favour of full time jobs even though these were frequently erratic, poorly paid or involved long hours (see Chapter 7). A pattern emerged whereby white working class boys in particular were drawn into a cycle of such jobs interspersed with short periods of unemployment, a cycle identified by Corrigan (1979) among boys from a northern town in Britain.

For working class girls the pattern was rather different and depended more on racial origins and levels of achievement. White, less-achieving, working class girls tended to secure permanent work and stick with it (or enter further education), but black, working class, less-achieving girls relied more heavily on YTS as a starting point and suffered more unemployment upon leaving or refusing schemes, a pattern referred to in Chapter 7. These differing routes (i.e. work/education versus YTS) disappeared when considering black and white achieving working class girls. Here, both black and white entered the 6th form in order to obtain additional qualifications and all informants in this group then proceeded to job and college destinations of their choice, indicating as Riley (1985b) suggests, that qualified black girls can hold their own in the labour market.

Conclusion

Taking Leafield life in school as a reference point, gender, race and class all played an important part in shaping classroom and other school experiences. Emanating from teachers came evidence that both sexual and racial discrimination were employed in the classroom and that working class interests were not accommodated in their teaching. Teachers also typified pupils according to broad racial and class stereotypes. The curriculum was also found to be primarily gender-biased whilst displaying insensitivity towards the interests and needs of both black and working class pupils. Careers advice was also restrictive, serving to limit the horizons of pupils primarily according to gender but also according to class.

From the perspective of the pupils, class informed their opinions of school such that working class pupils held predominantly anti-school attitudes. Class overrode gender and racial considerations in attitudes towards school, but gender rose above all other considerations in the area of pupil-pupil interactions which centered primarily on separateness and an element of competition and vying with the opposite sex, but also involved boys in direct harassment of girls both inside and outside lessons. Racial tensions were not present at Leafield, and racial prejudice in school was not an issue as far as black informants were concerned, but white racism lurked beneath the surface in the attitudes and beliefs of white pupils to an extent not recognised by black pupils. White racism transcended the class divide but there was some evidence that girls displayed greater sympathy and concern for the mal-treatment of black people than did boys. This is attributed to the socialised propensity in girls to develop a more 'caring' and 'nurturing' role towards others.

In the area of aspirations for the future, race did not appear to be a factor in what pupils ideally chose for themselves. However, race, or rather being black, interconnected with gender later in disfavouring black girls in the labour market. Class and gender were of crucial importance in job aspirations however, such that pupils simultaneously made both class-specific and gender-specific choices for the future. Of the two, gender overrode class inasmuch as traditionally 'male' and 'female' occupations were selected by all pupils irrespective of class position or academic ability. In addition, all female informants took into account the prospect of marriage and motherhood and this was incorporated in their aspirations, either by their interest in working with children or by their estimation of time spent out of the job market raising children.

Class background was also a powerful factor encouraging pupils to make realistic assessments of the job market and pragmatic choices in jobs based on the occupations of other members of the family and friends. Working class backgrounds could sometimes be negated by achieving pupils in conjunction with parental support for white collar, occupational goals but even so, there was evidence that academically able working class pupils did not harbour 'high-flying' ambitions and in fact under-aspired vis-á-vis their proven ability.

However, in the area of actual early destinations, race sprang to the fore as a major variable impeding the acquisition of desired employment. Here there was linkage between gender, race and class such that less-achieving working class black girls were the only informants to be unemployed when the study was concluded. In contrast, white, middle class pupils and achieving, black and white working class pupils aspiring to middle class occupations, were successful in matching their aspirations. Here, more girls than boys were upwardly mobile from working class origins.

Most white working class pupils found work in line with their choices but for some this involved accepting YTS placements in their chosen field, and for many their occupational choices were so flexible that it was not difficult to 'match' destinations with aspirations.

To summarise, class origins played a primary role in the formation of pupils' attitudes towards school and class, race and gender were involved in how teachers reacted to pupils. Gender considerations were of prime importance in how pupils interacted with each other. Class and gender were crucial to the occupational choices and career aspirations of pupils and race plus gender was crucial to whether these were achieved in the market place. The interaction of these variables in pupils' lives meant that white middle-class pupils thrived at school and were more likely to succeed in their chosen careers, but that white working class pupils found school irrelevant to their subsequent manual jobs. Girls and boys polarised both at school and in their job aspirations. Race provided an added dimension linked to gender such that black, working class, less-achieving girls were particularly disadvantaged in terms of actual destinations upon leaving school and gaining qualifications held the key to black, working class girls' success.

Put broadly the main impact of gender, race and class on Leafield pupils can be summarised as follows:

- class mostly informed attitudes to school, achievement and going out to work,

- gender mostly informed personal interactions and job choices,

- race mostly informed the degree of success in the labour market in connection with gender and achievement.

Appendix 1

Leafield 5th form pro-forma questionnaire

I am currently doing research into how pupils have got on at school, and what they have thought of it all, including their plans for the future. Your opinions are important and you can help me enormously in my work if you are willing to answer the following questions. All replies are strictly confidential to me and will not be seen by any member of staff, parent, or any other person.

Please hand this questionnaire back to me at the end of this session.

Thank you,

Amanda

1) Name:

2) Form:

3) Address:

4) When do you intend to leave school?

5) What would you most like to do when you leave?

6) What else are you prepared to do, if necessary?

7) Do you already have a job fixed up?   Yes/No

If so, please give type of work and employer's name:-

8) What have you done so far towards finding work, further training, etc?

(Please tick)

Attended school careers talks
Visited Careers Office
Requested career information
Written to employers
Attended interviews
Spoken with relatives
Spoken with friends

Other action (Please give details)

9) What work experience have you done?

10) What did you think of it?

11) Do you think your schooling has helped you to get a job?   Yes/No

Please give your reasons:-

12) What, if anything, have you liked about school?

13) What, if anything, have you disliked about school?

14) In your opinion, what could be done to improve schooling?

15) What do you think of the careers advice available in school?

16) What else could be done to help with advice on jobs?

17) How do you rate your chances of finding a good job?
    (Please tick)

Very good
Good
Fair
Poor

Appendix 2

Names and groupings of the twenty in-depth informants

The girls

White girls

Pauline	Middle class achiever
Sarah	Working class achiever
Lynn	Working class achiever
Natalie	Working class less-achiever
Tessa	Working class less-achiever
Shirley	Working class less-achiever

Black girls

Colette	Working class achiever
Sheilah	Working class achiever
Diane	Working class less-achiever
Delia	Working class less-achiever
Sonia	Working class less-achiever
Vanda	Working class less-achiever

The boys

White boys

Paul	Middle class achiever
Peter	Working class less-achiever
Philip	Working class less-achiever
Duncan	Working class-less-achiever

Black boys

Eric	Working class less-achiever
Bedford	Working class less-achiever
Winston	Working class less-achiever
Eddie	Working class less-achiever

Bibliography

Abrahams, R. (1972), 'Joking: The Training of the Man of Words in Talking Broad', in Kochman, T. (ed.) *Rappin' and Stylin' out*, University of Illinois Press, Champaign-Urbana, pp. 215-240.
Acker, J.R. (1980), 'Women and Stratification: a review of recent literature', *Contemporary Sociology*, January, pp. 25-35.
Allport, G.W. (1954), *The Nature of Prejudice*, Addison Wesley: London.
Anyon, J. (1983), 'Accommodation and resistance by working class and affluent females to contradictory sex-role ideologies', in Barton, L. and Walker, S. (eds.), *Gender, Class and Education*, Falmer Press: Lewes, pp. 19-37.
Austen, R. (1987) 'YTS, Black Girls and the Careers Service', in Cross, M. and Smith, D.I. (eds.), *Black Youth Futures*, National Youth Bureau: Leicester, pp. 59-72.
Bagley, C. (1971). 'A comparative study of social environment and intelligence in West Indian and English children in London', *Social and Economic Studies*, 20, pp. 420-430.
Ball, S.J. (1981), *Beachside Comprehensive: A Case Study of Secondary Schooling*, Cambridge University Press: Cambridge.
Baqi, L. (1987), 'Talking about YTS: the views of black young people', in Cross, M, and Smith, D.I. (eds.), *Black Youth Futures*, National Youth Bureau: Leicester, pp. 80-87.
Barnes, D. and Todd, F. (1977) *Communication and Learning in Small Groups*, Routledge and Kegan Paul: London.
Becker, H.S. (1952), 'Social class variation in pupil-teacher relationships' *Journal of Educational Sociology*, Vol. 25, No. 8, pp. 451-465.
Becker, H.S. (1963) *The Outsiders*, The Free Press: New York.
Bernstein, B. (1970), 'Elaborated and restricted codes: their social origins and some consequences', in Danziger, K. (ed.), *Readings in Child Socialisation*, Pergamon: Oxford, pp. 165-186.
Bernstein, B. (1975), *Class, Codes and Control*, Vol. 3, Routledge and Kegan Paul: London.

Bergqvist, K. and Saljo, R. (1987), 'What counts as valid talk? Communicating in the Comprehensive Classroom'. Paper presented at the conference on Ethnography and Inequality, St Hilda's College, Oxford, 14-16 September.

Beynon, J. (1984), ' "Sussing out" teachers: pupils as data gatherers', in Hammersley, M. and Woods, P (eds.), *Life in School*. Open University: Milton Keynes, pp. 121-144.

Beynon, J. and Atkinson, P. (1984), 'Pupils as data gatherers: mucking and sussing', in Delamont, S. (Ed), *Readings on Interaction in the Classroom*, Methuen: London, pp. 255-272.

Birksted, I.K. (1976), 'School performance viewed from the boys', *Sociological Review*, Vol. 24, No. 1, pp. 63-77.

Blackledge, D. and Hunt, B. (1985) *Sociological Interpretations of Education*, Croom Helm: London.

Bordieu, P. (1973), 'Cultural reproduction and social reproduction', in Brown, R.K. (Ed), *Knowledge, Education and Cultural Change*, Tavistock: London, pp. 71-112.

Bordieu, P. (1987), 'What Makes a Social Class?' *Berkeley Journal of Sociology*, Vol. XXXII, pp. 1-17.

Bowles, S. and Gintis, H. (1976), *Schooling in Capitalist America: Educational Reform and the Contradictions of Economic Life*, Routledge and Kegan Paul: London.

Brah, A.K. (1984), 'Unemployment and Racism: Asian Youth on the Dole', paper presented to the British Sociological Association annual conference, Bradford, 2-5th April.

Brewer, R.I. and Haslum, M.N. (1986), 'Ethnicity: the experience of socio-economic disadvantage and educational attainment', *British Journal of Sociology of Education*, Vol. 7, no. 1, pp. 19-34.

Brittan, E.M. (1976), 'Multiracial Education 2 - teacher opinion on aspects of school life: pupils and teachers', *Educational Research*, Vol. 18, No. 3, pp. 182-191.

Brown, P. (1987), *Schooling Ordinary Kids: Inequality, Unemployment and the new Vocationalism*, Tavistock: London.

Burgess, H. (1983), *An Appraisal of Some Methods of Teaching Primary School Mathematics*, Unpublished MA dissertation, University of London, Institute of Education.

Burgess, R.G. (1983), *Experiencing Comprehensive Education: A Study of Bishop McGregor School*, Methuen: London.

Burgess, R.G. (1984), *In the Field: An Introduction to Field Research*, George Allen and Unwin: London.

Burgess, R.G. (1986) *Sociology, Education and Schools: An introduction to the sociology of education*, Batsford: London.

Burgess, R.G. (1987), 'Something you learn to live with?: Gender and inequality in a comprehensive school'. Paper presented to the Ethnography and Inequality Conference, St Hilda's College, Oxford, 14-16 September.

Cameron, D. (1985), *Feminism and Linguistic Theory*, Macmillan: London.

Carby, H. (1981), 'White woman listen! Black feminism and the boundaries of sisterhood', in Centre for Contemporary Cultural Studies, *The Empire Strikes Back*, Hutchinson/CCCS, University of Birmingham: London, pp. 212-235.
Central Advisory Council for Education (1976), *Children and their Primary Schools*, Vol. 1. HMSO, London.
Cockburn, C. (1987), *Two-Track Training: Sex Inequalities and YTS*, Macmillan: Basingstoke.
Cohn, T. (1987), 'Sticks and stones may break my bones but names will never hurt me'. *Multicultural Teaching*, Vol. V, No. 3, pp. 8-11.
Cohn, T. (1988), 'Sambo - A study in name-calling', in Kelly, E. and Cohn, T. *Racism in Schools - New Research Evidence*, Trentham: Stoke-on-Trent, pp. 29-63.
Collier, K.G. (1978), 'School focussed INSET: questions posed by a three month consultancy'. *British Journal of In-Service Education*, Vol. 5, No. 1, pp. 43-49.
Corrigan, P. (1979), *Schooling the Smash Street Kids*, Macmillan: London.
Cowie, C. and Lees, S. (1981), 'Slags and Drags', *Feminist Review* No. 9, October 1981, pp. 17-31.
Crompton, R. (1976), 'Approaches to the study of white-collar unionism', *Sociology*, Vol. 10, No. 4, pp. 407-426.
Crompton, R. (1979), 'Trade unionism and the insurance clerk', *Sociology*, Vol. 13, No. 4, pp. 401-426.
Culley, L. (1988), 'Girls, Boys and Computers', in *Educational Studies*, Vol. 14, No. 1, pp. 3-8.
Curtis, L. (1984), *Nothing but the Same Old Story, The Roots of Anti-Irish Racism*, Information on Ireland: London.
Dalton, M. (1959), *Men Who Manage*, Wiley: New York.
David, M.E. (1985), 'Motherhood and social policy - a matter of education?'. *Critical Social Policy*, Issue 12, pp. 28-43.
Davies, L. (1979), 'Deadlier than the Male? Girls' Conformity and Deviance in School', in Barton, L. and Meighan, R. (eds.), *Schools, Pupils and Deviance*, Nafferton: Driffield, pp. 59-72.
Day, B. (1987), 'Rites of Passage: education policy from the perspective of school leavers', *Policy and Politics*, Vol. 15, No. 3, pp. 147-155.
Deem, R. (1978), *Women and Schooling*, Routledge and Kegan Paul: London.
Delamont, S. (1980), *Sex Roles and the School*, Methuen: London.
Department of Educations and Science (1986) *Statistics of Education, Vol. 2: School Leavers, CSE and GCE, England 1985*, HMSO: London.
Department of Employment (1984), 'Unemployment and ethnic origin', *Department of Employment Gazette*, June, pp. 260-264.
Dex, S. (1982), *Black and White school-leavers: the first five years of work*, (Research Paper No. 33), Dept. of Employment: London.
Dorn, A. and Hibbert, P. (1987), 'A comedy of errors: Section 11 funding and education', in Troyna, B. (ed.), *Racial Inequality in Education*, Tavistock: London, pp. 59-76.

Drew, D. and Jones, B. (1988), 'Ethnic Differences in the Youth Labour Market', *New Community*, Vol. XIV, No. 3, pp. 412-425.

Driver, G. (1980), *Beyond Underachievement: Case Studies of English, West Indian and Asian School-leavers at Sixteen Plus*, Commission for Racial Equality: London.

Dyhouse, C. (1977), 'Good Wives and little mothers: social anxieties and the schoolgirls' curriculum', *Oxford Review of Education*, Vol. 3, No. 1, pp. 21-25.

Eggleston, J., Dunn, D., Anjali, M., and Wright, C. (1986), *Education for Some: The Educational and Vocational Experiences of 15-18 year-old Members of Minority Ethnic Groups*, Trentham: Stoke-on-Trent.

Evans-Pritchard, E.E. (1940), *The Nuer: A Description of the Modes of Livelihood and Political Institutions of a Nilotic People*, Oxford Uniersity Press: Oxford.

Fawcett Society (The), (1984), *The Class of '84: A study of girls on the first year of the Youth Training Scheme*, The Fawcett Society: London.

Figueroa, P. and Swart, L.T. (1986) 'Teachers' and pupils' racist and ethnocentric frames of reference: a case study', *New Community*, Vol. XIII, No. 1, pp. 40-51.

Finn, D. (1984), 'Leaving school and growing up: work experience in the juvenile labour market', in Bates, I et al., *Schooling for the Dole? The New Vocationalism*, Macmillan: London, pp. 17-64.

Fuller, M. (1980), 'Black girls in a London Comprehensive School', in Deem, R. (ed.), *Schooling for Women's Work*, Routledge and Kegan Paul: London, pp. 52-65.

Furlong, A. (1986), 'Schools and the Structure of Female Occupational Aspirations', *British Journal of Sociology of Education*, Vol. 7, No. 4, pp. 367-377.

Furlong, J. (1984) 'Black resistance in the liberal comprehensive', in Delamont, S. (ed), *Readings on Interaction in the Classroom*, Methuen: London, pp. 212-236.

Garnsey, E. (1978), 'Women's work and theories of social stratification', *Sociology*, Vol. 12, No. 2, pp. 223-244.

Giddens, A. (1973), *The Class Structure of the Advanced Societies*, Hutchinson: London.

Goffman, E. (1963), *Stigma; Notes on the Management of Spoiled Identity*, Prentice-Hall: Englewood Cliffs.

Glass, D.V. (Ed), (1954) *Social Mobility in Britain*, Routledge and Kegan Paul: London.

Goldthorpe, J.H. (1980), *Social Mobility and Class Structure in Modern Britain*, Clarendon Press: London.

Goldthorpe, J.H. (1983), *Revised class schema 1983, based on OPCS Classification of Occupations 1980*, mimeo, Nuffield College: Oxford.

Goldthorpe, J.H. and Hope, K. (1974), *The Social Grading of Occupations: A New Approach and Scale*, Clarendon Press: Oxford.

Griffin, C. (1983), 'Women's Work, Men's Work: the great divide', in Wolpe, A. and Donald, J. (eds.), *Is there anyone here from education?*,

Pluto Press: London, pp. 71-75.

Griffin, C. (1985), *Typical Girls? Young Women from School to the Job Market*, Routledge and Kegan Paul: London.

Griffin, C. (1987), 'Young Women and the transition from school to unemployment: a cultural analysis', in Weiner, G. and Arnot, M. (eds.), *Gender under Scrutiny: New Inquiries in Education*, Hutchinson: London, pp. 213-221.

Halsey, A.H., Heath, A.F. and Ridge, J.M. (1980), *Origins and Destinations: Family, Class and Education in Modern Britain*, Clarendon Press: Oxford.

Hamblin, A. (1983), 'Is a feminist heterosexuality possible?', in Cartledge, S. and Ryan, J. (eds.), *Sex and Love: new thoughts on old contradictions*, Women's Press London, pp. 105-123.

Hammersley, M. (1981), 'Ideology in the Staffroom? A critique of false consciousness', in Barton, L. and Walker, S. (eds.), *Schools, Teachers and Teaching*, Falmer Press: Lewes, pp. 331-342.

Hanson, J. (1987), 'Muslim Girls', paper presented to the Ethnography and Inequality Conference at St Hilda's College, Oxford, 14-16 September.

Hargreaves, D.H. (1967), *Social Relations in a Secondary School*, Routledge and Kegan Paul: London.

Hargreaves, D.H. (1977), 'The process of typification in classroom interaction: models and methods', *British Journal of Educational Psychology*, Vol. 47, No. 3, pp. 274-284.

Hargreaves, D.H. (1978), 'Power and the paracurriculum', in Richards, D. (ed.), *Power and the Curriculum: Issues in Curriculum Studies*, Nafferton,: Driffied, pp. 97-108.

Hargreaves, D.H., Hestor, S.K. and Mellor, F.J. (1975) *Deviance in Classrooms*, Routledge and Kegan Paul: London.

Heath, A. (1981), Social Mobility. Fontana: London.

Heath, A. and Britten, N. (1984), 'Women's jobs do make a difference: A Response to Goldthorpe', *Sociology*, Vol. 18, No. 4, pp. 475-490.

Hubbuck, I and Carter, S. (1980), *Half a chance: report on job discrimination against young blacks in Nottingham*, CRC/CRE: Nottingham.

Humphreys, L. (1970), *Tearoom Trade*, Nelson: London.

Jackson, P. (1968), *Life in Classrooms*, Holt, Rinehart and Winston: London.

Jenkins, R. (1982), *Managers, recruitment procedures and black workers*, (Working Papers on Ethnic Relations, No. 18), RUER, University of Aston: Birmingham.

Johnson, M.R.D., Bewley, B.R., Banks, M.H., Bland, J.M. and Clyde, D.V. (1985), 'Schools and smoking: School features and variations in cigarette smoking by children and teachers', *British Journal of Educational Psychology*, Vol. 55, pp. 34-44.

Jones, C. (1985), 'Sexual Tyranny: Male violence in a mixed secondary school' in Weiner, G. (ed.), *Just a Bunch of Girls*, Open University: Milton Keynes, pp. 26-39.

Jones, M. (1980), 'Sugar and spice and all things nice? Career aspirations of girl school leavers', *Youth in Society*, February, pp. 13-15.

Karabel, J. and Halsey, A.H. (eds)., (1977), *Power and Ideology in Education*, Oxford University Press: Oxford.

Keddie, N. (1971), 'Classroom Knowledge', in Young, M.F.D. (ed.), *Knowledge and Control: New Directions for the Sociology of Education*, Collier Macmillan: London, pp. 133-160.

Keil, T. and Newton, P. (1980), 'Into Work: Continuity and change', in Deem, R. (ed.), *Schooling for Women's Work*, Routledge and Kegan Paul: London, pp. 98-111.

Kelly, E. (1988), 'Pupils, Racial Groups and Behaviour in Schools', in Kelly, E. and Cohn, T., *Racism in Schools - New Research Evidence*, Trentham: Stoke-on-Trent, pp. 5-28.

King, R. (1987), 'Sex and Social Class Inequalities in Education: a re-examination', *British Journal of Sociology of Education*, Vol. 8, No. 3, pp. 287-303.

Kirby, R. and Roberts, H. (1984), 'Y.B. on YTS? Why not?' Paper presented to the British Sociological Association annual conference, Bradford, 2-5th May.

Lacey, C. (1970), *Hightown Grammar: The School as a Social System*, Manchester University Press: Manchester.

Lambart, A. (1976), 'The Sisterhood' in Hammersley, M and Woods, P. (eds.), *The Process of Schooling*, Routledge and Kegan Paul: London, pp. 152-159.

Lee, G. and Wrench, J. (1987), 'Race and Gender Dimensions of the Youth Labour Market: From Apprenticeship to YTS', in Lee, G. and Loveridge, R., *The Manufacture of Disadvantage - Stigma and Social Closure*, Open University Press,: Milton Keynes, pp. 83-99.

Little, A. and Willey, R. (1981), *Multiethnic Education - The Way Forward*, (Schools Council Pamphlet 18), Schools Council: London.

Llewellyn, M. (1980), 'Studying girls at school: the implications of confusion', in Deem, R. (ed.), *Schooling for Women's Work*, Routledge and Kegan Paul: London, pp. 42-51.

Mahony, P. (1985), *Schools for the Boys?: Co-education re-assessed*, Hutchinson: London.

Main, B.G.M. (1987), 'The wage expectations and unemployment experience of school leavers', *Scottish Journal of Political Economy*, Vol. 34, No. 4, pp. 349-367.

Malinowski, B. (1922), *Argonauts of the Western Pacific*, Routledge and Kegan Paul: London.

Marsh, P., Rosser, E. and Harre, R. (1978), *The Rules of Disorder*, Routledge and Kegan Paul: London.

Marx, K. and Engels, F. (1965), *Manifesto of the Communist Party*, (translated from the German original of 1848), Foreign Languages Press: Peking.

Measor, L. (1984), 'Gender and the sciences: pupils' gender-based conceptions of school subjects', in Hammersley, M. and Woods, P.

(eds.), *Life in School: The Sociology of Pupil Culture*, Open University Press: Milton Keynes, pp. 89-105.

Meyenn, R. (1980), 'School girls' peer groups', in Woods, P. (ed.), *Pupil Strategies*, Croom Helm: London, pp. 108-142.

Modood, T. (1988), ' "Black", racial equality and Asian identity', *New Community*, Vol. XIV, No. 3, pp. 397-404.

Oakley, A. (1981), *Subject Women*, Martin Robertson: Oxford.

Office of Population, Censuses and Surveys (1982)a, *The 1981 Census of Population, County Report*, HMSO: London.

Office of Population Censuses and Surveys (1982)b, *The 1981 Census of Population, Small Area Statistics*, HMSO: London.

Parsons, T. (1959),'The school class as a social system', *Harvard Educational Review*, Vol. 29, pp. 297-318.

Phillips, E.J. (1984), *A longitudinal study of the effect of transitions on a fourth year tutor group in a Clwyd comprehensive school*, Unpublished M.Ed. dissertation, University College of North Wales: Bangor.

Pidgeon, D. (1970) *Expectations and Pupil Performance*, NFER: Slough.

Plewis, I. (1987), 'Social Disadvantage, Educational Attainment and Ethnicity: a comment', *British Journal of Sociology of Education*, Vol. 8, No. 1, pp. 77-82.

Pollard, A. (1985), 'Opportunities and Difficulties of a Teacher-Ethnographer. A Personal Account', in Burgess, R.G. *Field Methods in the Study of Education*, Falmer Press,: Lewes, pp. 217-234.

Purvis, J. (1984), 'Women and Education', Open University Course E205, *Conflict and change in Education: A Sociological Introduction*, Open University Press: Milton Keynes.

Raby, A.L. (1979), *Career aspirations and attitudes of middle and low stream pupils in an urban multiracial comprehensive school*, Unpublished Ph.D. thesis, University of Aston: Birmingham.

Raby, L. and Walford, G. (1981), 'Career related attitudes and their determinants for middle- and low-stream pupils in an urban, multiracial comprehensive school', *Research in Education*, No. 25, May, pp. 19-35.

Reeves, F. and Chevannes, M. (1981), 'The Underachievement of Rampton', *Multicultural Education*, Vol. 10, No. 1, pp. 35-42.

Reid, I. (1980), 'Teachers and Social Class', *Westminster Studies in Education*, Vol. 3, pp. 47-58.

Reid, I. (1986), *The Sociology of School and Education*, Fontana: London.

Richardson, E. (1973), *The Teacher, the School and the Task of Management*, Heinemann: London.

Riley, K.A. (1985a), 'Black Girls Speak for Themselves', in Weiner, G. (ed.), *Just a Bunch of Girls*, Oxford University Press: Oxford, pp. 63-76.

Riley, K.A. (1985b), *Attitudes and aspirations of secondary school girls of Afro-Caribbean origin*, Unpublished Ph.D. thesis; Bulmershe College of Higher Education: Reading.

Roberts, K., Noble, M. and Duggan, J. (1983), 'Young, black and out of work', in Troyna, B. and Smith, D.I. (eds.), *Racism, School and the Labour Market*, National Youth Bureau: Leicester, pp. 17-28.

Rosenthal, R. and Jacobsen, L. (1968), *Pygmalion in the Classroom*, Holt, Rhinehart and Winston: New York.

Rosser, E. and Harre, R. (1976), 'The meaning of "trouble"', in Hammersley, M. and Woods, P. (Eds), *The Process of Schooling*, Routledge and Kegan Paul: London, pp. 171-177.

Roy, D. (1970) 'The Study of Southern Labor Union Organising Campaigns', in Habenstein, R. (ed.), *Pathways to Data*, Aldine: Chicago, pp. 216-244.

Samuel, J. (1981), 'The teachers' viewpoint: Feminism and science teaching: some classroom observations' in Kelly, A. (ed.), *The Missing Half: Girls and Science Education*, Manchester University Press: Manchester, pp. 246-256.

Schatzman, L. and Strauss, A.L. (1973), *Field Research: Strategies for a Natural Sociology*, Prentice-Hall: Englewood Cliffs.

Sharp, R. and Green, A. (1975), *Education and Social Control*, Routledge and Kegan Paul: London.

Sharpe, S. (1976), *Just Like a Girl*, Penguin: Harmondsworth.

Shilling, C. (1988), 'School to Work Programmes and the Production of Alienation', *British Journal of Sociology of Education*, Vol. 9, No. 2, pp. 181-197.

Skeggs, B. (1988), 'Gender Reproduction and Further Education: Domestic Apprenticeships', *British Journal of Sociology of Education*, Vol. 9, No. 2, pp. 131-149.

Spender, D. (1980), *Man Made Language*, Routledge and Kegan Paul: London.

Spender, D. (1982), *Invisible Women: the Schooling Scandal*, Writers and Readers Publishing Co-operative: London.

Stanley, J. (1986), 'Sex and the Quiet Schoolgirl', *British Journal of Sociology of Education*, Vol. 7, No. 3, pp. 275-286.

Stanworth, M. (1981), *Gender and Schooling: A Study of Sexual Division in the Classroom*, Women's Research and Resources Centre: London. (Reprinted by Hutchinson, 1983).

Stebbins, R.A., Griffin, C. and Burgess, R.G. (1987), 'Review Symposium' review of McLaren, P. 'Schooling is a Ritual Performance', (1986), *British Journal of Sociology of Education*, Vol. 8, No. 1, pp. 83-86.

Swann, M. (1985), *Education for All: the Report of the Committee of Inquiry into the Education of Children from Ethnic Minority Groups*, HMSO: London.

Taylor, M. (1981), *Caught Between: A Review of Research into the Education of Pupils of West Indian Origin*, NFER-Nelson: Slough.

Troyna, B. (1984), 'Fact or Artefact? The 'educational achievement' of black pupils', *British Journal of Sociology of Education*, Vol. 5, No. 2, pp. 153-166.

Troyna, B. and Ball, W. (1985), *Views from the Chalk Face: School responses to an LEA's policy on multicultural education*, (Policy

Papers in Ethnic Relations, No. 1), CRER, University of Warwick: Coventry.

Verma, G.K. and Bagley, L. (1975), *Race and Education Across Cultures*, Heinemann: London.

Warr, P., Banks, M. and Ullah, P. (1985), 'The experience of unemployment among black and white urban teenagers', *British Journal of Psychology*, Vol. 76, pp. 75-87.

Weber, M. (1968), *The Sociology of Max Weber*, (translated from the French by Mary Ilford), Allen Lane: London.

Westergaard, J. and Resler, H. (1975), *Class in a Capitalist Society*, Penguin: Harmondsworth.

Whyte, W.F. (1955), *Street Corner Society*, (2nd Edition), University of Chicago Press: Chicago.

Willis, P. (1977), *Learning to Labour*, Saxon House: Farnborough.

Wolcott, H. (1975), 'Criteria for an ethnographic approach to research in school', *Human Organisation*, Vol. 34, No. 2, pp. 111-127.

Wood, J. (1987), 'Groping towards sexism: boys' sex talk', in Weiner, G. and Arnot, M. (eds.), *Gender Under Scrutiny, New Inquiries in Education*, Hutchinson: London, pp. 187-197.

Woods, P. (1979), *The Divided School*, Routledge and Kegan Paul: London.

Woods, P. (1983), *Sociology and the School*, Routledge and Kegan Paul: London.

Wrench, J. (1987), 'The unfinished bridge: YTS and black youth', in Troyna, B. (ed.), *Racial Inequality in Education*, Tavistock,: London, pp. 127-146.

Wright, C. (1985), 'The relations between teachers and Afro-Caribbean pupils: observing multiracial classrooms', in Weiner, G. and Arnot, M. (eds.), *Gender Under Scrutiny: New Inquiries in Education*, Hutchinson, London, pp. 173-186.

Wright, C. (1986), 'School Processes - An Ethnographic Study' in Eggleston, J. et al. *Education for Some: The Educational and Vocational Experiences of 15-18 year-old Members of Minority Ethnic Groups*, Trentham: Stoke-on-Trent, pp. 127-179.

Wright, C. (1987), 'Black students - White teachers', in Troyna, B. (ed.), *Racial Inequality in Education*, Tavistock: London, pp. 109-127.

Wright, E.O. (1978) 'Race, Class and Income Inequality', *American Journal of Sociology*, Vol. 83, No. 6, pp. 1368-1397.

Zweig, F. (1948), *Labour, Life and Poverty*, Gollancz: London.